A Guide to
European Community Law

LHBEC

AUSTRALIA
The Law Book Company
Sydney

CANADA
The Carswell Company
Toronto, Ontario

INDIA
N. M. Tripathi (Private) Ltd
Bombay

Eastern Law House (Private) Ltd
Calcutta

M.P.P. House
Bangalore

Universal Book Traders
Delhi

ISRAEL
Steimatzky's Agency Ltd
Tel Aviv

PAKISTAN
Pakistan Law House
Karachi

A Guide to European Community Law

by

P. S. R. F. Mathijsen

Professor of Law, University of Brussels.
Former Director-General with the Commission
of the European Communities

Fifth Edition

London
Sweet & Maxwell
1990

First Edition 1972
Second Edition 1975
Second Impression 1976
Third Edition 1980
Fourth Edition 1985
Fifth Edition 1990
Second Impression 1991

Published in Great Britain by
Sweet & Maxwell Limited
of South Quay Plaza, 183 Marsh Wall,
London E14 9FT
Computerset by
LBJ Enterprises Limited, Chilcompton, Somerset
Printed in Scotland

British Library Cataloguing in Publication Data
Mathijsen, P.S.R.F. (Petrus Servatius Renoldus
Franciscus)
    A guide to European Community law.—5th. ed.
    1. European Community. Law
    I. Title
    341.094

    ISBN 0–421–42810–4

To my daughters Claire
Bénédicte
Stéphanie
Valérie
Olivia
Daphné

ACKNOWLEDGEMENT

In the first place I wish to thank the publishers for having asked me, once again, to rewrite my "Guide". I do appreciate the freedom I have enjoyed in deciding on the new structure of this fifth edition, while abiding by their wish to maintain the introductory character of the work which also means a strict limit on the number of pages.

Then there are those who passively and actively were of direct assistance during the preparatory work.

Above all my wife Beverly who, for months, accepted that I spent practically every evening and weekend behind my desk and computer, intolerant of any interuption and unable to answer questions and requests. Without her support and acceptance things would have been quite different.

Then there is Mr. Tony Joris, assistant at the Law Faculty of the Vrije Universiteit van Brussel who not only helped me with advice and research, but read the manuscript and made invaluable comments. I am most grateful for his help.

I also wish to express my gratitude to the Publication Office of the European Communities and more especially to Mrs. J. Maas of the General Secretariat of the Commission. They keep me supplied with all the publications I need to remain informed of the Community developments. Without that, writing this book would have been much more difficult and complicated.

PREFACE

The first edition of this book covered the development of Community law up to the middle of 1972 and was published shortly before Denmark, Ireland and the United Kingdom joined the European Communities.

The second edition, which consisted mainly in an updating of the first, appeared in June 1975, after the negotiations regarding Britain's "continued" membership of the European Communities were concluded.

The third edition came out in 1980 just before the accession of Greece and was expanded to cover the first direct elections to the European Parliament, its new budgetary powers, the establishment of the Court of Auditors, the European Monetary System (EMS) and the Lomé Conventions with the African, Caribbean and Pacific States.

The forth edition, published in 1985 on the eve of the enlargement of the Communities to Portugal and Spain, included the institutional changes that followed. It also contained new chapters on Fisheries, on Industrial and Intellectual Property Rights and a special section on External Relations since the role of the EEC in those fields had dramatically increased.

As for this fifth edition (September 1990), it might seem an odd moment to publish it. Are we not in the middle of far-reaching transformations? The internal market should be completed within 18 months, while in December of this year two Intergovernmental Conferences will start work on drafting the Treaty amendments necessary to accommodate the Economic and Monetary Union (EMU) and the European Political Union (EPU). Why not wait till all the expected results have been achieved?

To do that would mean putting off any publication on the European Communities indefinitely. The pace of change both within and outside the EEC, *e.g.* Eastern Europe, has become so rapid that by the time it appears, the printed word will always be outdated in some respects. It seems nonetheless quite obvious that in order to grasp the meaning of all those future developments and their consequences for the Communities, a clear view of the points of departure and background is essential. Furthermore, so many changes have occured over the past five years that it has become imperative to record them and incorporate them in their proper place within the existing body of rules and regulations. The Commission White Paper on "1992", the Single European Act, the Court of First Instance, the Regulation on the control of concentrations and the fourth Lomé Convention are only a few examples of recent developments. When the new milestones will have been reached a new edition will also incorporate those.

I do find encouragement for continuing this work not only of course in the number of copies that have been sold (!) but also in the fact that several translations are in existence or are in preparation. What I wish I would get more of are comments from readers about the usefulness of this book (or lack of) for their work.

June 1990.   P.S.R.F. Mathijsen

CONTENTS

Contents

Contents

TABLE OF CASES

COURT OF JUSTICE OF THE EUROPEAN COMMUNITIES

Chronological List of Cases

xxvi   *Table of Cases*

COURT OF FIRST INSTANCE OF THE EUROPEAN COMMUNITIES

Alphabetical List of Cases

COMMISSION DECISIONS

NATIONAL COURTS

Belgium

France

TABLE OF TREATIES AND CONVENTIONS

TABLE OF SECONDARY LEGISLATION
OF THE EUROPEAN COMMUNITIES

Regulations

Commission Notices

TABLE OF NATIONAL LEGISLATION

ABBREVIATIONS

A.C.P.
African, Caribbean and Pacific countries, signatories to the Lomé Convention I and II.

Act of Accession
Act concerning the conditions of accession of Denmark, Ireland and the United Kingdom and the adjustments to the treaties establishing the ECSC, EEC and EAEC, annexed to the Treaty of accession. For texts see *Sweet & Maxwell's Encyclopedia of Community Law.*

Adaptation Decision
Council Decision of the European Communities of January 1, 1973, adjusting the instruments concerning the accession of Denmark, Ireland and the United Kingdom to the European Communities, O.J. 1973, L.2. These adjustments were necessary because Norway, although a signatory to the Treaty of accession, did not become a member of the European Communities.

Budgetary Treaties
Treaties of April 22, 1970 (and July 22, 1975) amending Certain Budgetary (Financial) Provisions of the Treaties establishing the European Communities and of the Treaty establishing a Single Council and a Single Commission of the European Communities.

Bull.
Bulletin of the European Communities edited by the Secretariat of the Commission; there are 11 issues per year (July-August are published together).

Bull. Suppl.	Supplement to the Bulletin.
C.M.L.R.	Common Market Law Reports.
C.M.L.Rev.	Common Market Law Review.
Competition Report	Report on Competition Policy.
Dec.	Decision.
Dir.	Directive.
E.C.R.	Official reports of cases before the Court of Justice in English.
ECSC	European Coal and Steel Community.
EEC	European Economic Community.
E.L.Rev.	European Law Review.
Euratom	European Community of Atomic Energy.
Gen.Rep.	General Report on the activities of the Communities, published yearly by the Commission. The year mentioned after the word Report refers to the period covered by the Report.
J.O.	*Journal Officiel:* French edition of the *Official Journal of the European Communities.* *Remarks* 1. This Journal was published under the name *Journal Officiel de la Communauté Européenne du Charbon et de l'Acier* from 1952 to April 19, 1958; on April 20, 1958, the first issue of the *Journal Officiel des Communautés Européennes* appeared, without modifying the structure of the Journal itself; this lasted until December 31, 1967.
	References to publications in the *Journal Officiel* for the period 1952 to July 1, 1967, are made by mentioning the page and the year or vice versa such as J.O. 849/65. Between July 1 and December 31, 1967, each issue is paged separately.

2. After January 1, 1968 (see O.J. 1968, L.30), the Journal was divided into two separate editions designated by the letters "L." (legislation) and "C." (communications).

Legislative texts are published in the edition marked "L." and are again subdivided in two categories:

   I. Acts for which publication is a condition for their application (see EEC, Art. 191);

  II. Acts for which publication is not required.

All other texts appear in the edition marked "C."

References to publications in the *Journal Officiel* after January 1, 1968, are made by mentioning the letter "L." or "C.", the year, the No. of the issue and the page, *e.g.* J.O. 1970, 31/1.

3. Starting on January 1, 1973, the Journal is also published in the Danish and English languages.

4. In accordance with Article 155 of the Act of Accession, provision was made in Council Regulation 857/72 of April 24, 1972, for Special Editions of the *Official Journal* for the publication *inter alia* of the English text of acts of the institutions of the Communities adopted and published before accession. Consequently an authentic English translation now exists of the most important Community acts.

This special edition was published in November and December 1972 and a subsequent edition was published in 1974 (see O.J. 1972, L.101/1). All references to an O.J. publication prior to January 1, 1973 are necessarily in the Special Edition.

5. The numbering of the pages is the same in the French, English and other language editions.

6. Starting on January 1, 1981, the Official Journal is also published in Greek.

Merger Treaty	Treaty of April 8, 1965, establishing a Single Council and a Single Commission of the European Communities.
O.J.	*Official Journal of the European Communities;* see J.O. above.
Rec.	*Recueil de la Jurisprudence de la Cour,* Official Court Reports.
Reg.	Regulation.
Rules	Rules of Procedure of the Court of Justice (O.J. 1975, L.102/1).

CHAPTER 1

THE EUROPEAN COMMUNITIES

When the European Coal and Steel Community was established in 1952, the drafters of the Treaty coined the word "supranational" to indicate the particular character of their creation and the law it embodied. Although it was set up by an international agreement similar to many others concluded between sovereign states, the signatories were conscious of having drafted something that was different from international law, the law of nations. They were not, like so many countries before them, merely creating mutual obligations[1]; they were doing much more: they were limiting their own sovereign rights, transferring them to institutions over which they had no direct control and endowing them with powers they did not always possess themselves. Furthermore they were not only binding the states they represented to assume new rights and obligations, they were also directly including their citizens, who became subjects of the Community.

By contrast with ordinary international treaties, the European Treaties have thus created their own legal system to which the term "international" could not apply; the term "supranational" would therefore indicate the difference: the law of the Community is not international law.

On the other hand, the terms and the spirit of the European treaties make it impossible for the Member States, as a corollary,

---

[1] Case 26/62 *Van Gend en Loos* v. *Nederlandse Administratie der Belastingen* [1963] E.C.R. 1 at 12.

to accord precedence to their national law over a legal system accepted by them on a basis of reciprocity. The executive force of Community law cannot vary from one state to another in deference to domestic laws without jeopardising the attainment of the objectives of the treaties.[2] The law of the European Communities cannot therefore be regarded as national law. It is different and independent, it stands apart, it is not national law; since it is common to 12 nations, it is "supranational."

The term has now fallen into disrepute and is no longer used. This does not change the specific nature of the law created by the Treaties; more important, the concept is now universally accepted and expressed by the words "Community law."

Community law is to be found mainly in the European Treaties and the secondary legislation. Originally there were the treaties setting up the European Coal and Steel Community (ECSC), the European Atomic Energy Community (Euratom) and the European Economic Community (EEC). The first two can be designated as sectoral Treaties while the third one, the EEC Treaty, covers the economy in general (hereinafter "the Treaty" means the EEC Treaty signed in Rome in 1957). Reference must also be made to the successive texts which implemented and amended the basic texts: the Convention on certain institutions common to the three Communities; the Treaty establishing a single Council and a single Commission, the Decision creating the Communities' own resources, the Treaty amending certain budgetary provisions, the Treaty of accession of Denmark, Ireland and the United Kingdom, the Treaty amending certain financial provisions, the Act concerning direct elections for the European Parliament, the Treaty concerning Greek accession, the Treaty amending the original Treaties with regard to Greenland,[3] the Treaties concerning Portuguese and Spanish accession and, finally, the Single European Act. However those only constitute the charter, the point of departure.

Community law has gradually evolved and developed over the past 38 years, from the 100 Articles of the Coal and Steel Treaty,

[2] Case 6/64 *Costa* v. *ENEL* [1964] E.C.R. 585 at 594.
[3] See O.J. 1985, L. 29/1.

into an impressive body of law comprising thousands of Regulations, Directives, Decisions, Resolutions, Agreements, Programmes and other measures, and above all the case law of the
Court of Justice.

It is impressive, not because of its sheer volume but because of
its original character and its growth potential. It is worthwhile
considering this particular nature of the body of Community law:
except for the basic treaties mentioned earlier, none of the
Communities' acts find their origin in the traditional institutions,
bodies and organs with which lawyers and citizens are familiar
and over which they exercise, through democratic elections, some
sort of control. Community regulations, directives, decisions,
etc., are issued outside most citizens' own countries, according to
procedures they often cannot grasp and are too remote to be
controlled; they are nevertheless directly involved. Not only do
those measures impose obligations upon them, without the
possibility of their national authorities controlling either their
implementation or their enforcement, but they confer upon them
rights which they in turn can ask their national courts to uphold
against fellow-citizens, undertakings and even their own government. And indeed, these rights arise not only where they are
expressly granted by the Treaty, but also as a consequence of the
obligations which the Treaty, in a clearly defined way, imposes
upon individuals as well as upon the Member States and the
institutions of the Community.[4] Citizens can also challenge the
legality of Community measures in the Community Court, when
they are directly and individually concerned.

The apparent aloofness of the European authorities combined
with this direct involvement is sometimes bewildering, although
the direct election of the Members of the European Parliament
has made most people in the Member States familiar with at least
some of the aspects of Commuity law. But, if democratic control
through directly elected representatives is to become a reality,
some knowledge of the basic rules and procedures of the Community is required.

---

[4] See n. 1, above.

Since all the citizens are concerned, it seems that not only the law student but also the practitioner, the politician and the general public must understand what it is all about. Unless one realises what the objectives are and what means and procedures have been provided to attain them, no participation is possible, no criticism is justified, no suggestion can be pertinent. The objectives are clearly set out in the Treaty: to promote throughout the Community harmonious development of economic activities, a continuous and balanced expansion, an increase in stability, an accelerated raising of the standard of living and closer relations between the Member States.[5] The means provided by the Treaty seem rather limited; there is first the establishment, functioning and development of a common market and second the progressive approximation of the economic policies of the Member States. But while the Treaty provides precise rules and timetables for the former, the second is described in very general terms. However, notwithstanding this vagueness, Community activities have penetrated more and more social, economic and related domains, some of which were not, until recently, explicitly provided for in the Treaty. This was the case for regional policy, the European Monetary System, Economic and Monetary Union and Political Co-operation. The Single European Act introduced all those policies into the Treaty, thereby providing the necessary legal basis for Community measures in those fields.

Community law is therefore also impressive because of its continuous growth since, next to the coal and steel and nuclear sectors, the EEC Treaty aims at integrating the entire economies of the Member States.

The dynamics of the Communities are not the only proof of their vitality; notwithstanding a decade of economic recession and political crises of all kinds, they not only held together but expanded both geographically and politically, which seems to indicate that they fulfill a basic need and respond to a profound aspiration.

[5] EEC, Art. 2.

CHAPTER 2

HISTORY

Every institution is the product of a series of historical events and at the same time reflects the convictions, hopes and concerns of those who were instrumental in establishing it. The European Communities are no exception to this. For a full understanding and correct interpretation of the European treaties some knowledge of the historical background seems necessary.

Although the expression "United States of Europe" was already used by Victor Hugo in 1849,[1] there is no need to go that far back! The end of the Second World War seems a fair starting point, notwithstanding the existence before that of a very active but not too influential Pan-European Movement inspired by Count Coudenhove-Kalergi.

1. Churchill's speech

The agreement made at Yalta in 1945 by the United Kingdom, the United States and the U.S.S.R. left Europe more divided than ever and the growing antagonism among the victorious "Allies" spelt only more tensions and catastrophies. It was on September 19, 1946, in a speech at Zurich University, that Winston Churchill proposed a "sovereign remedy," *i.e.* to "recre-

---

[1] See Henri Brugmans, *L'Idée Européenne*, 1920–1970 (Bruges, 1970).

5

History

ate the European family, or as much of it as we can, and provide it with a structure under which it can dwell in peace, in safety and in freedom. We must build a kind of United States of Europe." And he went on to "say something that will astonish you. The first step in the recreation of the European family must be a partnership between France and Germany"; at that time it needed a lot of courage and foresight to make such a suggestion. As will be seen, it was this (British) idea which also inspired the French Government in 1950 to propose the establishment of the European Coal and Steel Community. Towards the end of his Zurich speech, Churchill also proposed to start by setting up a regional structure and to form a Council of Europe.[2]

2. Marshall Plan-OEEC

If Churchill's words were well received, the European states in those days lacked the necessary stamina to proceed with such far-reaching plans, since they were preoccupied with their daily fight for economic survival. Once again the United States came to the rescue. In another famous university speech, at Harvard this time, George Marshall, United States Secretary of State, announced on June 5, 1947, that the United States would do "whatever it is able to do to assist in the return of normal economic health in the world." This offer was accepted by 16 European countries on July 15, 1947, and so the Marshall Plan was born; but more important for the future of European integration was the setting up of the Organisation of European Economic Co-operation (OEEC)[3] in 1948; this was in response to the American request for an agreement among Europeans.

3. Robert Schuman: May 9, 1950

In the meantime, Churchill's words about a partnership between France and Germany had not been forgotten and on May 9,

---

[2] The Treaty establishing the Council of Europe was signed in London on May 5, 1949.

[3] In 1961, it became the Organisation for Economic Co-operation and Development (OECD), with the participation of the U.S.A. and Canada.

1950, Robert Schuman, French Foreign Minister, declared that a united Europe was essential for world peace and that a gathering of the European nations required the elimination of the century-old opposition between France and Germany. As a first practical step towards this end he proposed "to place the whole Franco-German coal and steel production under one joint High Authority, in an organization open to the participation of the other countries of Europe." He described this pooling of production as the "first stage of the European Federation." Germany, the Netherlands, Belgium, Luxembourg and Italy accepted in principle and negotations started at once.

4. European Coal and Steel Community

The negotiations progressed rapidly and were simplified by the fact that all the future partners had accepted the proposed principles; the work consisted mainly in giving them legal form. A sense of urgency was probably added to the existing goodwill by the communist invasion in South Korea. The Treaty establishing the European Coal and Steel Community (ECSC) was signed in Paris, on April 18, 1951. Ratification by the national parliaments met with little opposition and on July 25, 1952, the Treaty entered into force.

5. European Defence Community

The following two years were difficult. It has been said that the easing of the international political situation—Stalin died on March 5, 1953, and July 27, 1953 marked the end of the Korean war—diminished the necessity for "closing the ranks." In any case, two additional proposals for close co-operation among the "Six"—in the form of a European Defence Community and a European Political Community—failed miserably.

6. EEC and Euratom

Undaunted by those setbacks, the Benelux countries proposed in 1955, to their partners in the Coal and Steel Community, to take another step towards economic integration by setting up a common market and jointly developing transportation, classical and atomic energy. This led to the conference of Messina in the same year, at which Mr. Spaak was asked to report on the feasibility of those plans. At that time an invitation was issued also to the British Government to join the negotiations of the Six; alas, to no avail.[4]

The "Spaak Report" was ready in 1956, and was discussed in Venice, where the decision was taken to start negotiations for drafting treaties that would establish a "common market" and an Atomic Energy Community. With incredible speed (June 1956–February 1957) these two complex treaties were prepared for signature in Rome on March 25, 1957, and on January 1, 1958, the European Economic Community (EEC) and the European Atomic Energy Community (Euratom) became a reality. In 1961, the British Government decided to apply for negotiations to determine whether satisfactory arrangements could be made to meet the needs of the United Kingdom, of the Commonwealth and of EFTA. The Government were "baulked in their objective, so that it was not possible to determine whether satisfactory conditions of entry could be obtained."[5]

7. Merger Treaty

On April 8, 1965, the institutional set-up of the Communities was simplified by the Treaty establishing "a Single Council and a Single Commission of the European Communities," commonly referred to as the "Merger Treaty." This treaty became effective on July 1, 1967; as from that date there was therefore one Council, one European Commission, one European Court and one Assembly for all three Communities.[6]

---

[4] See Hans Joachim Heiser, *British Policy with regard to the unification efforts on the European Continent* (Leyden, 1959), p. 96.
[5] *The United Kingdom and the European Communities*, 1971 (Cmnd. 4715), para. 6.
[6] See below.

8. The Customs Union

The Customs Union was fully operative in the EEC on July 1, 1968. It meant that tariff and quota restrictions between Member States had by then been completely abolished and that the replacement of the national external tariff by the common external tariff had been completed. The Community was 18 months ahead of the schedule laid down in the Treaty.[7]

9. Community's Own Resources

The Replacement of Financial Contributions from Member States by the Community's Own Resources[8] inaugurated a new era in the history of the Community. It became, in a certain way, financially independent and the Treaty amending Certain Budgetary Provisions of the ECSC, EEC and Euratom Treaties and of the Merger Treaty, conferred specific budgetary powers upon Parliament. The own resources are provided by the agricultural levies, the customs duties, a percentage of the VAT collected by the Member States and, since February 1988,[9] a rate applied to an additional base, representing the sum of the GNP at market prices.

10. British, Danish and Irish membership

After a debate in both Houses of Parliament, at the end of which the Government's decision was approved in the Commons by a

---

[7] Twelve years, see EEC, Art. 8 and Acceleration Decisions (J.O. 1960, 1217 and J.O. 1962, 1284).

[8] Decision 70/243 of April 21, 1970 (J.O. 1970, L. 94/19; O.J. 1970(I), 224). It became effective on January 1, 1971, after ratification by the six national Parliaments.

[9] Bull. 2–1988, 13.

majority of 426, the British Government applied for membership of the Communities on May 10, 1967. By December of the same year it was clear however that the "Six" could not reach the unanimity necessary under the Community Treaties to return a reply to Britain's application. Thus ended the second endeavour of the United Kingdom to enter "Europe." The British Government, however, decided to maintain their application for membership and it was discussed at many meetings of the Council of the Communities in the following two years.

At the meeting of Heads of State or Government, on December 1 and 2, 1969, at The Hague, it was finally agreed to open negotiations between the Communities and the States which had applied for membership. Other important decisions taken at this "Summit" concerned the economic and monetary union and the Community's own resources, *i.e.* Community's direct income system.

The Treaty of Brussels relating to the accession of the United Kingdom, Ireland, Norway and Denmark was signed on January 22, 1972; this Treaty entered into force on January 1, 1973, except for Norway which, as a result of a referendum on the subject, did not ratify the Treaty. Consequently, several provisions of this Treaty and of the "Act concerning the conditions of accession and the adjustments to the Treaties" attached thereto were modified by the Council Decision of January 1, 1973, adjusting the documents concerning accession of the new Member States to the European Communities (hereinafter referred to as the "Adaptation Decision").

11. Further enlargement

On June 12, 1975, Greece applied for membership to the European Communities and the Treaty of Accession, together with an Act concerning the conditions of accession and the adjustments to the Treaties were signed at Athens on May 28, 1979[10]; it was ratified by the Greek Parliament on June 28, 1979.

[10] O.J. 1979, L. 291/1.

On March 28, 1977, Portugal[11] and on July 28, 1977, Spain[12] applied for membership. Formal negotiations with Portugal started on October 16, 1978, and with Spain on February 5, 1979. They were successfully concluded at the European Council of March 29 and 30, 1985 and the third enlargement became effective on January 1, 1986, bringing the total of Member States to 12.

12. Direct election of Parliament, Declaration on Democracy and Fundamental Rights

On September 20, 1976, the representatives of the Member States in Council agreed on the conditions for direct election and signed an Act concerning the Election of the Representatives of the Assembly by Direct Universal Suffrage[13] which was subsequently ratified by the then nine national parliaments. The first elections were held in June 1979,[14] giving the European Communities their democratic legitimacy.

On April 5, 1977 the European Parliament, the Council and the Commission issued a Joint Declaration on Fundamental Rights[15] with which the Heads of State and of Government associated themselves in their Declaration on Democracy in which they confirmed their will to ensure that the values of their legal, political and moral order are respected and to safeguard the principles of representative democracy, of the rule of law, of social justice and of respect for human rights. They stated that the application of these principles implies a political system of pluralist democracy.[16]

On June 19, 1983, the ten Heads of State and Government signed the Solemn Declaration on European Union expressing

[11] Bull. 3–1977, 8 and Suppl. 5/78.
[12] Bull. 7/8–1977, 6 and Suppl. 9/78.
[13] O.J. 1976, L. 278/1.
[14] See below, European Parliament.
[15] O.J. 1977, C. 103/1.
[16] Bull. 3–1978, 5; in other words a State without pluralistic democracy cannot be a member of the European Communities.

inter alia their determination "to achieve a comprehensive and coherent common political approach" and their will to transform the whole complex of relations between their States into a European Union.[17]

13. Secession of Greenland

On February 1, 1985, Greenland ceased to be part of the European Communities to which it had belonged since January 1, 1973, as part of the Kingdom of Denmark. Greenland has enjoyed a special status within the Kingdom since the Home Rule Act of 1979 and the Greenland Government has exclusive competence *inter alia* for fishing, agriculture and stock farming.

Greenland's special features, *i.e.* remoteness, climatic conditions and the cultural particularities of its non-European population pleaded in favour of new arrangements after the people of the island had decided in 1982 by referendum to withdraw from the Community and to seek a new type of relationship. The Treaty provisions applicable to overseas countries and territories provided an appropriate framework for these relations, although additional specific provisions were needed.[18]

14. The Completion of the Internal Market by 1992

In June 1985, the Commission sent a White Paper to the European Council entitled "Completing the Internal Market." This was the beginning of Operation 1992. It lays down a programme and timetable for the abolition of barriers of all kinds in inter-state trade, the harmonisation of rules, the approxima-

---

[17] Bull. 6–1983, 24. See also Draft Treaty establishing the European Union, Bull. 2–1984, 7.

[18] See Commission opinion on the status of Greenland (Bull. 1–1983, 13) and text of amending treaty with various Council regulations (O.J. 1985, L. 29/1).

tion of legislation and tax structures and the strengthening of monetary co–operation. To complete the internal market, the White Paper provides for removal of physical, technical and fiscal barriers. It was *inter alia* to make the implementation of this comprehensive programme possible that the Member States decided to amend the existing Treaties through the Single European Act.

15. The Single European Act (SEA)

The SEA entered into force on July 1, 1987. The main features of the SEA are, in order to achieve a completely free market, the strengthening of the decision-making power of the Community by extending qualified majority voting, the inclusion in the Treaty of Chapters on Economic and Social Cohesion (Regional Development Fund), Research and Technological Development and Environment. It also provides for closer involvement of Parliament in the legislative procedures. Finally the SEA makes reference to a Treaty on Economic and Monetary Union.

16. Economic and Monetary Union (EMU)

In 1988 the European Council set up a Committee composed of the Governors of the Central Banks and monetary experts under the chairmanship of the President of the Commission. It produced a report in 1989[19] proposing *inter alia* three stages for the establishment of the EMU. The first stage would consist in strengthening economic and monetary co-ordination within the existing institutional framework and preparation and ratification of the amendments to the Treaty. In June 1989, the European Council decided that this first stage would start on July 1, 1990

---

[19] Bull. 4–1989, 8.

and that an Intergovernmental Conference would meet before the end of that year to lay down the subsequent stages.

CHAPTER 3

THE INSTITUTIONS AND OTHER ORGANS OF THE COMMUNITY

Among the various bodies established by, or in pursuance of, the European Treaties,[1] four are referred to as "institutions": the European Parliament, the Council, the Commission and the Court of Justice.[2] What distinguishes an institution from another Community body is the fact that, generally speaking, it is empowered to take decisions binding upon Member States, institutions or persons (natural or legal). The other bodies, with the exception of the European Investment Bank and Euratom's Supply Agency, act in an advisory capacity.

Only the Community itself, the Bank and the Agency[3] have legal personality and capacity[4]; when the Community acquires or

---

[1] For bodies set up by the Treaties see, *e.g.* the Consultative Committee (ECSC, Art. 18), the Scientific and Technical Committee (Euratom, Art. 134), the Economic and Social Committee (Euratom, Art. 3 and EEC, Art. 4), the Court of Auditors (ECSC, Art. 7, Euratom, Art. 3 and EEC, Art. 4), the European Investment Bank (EEC, Art. 3(j)), the Monetary Committee (EEC, Art. 105) and the Committee of Permanent Representatives (Merger Treaty, Art. 4).

For bodies set up by the institutions in pursuance of powers conferred upon them by the Treaties see, *e.g.* the Committee for medium-term economic policy (Dec. 64/47, J.O. 1964, 1031).

[2] EEC, Art. 4.

[3] Euratom, Art. 54; see Ruling 1/78 [1978] E.C.R. 2151.

[4] EEC, Arts. 210 and 211; see Joined Cases 43/59 etc. *Lachmüller* v. *Commission* [1960] E.C.R. 463 at 472 ("that personality is one of public law"); in its judgment in Case 22/70 *Commission* v. *Council* (better known as the ERTA case) [1971] E.C.R. 263 at 274(14), the Court decided that having this legal personality means that, in its external relations, the Community enjoys the capacity to enter into international commitments; for the EIB see EEC, Art. 129.

disposes of property or is party to legal proceedings (outside the Court of Justice) it is represented by the Commission. On the other hand, agreements with one or more States or an international organisation are concluded by the Council.[5]

The first European institutions, *i.e.* the High Authority, the Common Assembly, the Special Council of Ministers and the Court of Justice, were set up by the Treaty of Paris of 1951 establishing the European Coal and Steel Community.[6] Similar institutions, the Assembly, the Council, the Commission and the Court of Justice were created by the EEC and by the Euratom Treaty. Theoretically, the result would have been twelve institutions; three of each kind, had not a Convention, annexed to these Treaties, provided for a single Assembly and a single Court of Justice for the three Communities.[7]

Nonetheless this left three Councils and three Commissions (High Authority), besides the one Assembly and the one Court, a total of eight institutions. A further rationalisation was introduced by the Merger Treaty of 1965[8] establishing "a Council of the European Communities" and "a Commission of the European Communities," to replace the existing Councils, Commissions and High Authority of the ECSC, EEC and Euratom. The four single institutions now exercise the powers and jurisdiction conferred on the institutions they replaced, in accordance with the provisions of the relevant Treaties.[9]

It might be interesting to note that according to the Preamble of the Merger Treaty, the merger of the institutions is seen as a step in the direction of the "unification of the three Communities."

I. THE EUROPEAN PARLIAMENT

Until recently all the European Treaties referred to this institution as the "Assembly"[10] and there always was strong opposition

---

[5] EEC, Art. 228(1).
[6] ECSC, Art. 7.
[7] Convention relating to certain institutions common to the European Communities, of March 25, 1957, annexed to the EEC and Euratom Treaties.
[8] This Treaty came into force on July 1, 1967 (J.O. 1967, 152/2).
[9] Convention of March 25, 1957, Arts. 1 to 4 and Merger Treaty, Arts. 1 and 9.
[10] Or "Common Assembly," ECSC, Art. 7.

from the Council and several Member States to calling it the "Parliament."

It was the Assembly which, back in 1962, decided to call itself the "European Parliament."[11] All the institutions, including the Court, except for a while the Council,[12] have adopted that denomination; the official acts of the Community which require consultation of the Assembly refer, apart from a few years, to the "opinion of the European Parliament."[13]

The name was formally changed, albeit in an unclear and indirect way, by the Single European Act, which refers to the institutions "designated as referred to hereafter" and the reference is always to the "European Parliament"![14]

Whether the Assembly was well advised in changing its name can be questioned, not so much because this institution does not have the powers which are characteristic of democratic parliaments, *i.e.* the powers to legislate and to raise taxes, but because by calling itself a parliament it has created the illusion that democratic control already exists within the European Communities. And although the SEA has conferred upon the European Parliament, as will be seen hereinafter, a larger role in the legislative process of the Community, there is, strictly speaking, no question yet of legislative power.

1. Members of Parliament

According to the Treaty, Parliament consists of "representatives of the peoples brought together in the Community"[15] and exercises advisory and supervisory powers.

---

[11] Resolution of March 30, 1962 (J.O. 1962, 1045). On March 20, 1958, the Assembly had decided to call itself "European Parliamentary Assembly."

[12] See, *e.g.* answer to question No. 398/77 in which the Council stated that the denomination of any one of the institutions could only be amended by a Treaty amending the existing Treaties (O.J. 1977, C. 270/18).

[13] See, *e.g.* Reg. 214/79 concerning the European Regional Development Fund (O.J. 1979, L. 35/1).

[14] SEA, Art. 3(1).

[15] EEC, Art. 137. It will be noted that the Treaty refers to "representatives" in Art. 137 and to "delegates" in Art. 138. The Act concerning the direct elections refers only to "representatives" (O.J. 1967, L. 278/1).

(1) *Election of Members*

Until June 1979, *i.e.* the date of the first direct elections for Parliament, the members were simply designated by the respective national Parliaments from among their members in accordance with the procedure laid down by each Member State.[16] It was not until September 20, 1976 that the Act concerning the Election of the Representatives of the Assembly by Direct Universal Suffrage was finally adopted by the Representatives of the Member States in Council.

Elections by direct universal suffrage must be held "in accordance with a uniform procedure in all Member States,"[17] but agreement on such procedure has not been reached yet and all the elections until now were held in accordance with the method of voting decided nationally.[18]

Presently, Parliament is composed of 518 representatives distributed nationally as follows: 81 each for the larger Member States (Germany, France, Italy and the United Kingdom), 60 for Spain, 25 for the Netherlands, 24 for Belgium, Greece and Portugal, 16 and 15 respectively for Denmark and Ireland and 6 for Luxembourg.[19]

(2) *Member's Mandate*

Members of the European Parliament (MEPs) are elected for a term of five years. Anybody can stand for Parliament,[20] it being

---

[16] EEC, former Art. 138; this Art. lapsed on July 17, 1979 in accordance with Art. 14 of the Act concerning the election. The method of "designating" the members was intended as a temporary procedure—although it lasted 27 years! Already Art. 21(3) of the ECSC Treaty provided for election by direct universal suffrage. Agreement concerning the implementation of this provision was finally reached at the Summit Conference (forerunner of the European Council) held in Paris in 1974.

[17] EEC, Art. 138(3) and Act concerning the election, Art. 7(1) and (2).

[18] All Member States, except the United Kingdom, apply with some variations a proportional representation system via party lists.

[19] EEC, Art. 138(2), as last modified by Art. 10 of the Act of Accession ESP /PORT.

[20] Including, *e.g.* in the UK, peers and ministers of religion who are excluded from election to Westminster.

understood that upon election the rules concerning incompatibility[21] apply. Under the old rules, MEPs had to be members of a national parliament, now the Act concerning direct election simply states that there is no incompatibility between the two offices.[22] Although it must be admitted that fulfilling two mandates is a nearly impossible task, it seems that the disjunction between the two—only very few MEPs still have a double mandate—has estranged the European Parliament from the national ones, thereby eliminating a good chance for political integration.

During the sessions of Parliament, the representatives enjoy the privileges and immunities accorded to members of national parliaments when in their own country, and immunity from detention and legal proceedings when on the territory of another Member State.[23]

2. Tasks and powers

According to the Treaty, Parliament exercises only "advisory and supervisory" powers and, although the SEA has introduced a "co-operation procedure" between the Council, Commission and Parliament for the adoption of certain Community acts, the tasks and powers have, on the whole, remained unchanged. It should be noted however that the Treaty of April 22, 1970 amending certain budgetary provisions of the original three Treaties and of the Merger Treaty, did confer upon Parliament certain budgetary powers.[24] Nonetheless, Parliament does not exercise the main

---

[21] Act concerning direct election, Art. 6(1) and (2). Where an elected candidate does not wish to relinquish an office which is incompatible with that of an MEP, he will be replaced, pending the entry into force of the uniform electoral procedure, in accordance with procedures laid down by each Member State.

[22] *Ibid.,* Art. 5.

[23] Protocol on the privileges and immunities of the European Communities of April 8, 1965, Art. 10. See, *e.g.* Case 149/85 *Wybot* v. *Faure*, [1986] E.C.R. 2403; it follows that Parliament is always "in session."

[24] EEC, Art. 203 as amended.

attributes of an elected representative body, *i.e.* legislation and the raising of taxes.

The tasks of Parliament, as defined in the Treaty, are as follows:

— to participate in the legislative procedure;
— to put questions to the Council and the Commission;
— to adopt a motion of censure where it disapproves of the activities of the Commission.
— to discuss the annual General Report submitted to it by the Commission;
— to participate in the budgetary procedure;
— to initiate procedures in the Court of Justice against the Council or the Commission in case they fail to act, or to protect its own rights and to intervene in other cases;
— to participate in other activities of the Communities.

(1) *Participation in the legislative procedure*

It is in this area that the SEA introduced the most far-reaching changes by providing for a "co-operation procedure" and by slightly increasing the cases wherein Parliament must be consulted by the Council as part of the process leading up to the adoption of a regulation, directive or decision. Until recently there were 27[25] such instances in the Treaty. Generally speaking the Treaty provides for consultation on all important matters such as Community policies (*e.g.* agriculture, transport, competition) and association agreements.[26] But, there was no consultation provided, for instance, on economic policy, social policy and the admission of new members.

[25] See EEC, Arts. 7, 14(7), 43(2), 49, 54(1), (2), 56(2), 57(1), (2), 63(1), (2), 75(1), 87(1), 99, 100, 126, 127, 201, 212, 228(1), 235, 236 and 238. See, *e.g.* modifications introduced by the SEA in Arts. 237 (new members) and 238 (association agreements).
[26] See request of Parliament to be consulted (O.J. 1982, C. 66/50). The Council agreed in 1973 to a greater participation of Parliament in the conclusion of commercial agreements; Seventh General Report (1973), 64.

However, the Council has, for many years, agreed to consult Parliament in cases where it is not specifically provided for. A further change was, as already indicated, introduced by the SEA. The latter not only extended the number of subjects on which consultation is required, but upgraded the role of Parliament in certain areas, by providing for the "assent of the European Parliament"[27] or for a "co-operation procedure." The latter applies for all matters concerned with the completion of the internal market.

Roughly speaking, the co-operation procedure means that after having consulted Parliament on a Commission proposal, the Council adopts a "common position" (instead of a decision, which would normally be the case) and this common position is then communicated to Parliament. The latter can:

(1) approve it or take no decision, after which the Council adopts the act in accordance with the common position; or

(2) propose amendments by an absolute majority and the Commission then re-examines its original proposal in the light of these amendments and re-transmits its proposal to the Council together with the amendments of Parliament it has not accepted and its opinion on them; the Council then takes its final decision; or

(3) Parliament can reject the common position and the Council then can nonetheless take a decision, but unanimously.

The Treaty also provides for time-limits within which the institutions must take their decisions.[28]

When the Council enacts regulations, directives or decisions on the basis of proposals submitted to it by the Commission,

---

[27] EEC, Arts. 237 (accession of new members to the Community) and 238 (international agreements); in 1988 this new procedure was applied 14 times, in 1989, three times.

[28] EEC, Art. 149(2); see SEA, Art. 6(1) for a list of Treaty Arts. affected by this new procedure.

consultation of Parliament is initiated by the Council on the basis of those proposals. As long as the Council has not acted, the Commission may alter its original proposal, in particular, when Parliament has been consulted on the proposal.[29]

Parliament's opinions have no binding force. However, mention must be made, in the acts, of the fact that Parliament was consulted. On the other hand, the Treaty does not require the Council to mention whether the expressed opinion was favourable or not, nor to refute in the latter case the arguments brought forward by Parliament.[30] It should also be noted that the Council can always adopt an act constituting an amendment to the Commission's proposal, but only with an unanimous vote.[31]

Finally, mention must be made of the fact that when provided for by the Treaty, consultation of Parliament constitutes an "essential procedural requirement" and failure of the Council to comply with it may become a ground for annulment of the Council's act by the Court.[32]

Notwithstanding the modifications introduced by the SEA, Parliament's participation in the legislative process remains limited to issuing an opinion or proposing amendments. To give more weight to the opinions, a "conciliation procedure" was introduced in 1977 to be used when the Council departs from the opinion of Parliament. This procedure was instituted by a Joint Declaration of the Parliament, the Council and the Commission.[33] The aim was to give Parliament a more effective participation in

---

[29] EEC, Art. 149(2).
[30] See Case 6/54 *Government of the Kingdom of the Netherlands* v. *High Authority* [1954–56] E.C.R. 103 at 111. The Commission undertook, starting with the July 1973 session of Parliament, systematically to inform it of actions taken on its opinions.
[31] EEC, Art. 149; renewed consultation of Parliament in such cases is only required if the modifications introduced by the Council do affect the essence of the Commission's proposal; see Case 41/69 *ACF Chemiefarma* v. *Commission* [1970] E.C.R. 661 at 689(69).
[32] See Case 138/79 *Roquette Frères* v. *Council* and Case 139/79 *Maizena* v. *Council* [1980] E.C.R. 3333 and 3393, where the Court annulled a Regulation because the Council, although it had transmitted the Commission's proposal to Parliament, adopted the Regulation without waiting for the opinion of Parliament.
[33] O.J. 1975, C. 98/1.

the procedure for preparing and adopting acts of general application which give rise to important expenditure or revenue. The conciliation procedure should normally not take more than three months.

Irrespective of the opinions issued following consultation by the Council, Parliament has always felt free to formulate other resolutions whenever it considered it necessary.[34] The Rules of procedure provide only that such resolutions must concern matters falling within the activities of the Community.

(2) *Parliamentary questions*

In accordance with the Treaty, the Commission must reply orally or in writing to questions put by Parliament or its members.[35] This obligation, originally provided only for the Commission, is an important aspect of the supervisory powers of Parliament. This right of Parliament to obtain answers to its questions is widely used[36] and has been extended considerably over the years. In the first place, although the Treaty only imposes the obligation to answer on the Commisson, Parliament itself extended it to the Council[37] in 1958 and the latter agreed. Secondly, in 1962, Parliament introduced the procedure of oral questions followed by a debate[38] which was accepted by the Council and by the Commission with the proviso that, where the Council is con-

---

[34] Rules of procedure, Art. 47 (O.J. 1981, C. 90/49, 65); in 1989, for instance, Parliament adopted 605 resolutions of which only 190 embody opinions. This ratio raises the question of whether or not Parliament is dispersing itself too much. It might do better to concentrate more on Community legislation which often has to wait for Parliament's opinion. Parliament even made proposals for legislation; see Resolution of May 11, 1979, containing a draft proposal for a regulation on fishfarming (O.J. 1979, C. 140/117).

[35] EEC, Art. 140(3).

[36] During 1989 a total of 1,969 written questions were tabled, 1,711 to the Commission, 144 to the Council and 114 to the Conference of Ministers of Foreign Affairs (Political Co-operation). Oral questions numbered 883, 581 to the Commission, 172 to the Council and 130 to the Conference of Ministers of Foreign Affairs (question time) and another 196 oral questions; see General Report (1989), 38.

[37] Rules, Arts. 44, 45 and 46.

[38] Rules, Art. 47.

cerned, the debate may not be concluded by a vote on a resolution concerning the debated question. Thirdly, in 1973, Parliament introduced the question time in which Council and Commission agreed to participate.[39] Here also a difference is made between the latter two institutions, since only the answers from the Commission can give rise to a debate. This distinction between the Council and the Commission corresponds to the difference in relationship which exists between Parliament and each of these institutions: the supervisory powers conferred upon Parliament concern only the Commission which is indeed under the political control of Parliament. The relationship with the Council is rather one of political co-operation and partnership and tends to find expresson in a dialogue between the two institutions:

— once a year Parliament meets with the President of the Council, in the presence of the Commission, to discuss matters of general interest on which the Council has not yet decided, the so-called "colloquies."

— similarly, a representative of the Council presents an oral report to Parliament three times a year on the activities of the Council, and the President of the Council makes a statement to Parliament on the outcome of each meeting of the European Council[40]

— furthermore, a "programme of the Presidency" is presented by the incoming President of the Council every six months, at the beginning of his six months term, and a survey of significant developments at the end of the Presidency.[41]

— finally, in pursuance of the SEA, Parliament is closely associated with the European Political Co-operation.[42] To that end the Presidency regularly informs Parliament of the foreign policy issues which are being

---

[39] Rules, Art. 47 *bis*.
[40] See, *e.g.* Bull. 12–1988, 143.
[41] *Ibid.*, 144.
[42] See SEA, Art. 30(4).

examined within the framework of the Political Co-operation.

These addresses, more than any other form of co-operation give the members of Parliament an opportunity to impress upon the Council their views on the future developments of the Community.

(3) *The motion of censure*

If Parliament were to disagree with activities of the Commission, it could adopt a "motion of censure," thereby forcing the members of the Commission to resign as a body.[43] This is by far the most impressive power vested in Parliament, but although some motions have been tabled in the past,[44] never yet has one been carried. The procedural requirements are cumbersome. First, the Treaty prescribes a "reflection time" of three days between the time the motion is tabled and the actual open vote. Secondly, the Treaty requires that a majority of the representatives cast their vote and that two thirds of them vote for the motion. Finally, the motion must be moved either by a political group or by one tenth of the Members of Parliament.

It must be underlined, however, that this censure only affects the Commission. The Council, which is the decision making body within the Community, remains outside the reach of Parliament. Whether the motion of censure will have much practical effect depends on the reaction of the members of the Commission since "they shall continue to deal with current business until they are replaced in accordance with Article 158."[45] From there on, the decisions are no longer influenced by Parliament; it has no say in the choice of the new Commissioners. The Member States could

---

[43] EEC, Art. 144.

[44] The first time was in November 1972 and was based on the failure of the Commission to submit proposals concerning the reinforcement of the budgetary powers of Parliament; it was later withdrawn.

[45] Merger Treaty, Art. 11 provides that the members of the Commission are appointed by common accord of the governments of the Member States.

very well re-appoint the same (or some of the) members, for instance on political grounds. But, whoever the members of the new Commission are, they will not forget lightly the reaction of Parliament. Therefore, whatever its ultimate effect, the motion of censure remains the clearest symbol of parliamentary control within the Communities. Finally, it should be noted that the real influence of an institution cannot, of course, be judged on the basis of the legal provisions alone; it depends in great part on the expertise of its members and their powers of persuasion. This requires concentration on internal Community affairs; after all, Parliament's creditability will depend on the influence it exercises on the development of the Community.

(4) *The General Report*

Each year the Commission must publish and submit to Parliament a General Report on the activities of the Community not later than one month before the opening of its session.[46] This report is discussed in open session. There exists an obvious link between the General Report and the motion of censure on the activities of the Commission,[47] but Parliament would certainly not wait for the publication of the report to censure the Commission.

The discussion by Parliament of the General Report gives rise to a general debate on all the facets of Community life, since the Report covers all the activities of all the institutions and bodies. However, the work of the Council and the European Investment Bank, for instance, is described in detail in their own annual reports.[48]

The General Report is supplemented by an annual Report on the Agricultural situation in the Community,[49] a Report on the

---

[46] Merger Treaty, Art. 18. According to EEC, Art. 139(1), Parliament convenes for its annual session on the second Tuesday in March. The Commission has always scrupulously respected this obligation.

[47] In the ECSC Treaty both subjects are provided for in the same article Art. 24.

[48] See the "Reviews" of the Council's work published by the Secretariat-General of the Council and the Annual Reports of the EIB.

[49] See Declaration on the System for Fixing Farm Prices contained in the Accession Documents of January 22, 1972 (J.O. 1972, L. 73/200).

Development of the Social Situation in the Community,[50] and a Report on Competition Policy.[51] The Commission also presents an annual Report on the Regional Fund,[52] on the State of the Environment[53] and on Consumer Protection and Information Policy.[54] All those Reports constitute an invaluable source of information on the activities of the Community, the problems they encounter and the proposed and adopted solutions. They are less important for the supervisory function of Parliament since it is kept well informed by the permanent contacts it maintains mainly with the Commission through the work of the parliamentary Committees in which the Commission always participates. More important, however, is the programme-address which the President of the Commission presents to Parliament at the beginning of every year and which gives rise to a general debate.

(5) *Participation in the budgetary procedure*

The budgetary procedure and the role of Parliament in it can be summarised as follows.[55]

The Commission draws up a "preliminary draft budget" covering all the expenses and revenues of the whole Community, and sends it to the Council, not later than September 1. The Council establishes a "draft budget" and sends it to Parliament, not later than October 5.

Parliament can then take one of several actions:

(a) approve the draft budget within 45 days; the budget then stands as finally approved;

(b) refrain from amending it or from proposing modifications within 45 days; the budget is then deemed to be approved;

---

[50] EEC, Art. 122.
[51] Undertaking given by the Commission to Parliament on June 7, 1971; see Resolution concerning the competition rules (O.J. 1971, C. 66/11).
[52] Reg. 2052/88, Art. 416 (O.J. 1988, L. 185/9).
[53] The first Report was published in 1977.
[54] *Ibid.* (As far as could be ascertained there have not been any since!)
[55] EEC, Art. 203.

   (c) adopt amendments and/or propose modifications

      (i) with regard to expenditure necessarily resulting from the Treaty or from acts adopted in accordance therewith ("obligatory expenditure"),[56] Parliament, acting by an absolute majority of the votes, may only propose modifications;

     (ii) with regard to other expenditures, Parliament may, acting by a majority of its members, amend the draft budget, but within a maximum rate of increase communicated by the Commission[57];

     the draft budget, together with the amendments and proposed modifications, is then forwarded to the Council.

If option (c) is adopted, the Council, after consulting the Commission and any other concerned institution, can then act under the following conditions:

—   with regard to the proposed modifications, the Council may reject them by a qualified majority (generally referred to as a "reversed majority");

—   with regard to the amendments (expenditure not necessarily resulting from legal provisions), it may modify them within 15 days by a qualified majority; in the absence of such majority the amendments stand.

If the Council accepts the proposed modifications and does not modify the amendments, the budget is deemed to be finally adopted and Parliament is informed accordingly. If, on the other hand, one or more proposed modifications are rejected or modified or amendments have been modified, the modified draft budget is returned to Parliament.

---

[56] Also referred to as "compulsory expenditure." See below "Financing Community Activities."

[57] This maximum rate of increase results from the trend of GNP within the Community, the average variations in the national budgets and the trend of the cost of living; see EEC, Art. 203(9). See Case 34/86 *Council* v. *Parliament* [1986] E.C.R. 2188 at 2210: power to increase non-compulsory expenditure.

At this stage the powers of Parliament are limited to the expenditures other than those resulting from the Treaty or from acts adopted by the institutions, and for which it has a right of amendment as described above. Parliament may within 15 days, amend or reject the modifications made by the Council to its amendments, acting by a majority of its members and three-fifths of the votes cast. Parliament then adopts the budget and the President of Parliament declares that the budget has been finally adopted.[58]

However, Parliament may, if there are important reasons, reject the draft budget acting by a majority of its members and two-thirds of the votes cast.[59]

It follows from this lengthy procedure that Parliament now has the final word, within the limits of the maximum amount of increase, with regard to the non-obligatory expenditure[60] and actually adopts the budget. On July 1, 1988 an Interinstitutional Agreement[61] came into force which covers budgetary discipline and improvement of the budgetary procedure; consequently the powers of Parliament in this field were somewhat limited.

Parliament's role does not end with the adoption of the budget; it also exercises control over its implementation. In this task it is assisted by the Court of Auditors.[62] Parliament gives a discharge to the Commission in respect of the implementation of the budget. To this end the Commission submits annually to Parliament and to the Council the accounts of the preceding financial year together with a financial statement of the assets and liabilities of the Communities.[63] The Council and Parliament, in

---

[58] See Case 34/86 *Council* v. *Parliament* (n. 57 above).
[59] EEC, Art. 203(8); this happened in 1979, see Bull. 12–1979, 93 and 120, and in 1984, see Bull. 12–1984, 28.
[60] Those non-obligatory expenditures have increased over the years from a very small percentage of the budget to nearly 25 per cent. in 1989; according to the "Financial perspective 1988–92" they will reach 40 per cent. in 1992.
[61] O.J. 1988, L. 185 and Bull. 6–1988, 112–114 and 121. The Agreement was approved by Parliament in June 1988.
[62] See below, "Other bodies of the European Communities."
[63] Treaty amending certain financial provisions, Arts. 14 and 17 and EEC, Arts. 205A and 206. For 1977, for instance, see O.J. 1979, L. 331/1. In 1984, Parliament refused to discharge the Commission with regard to the 1982 budget implementation; see Bull. 11–1984, 67.

turn, examine the accounts and statement together with the annual report of the Court of Auditors. In giving a discharge to the Commission, Parliament acts on a recommendation from the Council.

(6) *Procedures in the Court of Justice*

Apart from intervening in cases before the Court,[64] instituting third party proceedings to contest a judgment and applying for interpretation of a judgment, Parliament may bring an action before the Court against the Council and/or the Commission for failure of these institutions to act in infringement of the Treaty.[65]

Parliament however is much more interested in actions brought against acts of the Council or the Commission since this would allow it to challenge these institutions more effectively. Unfortunately for Parliament, the Treaty only confers upon the Council and the Commission the right to ask the Court to review the legality of such acts.[66] However, in May 1990, the Court accepted the admissibility of an action brought by Parliament against a Council measure on condition that the action aims at preserving Parliament's prerogatives.[67]

(7) *Participation in other Community Activities*

Several agreements of association between the Community and third States provide for a joint Parliamentary Committee. This is the case, *e.g.* for the EEC–Turkey Association. [68] Eighteen representatives of Parliament sit on each one of these commit-

---

[64] See, *e.g.* Resolution of December 14, 1979 (O.J. 1980, C. 4/52) to intervene in Case 138/79 *SA Roquette Frères* v. *Council* [1980] E.C.R. 3333 and in Case 139/79 *Maizena* v. *Council* [1980] E.C.R. 3393.

[65] EEC, Art. 175(1) and (2). See Case 13/83 *Parliament* v. *Council* [1985] E.C.R. 1556.

[66] EEC, Art. 173. See Case 302/87 *Parliament* v. *Council*, judgment of September 27, 1988 (not yet published). The Court stated that no parallel can be drawn between the capacity of a defendant and that of an applicant for judicial review.

[67] Case 70/88 *Parliament* v. *Council* May 22, 1990, not yet published).

[68] See Art. 27 of the Agreement (O.J. 1964, 3687).

tees. Similarly the ACP-EEC Convention[69] provides for a Consultative Assembly of which several representatives of Parliament are members. Finally, it should be noted that Parliament holds an annual joint meeting with the Consultative Assembly of the Council of Europe.[70]

3. Internal organisation

The internal organisation of Parliament is broadly comparable to that of any national Parliament. It is based on a double structure; the political parties (called "groups") and the parliamentary committees.

(1) *Political groups*

Representatives sit in eleven multinational political groups.[71] However, the Act concerning the elections stipulates that representatives shall vote on an individual basis and that they shall not be bound by any instruction nor receive a binding mandate.[72]

The Rules of procedure of Parliament require for the formation of a political group 21 representatives when they belong to

---

[69] See Fourth ACP-EEC Convention, Art. 32 (The Courier No. 120—March -April 1990, 16).
[70] See Bull. 1–1978, 74.
[71] Situation on January 1, 1990:

Socialists	180
European People's Party	121
Liberal, Democratic and Reformist Group	49
European Democratic Group	34
Greens	29
European Unitarian Left	28
European Democratic Alliance	22
Technical Group of the European Right	17
Left Unity group	14
Rainbow Group	14
Non-affiliated	10

[72] Act concerning direct election, Art. 4(1). There are no Party whips in the European Parliament.

one single Member State, 15 when they come from two Member States and 10 when the number of Member States is three or more[73]; clearly this rule was made to encourage the formation of trans-national groups which is one of the main characteristics of the European Parliament.

(2) *Parliamentary committees*

The rules of procedure provide that Parliament can set up standing or temporary, general or special committees and determine their task.[74]

Generally speaking the committees prepare the resolutions to be adopted by Parliament in plenary session; when Parliament is consulted by the Council on Commission proposals, they are examined by the relevant committee(s) which report(s) back to Parliament. The latter expresses its "opinion" in the form of a "Resolution."[75]

(3) *Bureau*

Parliament elects a President and 12 vice-Presidents which together constitute the "Bureau," *i.e.* the executive body. This Bureau drafts the agenda of the sessions, decides on matters of competence and makes up the preliminary draft of Parliament's budget.[76] The rules also provide for an "enlarged Bureau"

[73] Rules, Art. 36.
[74] At the beginning of 1990, the Parliament's committees numbered 18: Political Affairs (56 members), Agriculture, Fisheries and Rural Development (47), Budgets (32), Economic and Monetary Affairs and Industrial Policy (52), Energy, Research and Technology (34), External Economic Relations (29), Legal Affairs and Citizens' Rights (34), Social Affairs, Employment and Regional Planning (38), Transport and Tourism (30), the Environment, Public Health and Consumer Protection (51), Youth, Culture, Education, the Media and Sport (31), Development and Co-operation (43), Budgetary Control (28), Institutional Affairs (38), the Rules of Procedure, the Verification of Credentials and Immunities (27), Women's Rights (33), Petitions (25).
In January 1988 Parliament set up a committee of inquiry into the affair surrounding the nuclear power plant in Mol, Belgium.
[75] Rules, Arts. 37–44.
[76] Rules, Arts. 5–7, 12 and 50.

consisting of the Bureau and the Presidents of the political groups; it is the enlarged Bureau which in fact constitutes the ultimate centre of decision-making for all internal matters.

Parliament has its own staff of about 3000 permanent and 400 temporary posts grouped in a "Secretariat" headed by a Secretary-General.

(4) *Sessions and meeting place(s)*

Parliament holds annual sessions, *i.e.* lasting 12 months, but only sits during 12 part-sessions which last 5 days.[77] It meets without requiring to be convened on the second Tuesday in March. Parliament may also meet in extraordinary session. All meetings are held in Strasbourg, although Parliament is trying hard to get away from there for the sake of efficiency.[78]

Members of the Commission may attend all meetings and the Council has agreed to be represented at all the plenary sessions.

The minutes of the meetings are published in the Official Journal and the full debates are published in an annex thereto.

Except for the adoption of the motion of censure and the budgetary procedure,[79] Parliament acts by a majority of the votes cast. There is a quorum when the majority of the representatives are present.[80]

---

[77] Parliament is understood to be "in session," even if not actually sitting, until the session is declared closed. See Case 101/63 *Wagner* v. *Fohrman and Krier* [1964] E.C.R. 195 and Case 149/85 *Wybot* v. *Faure* [1986] E.C.R. 2391.

[78] This is understandable since the Secretariat is located in Luxembourg, the Committees always meet in Brussels and only the part-sessions are held in Strasbourg. Parliament's decision to hold its sessions wherever it decides was attacked by Luxembourg; see Case 230/81, *Luxembourg* v. *Parliament* [1983] E.C.R. 255; Case 108/83, *Luxembourg* v. *Parliament* [1984] E.C.R. 1945 (Parliament has no right to decide on the location of its departments); and Case 358/85, *France* v. *European Parliament* (Resolution on the infrastructure necessary to hold meetings in Brussels) [1986] E.C.R. 2149 (not a decision on the merits of the case).

[79] For the motion, see EEC, Art. 144 and for the budget see EEC, Art. 203(6) and (8).

[80] Under Art. 33(3) of the Rules, votes (except nominal votes) are always valid as long as the President has not been formally requested, before the vote, to ascertain the number of members present.

4. Conclusion

Before 1979, the year of the first direct elections, the increasingly important role played by Parliament within the institutional system of the Community was mainly due to the quality of its members and the dual membership which gave them a political power base in their own country; in most cases the latter has disappeared with the direct elections.

In the second edition of this book it was stated that "election by universal suffrage only has sense if at the same time the formal powers of the Assembly are increased."[81] Since then Parliament has obtained a limited co-decision right in budgetary matters, the so-called "conciliation procedure" and now the "co-operation procedure" in the legislative field, but as was pointed out above, Parliament still does not enjoy the normal Parliamentary prerogatives. Before this can change its members will, at least, have to become directly responsible towards a well-defined electorate.

II. THE COUNCIL

To attain the objectives assigned to the Community, the Treaty provides for two means: the establishment of the common market and the progressive approximation of the economic policies of the Member States.[82] To implement the second of those two means is the proper task of the Council, as defined by the Treaty: "ensure co-ordination of the general economic policies of the Member States."[83] At first, the Treaty rules concerning economic policies were very general indeed; they were however complemented by the SEA which, as will be seen, added a chapter on "co-operation in economic and monetary policy," one on "economic and social cohesion" and one on "research and technological development." Nonetheless these provisions do not impose

[81] *A Guide to European Community Law* (1975), p. 173.
[82] EEC, Art. 2.
[83] EEC, Art. 145.

very precise obligations upon the Member States. It is in the course of the elaboration of the necessary policies that more concrete rules are formulated by the Council. In doing so the latter somehow continues the legislative work of the drafters of the Treaties establishing the Communities.

1. Organisational aspects

(1) *Members of the Council*

The Council consists of representatives of the Member States, each government delegating to it one of its members.[84] Being representatives of their respective countries, the members of the Council act on the basis of instructions or mandates received from their governments. They do not, however, constitute a conference of government representatives comparable to those existing in international organisations[85]; neither are they designated to fulfil a Community function in the sense MEPs, Commissioners and Judges are. They constitute an institution of the Community and as such they must always act in the Community interest. It is not evident that this is always clearly perceived by all participants at the Council meetings.

It is left to the governments to decide which one of their members they send to the Council meetings, and although the Treaty refers to "one" member, often two or more members of a government are present at the same session; only one of them has the right to vote. Besides the "general" Councils which are composed of the Ministers of Foreign Affairs, specialised Council meetings take place to deal with specific subjects such as agriculture, economy and finance (the so-called "ecofin"), social affairs, environment, etc. Those Council meetings are attended by the Ministers nationally responsible for these matters. Consequently,

---

[84] Merger Treaty, Art. 2(1).
[85] *e.g.* the Committee of Ministers of the Council of Europe, Statute, Art. 13 *et seq.*, or the Council of the Organisation for Economic Co-operation and Development, Convention, Art. 7.

it is not unusual to have various Council meetings in session at the same moment.

When no member of a government can be present at a Council meeting, the Member State in question may send a civil servant[86]; the latter, however, has no vote. But, in case of absence, a member may ask another member to vote on his behalf; no member may act on behalf of more than one other member.[87]

Neither the Treaty, nor the Rules of Procedure[88] require a quorum. However, since the Council can only, in the simplest of cases, act by a majority of its members[89] (at present 12), no decision can be taken unless seven votes are cast, which means that a minimum of four members must be present.[90]

Council meetings are convened by the President on his own initiative or at the request of one of the members or of the Commission.[91] The office of President is held for a term of six months by each member of the Council in turn, according to an alphabetical order. Every six years this order is changed in such a way as to allow the Presidencies which normally start on January 1, to start on July 1.[92] The same rotation applies to all the subordinate bodies such as the Committee of Permanent Representatives,[93] the Council working groups and other meetings of Ministers such as those on Political Co-operation.[94] The meetings of the Council are attended by the Commission[95] represented by

---

[86] Rules of procedure, Art. 4 (O.J. 1979, L. 268/1); usually this is the Permanent Representative, see below.

[87] EEC, Art. 150.

[88] The rules of procedure were adopted by the Council on April 15, 1958; see Merger Treaty, Art. 5.

[89] EEC, Art. 148(1); for further details, see below, "Voting Procedure."

[90] When unanimity is required, the quorum obviously becomes six although abstention by members present or represented does not prevent the adoption of acts requiring unanimity; see EEC, Art. 148(3).

[91] Merger Treaty, Art. 3.

[92] The office of President is held in the following alphabetical order corresponding to the first letter of each country's name in the national language: Belgium, Denmark, Germany, Greece, Spain, France, Ireland, Italy, Luxembourg, Netherlands, Portugal and United Kingdom (EEC, Art. 148(2)).

[93] See below.

[94] *Ibid.*

[95] Rules of procedure, Art. 4(a), (b).

its President and/or those Commission members who are more particularly responsible for the subjects under discussion.

(2) *Voting procedure*

The basic rule with regard to voting is that the Council acts by a majority of its members,[96] except where otherwise provided in the Treaty.[97] Since most Treaty provisions do provide otherwise, the general rule is in fact the exception. The other voting procedures are:

(a) *Qualified majority when the Council is acting on a proposal from the Commission*; this is usually the case[98]; for this purpose the votes of the members are weighted, and out of a total of 76[99] at least 54 votes in favour are required to adopt an act. This means *inter alia* that the four largest members (Germany, France, Italy and the United Kingdom) cannot impose their will on the other members, but that the latter, acting together, or two large Member States, can block qualified majority decisions.

(b) *Qualified majority when the Council acts without a proposal from the Commission*[1]; in this case the additional

---

[96] Since there are presently 12 members, the majority is seven.

[97] EEC, Art. 148(1).

[98] See, *e.g.* EEC, Arts. 20, 28, 38(3), 43(2), 44(5), 54(2), 57, 63(2), 69, 75(1), and 101. The SEA added to this list *inter alia* Arts. 59(2), 70(1), 84(2), 100a, 100b, 118a, 130c, 130e, 149(2)(a) and (e).

[99] EEC, Art. 148(2):

Belgium	5	Ireland	3
Denmark	3	Italy	10
Germany	10	Luxembourg	2
Greece	5	Netherlands	5
Spain	8	Portugal	5
France	10	United Kingdom	10

[1] See, *e.g.* EEC, Arts. 73(2), 106(2), 108(2), (3), 109, 111, 113, 114, 154, 204 and 206.

condition applies that the 54 votes must be cast by at least eight members; concretely speaking this means that a two-thirds majority of the members is required to pass the act.

(c) *Unanimous vote*; this had become the common practice, although it is only required by the Treaty in a limited number of cases[2] and each time the Council, acting on a proposal from the Commission, wants to adopt an act constituting an amendment to that proposal.[3] This practice finds its origin in the Arrangement regarding majority voting adopted by the Council at its meeting of January 28 and 29, 1966, in Luxembourg, improperly referred to as the "Luxembourg Agreement" or "Accord"; this arrangement ended the most serious crisis the Community has known and which was started by the oversensitive and nationalistic government of General De Gaulle.

Although the SEA not only makes no reference to the arrangement but can be considered as having pre-empted it by clearly indicating when majority voting applies, it might be useful to reproduce here part of the terms of the arrangement.

1. Where, in the case of decisions which may be taken by majority vote on a Commission proposal and very important interests of one or more partners are at stake, the members of the Council will endeavour, within a reasonable time, to reach solutions which can be adopted by all the members of the Council while respecting their

---

[2] EEC, Arts. 14(7), 45(3), 76, 93(2), 136, 188, 200(3), 223(3), 227(2), 237, 238. In many cases the Treaty provides for a unanimous vote during a certain period after the entry into force of the Treaty (all those time periods have now elapsed) and a qualified majority afterwards; see EEC, Arts. 28, 33, 42–44, 54, 56, 57, 63, 69, 75, 87, 101 and 111–114. The SEA added to this list Arts. 130d, q and s, 145, 149(2) (d), (e), 168a (1), (4).

[3] EEC, Art. 149.

   mutual interests and those of the Community, in accordance with Article 2 of the EEC Treaty.

2. With regard to the preceeding paragraph, the French
   delegation considers that, where very important interests
   are at stake, the discussion must be continued until
   unanimous agreement is reached.

3. The six delegations note that there is a divergence of
   views on what should be done in the event of failure to
   reach complete agreement.

The main question was therefore: what happens in the case of
such a failure? For five delegations the rules of the Treaty then
apply and decisions can be taken by qualified majority; for
France, discussions should continue until unanimity is reached.
Fortunately, this quarrel is now considered by most as belonging
to the past and the decisions taken at the European Council,
meeting at Strasbourg in December 1989, concerning the Economic and Monetary Union and the Social Charter, against an
oversensitive and nationalistic British Prime Minister, indicate
that progress in the Community can no longer be blocked by a
single Member State. The Luxembourg Arrangement is dead
indeed!
   A final observation worth noting concerning the voting procedure of the Council is that acts on an urgent matter may be
adopted by "written procedure."[4]

(3) *Committee of permanent representatives—Coreper*[5]

The creation of this committee stems from the fact that the
Council meets no more than a few days a month and that with
the increase of Community business a more permanent presence

---

[4] Rules of Procedure, Art. 6.
[5] COmité des REpresentants PERmanents. It is subdivided into Coreper I
composed of the deputy Permanent Representatives, which handles *inter alia*
agriculture, and Coreper II formed by the Ambassadors.

seemed required. The Permanent Representatives—high level civil servants with the rank of ambassador—follow the various Community activities practically on a day-to-day basis. They are not however empowered to take decisions; they constitute a subordinate organ of the Council and are not a gathering of deputies of the members of the Council; indeed, the latter (like the other institutions) may not delegate their power of decision. The powers delegated by the Council to the Commission under Article 155 are powers of implementation.

Nevertheless, once Coreper has reached agreement, for instance on a proposal from the Commission, the decision of the Council can, for all practical purposes, be considered as having been adopted. This is expressed by the fact that in such a case the matter is put on the agenda of the next Council meeting as an "A point."[6] The practice is that the Council accepts all such points at the beginning of its meeting and thereby transforms them into binding legal acts as provided for in the Treaty. It must, however, be emphasised that the Council is in no way bound to accept these "A points" and any Council member is free to ask for a discussion on the subject, in which case it is placed on the agenda of the next meeting, but then as a "B point."

When no agreement can be reached on a subject at Coreper level, but it is thought that a solution can be found at ministerial level, or such is explicitly requested by one of the Permanent Representatives, the subject is placed on the Council's agenda as a "B point," *i.e.* a point on which discussion is needed, since no solution has been found.

Coreper is assisted in its work by a whole series of working groups, which, in turn, prepare its work and indirectly the work of the Council. These working groups are composed of senior national civil servants and convene whenever necessary to examine subjects which fall within their competence nationally. When a Commission proposal is sent to the Council, it is examined in the first place by Coreper which decides either to examine it further or ask one of the working groups to examine it and report

---

[6] Rules of Procedure, Art. 2(6).

to the Committee; at least that is the theory. In fact the attribution of dossiers to the various working groups is decided by the Presidency, for which read the Secretary-General.

Practically all the meetings of the Council, Committee and working groups are attended by the Commission. Each one of these meetings is presided over by a national of the Member State which holds the office of President.[7]

The great advantage of having those working groups, composed of national civil servants, is that the national view is clearly expressed in Brussels, while the national administrations are informed, through these direct contacts, of the opinion of the Commission and the other Member States.

In the same way it can be said that the Permanent Representatives fulfil a double function: they defend the national interests within the Community and at the same time represent the Community's point of view at home. They thus constitute a precious link between the national administrations and the European institutions.

(4) *The European Council*

When important decisions were no longer taken by qualified majority and when the subjects to be decided upon became more and more political because they were vital for the general economic development of the Member States, the decision-making process within the Community came virtually to a halt. It became obvious that new impulses had to be given and new methods of decision-making had to be provided. Since the Council is already a gathering of high level politicians, the solution was sought more and more in the Conferences of Heads of State or of Government[8] which would take the necessary decisions at the highest political level. At the 1974 Summit meeting, the participants

---

[7] See Merger Treaty, Art. 2.
[8] The first such conference was held at Paris on February 10 and 11, 1961 (see Communiqué in Bull. 3–1961, 13); and the second at Bonn on July 19, 1961, where it was decided to hold such meetings at regular intervals (see Communiqué, Bull. 7/8–1961, 40).

"recognised the need for an overall approach to the internal problems involved in achieving European unity and the external problems facing Europe—consider it essential to ensure progress and overall consistency in the activities of the Communities and in the work on political co-operation—and [have] therefore decided to meet, accompanied by the Ministers of Foreign Affairs, three times a year and, whenever necessary, in the Council of the Communities and in the context of Political Co-operation."[9]

Consequently, since 1975, the Heads of State[10] or of Government meet three[11] times a year as the "European Council." It is presided over by the "Head" whose representative holds the office of President of the Council; the secretariat is provided for by the Secretaries General of the Council and the Commission. The President and the senior vice-President of the Commission are always present.

The European Council has, to date, mainly confined itself to issuing general guidelines which have then been acted upon by the Council and the Commission.[12] Notwithstanding the fact that "the prospect of regular European Council meetings acted as a catalyst, expediting certain Council work at ministerial level,"[13] it does happen that matters are simply not decided at Council level, but left to fill the agenda of the European Council; fortunately, the latter has always refused to decide on technical matters and limited itself, generally speaking[14], to broad policy lines. The European Council could however, if it decided to do so, meet as the Council and, as such, take binding decisions, on the condition

[9] Eighth General Report (1974), 297.
[10] The mention of the "Head of State" was necessary to recognise the participation of the French President who also functions as "Head of Government"; all the other Member States are represented by their "Prime Minister."
[11] This has been tacitly reduced to two, to correspond to the end of each semester of the Council Presidency.
[12] Ninth General Report (1975), 19.
[13] *Ibid.*
[14] *e.g.* in March (Brussels) and June (Fontainebleau) 1984, detailed budgetary matters were discussed; see Bull. 3–1984, 7 and 6–1984, 7.

of course that all the rules of the Treaty applying in such a case be observed, *i.e.* proposal from the Commission and consultation of Parliament if provided for. The existence of the European Council has been formally recognised by the SEA:

> "The European Council shall bring together the Heads of State or of Government of the Member States and the President of the Commission of the European Community. They shall be assisted by the Ministers for Foreign Affairs and by a member of the Commission. The European Council shall meet at least twice a year."[15]

The European Council also meets in the context of the Political Co-operation[16]; although the latter was formalised by the SEA, the European Council is not mentioned as such in this regard.[17] In this capacity, it functions as an informal gathering of top politicians where all major political problems can be freely discussed.

At the European Council meeting in London on June 29 and 30, 1977, agreement was reached on a framework for the organisation of the meetings.[18] It was also agreed that for "discussions aimed at reaching decisions or issuing statements there should be a record of conclusions, which should be issued on the authority of the Presidency."[19]

Notwithstanding the existence of some unresolved problems with regard to the relations between the European Council and the other Institutions, particularly Parliament, this new Community organ fulfils an extremely important role in determining policies, both within the Community and towards third countries.

---

[15] SEA, Art. 2.
[16] See below Chap. V, Part Three.
[17] See SEA, "Provisions on European co-operation in the sphere of foreign policy," Art. 30. This part of the Act is drafted as a separate instrument in the form of an international agreement; it was however decided not to make two acts but a "Single" one.
[18] See Bull. 6–1977, 83.
[19] Those "conclusions" are published in the Bulletin of the European Communities. The preamble of the SEA refers to several of those meetings.

(5) *Representatives of the Member States in Council*

In accordance with the Treaty, certain decisions must be taken by the Member States acting by "common accord"[20]; in such cases the members of the Council meet as a "conference of representatives of the governments of the Member States."[21] This kind of conference and the acts it issues are to be distinguished from the meetings of the "representatives of the governments of the Member States meeting within the Council," which are not provided for in the Treaty. The legal character of such meetings within the Council (not "of" the Council), and of its decisions raises the same problems as the European Council and its decisions. In practice, meetings within the Council deal with matters for which the Community itself lacks competence, but which, directly or indirectly, affect Community powers[22] or are connected with its activities.[23]

2. Tasks and powers of the Council

(1) *Decision-making*

The Council is the central institution of the Community endowed with the "power to take decisions."[24] However, the balance of powers is such that, in most cases, the Council can only act on the basis of a proposal from the Commission and under the

---

[20] See EEC, Art. 167; Merger Treaty, Art. 11.

[21] See EEC, Art. 236.

[22] See Resolution of the Council and the Ministers of Education meeting within the Council of February 9, 1976, on the action programme in the educational field (O.J. 1976, C.38/1).

[23] As stated in the Act of Accession, Art. 3(1) "The new Member States accede by this Act to the decisions and agreements adopted by the Representatives of the Governments of the Member States meeting in Council. They undertake to accede from the date of accession to all other agreements concluded by the original Member States relating to the functioning of the Communities or connected with their activities."

[24] EEC, Art. 145. It should be noted that the Commission also has powers to take decisions; see below, "Commission."

judicial control of the Court of Justice. Particularly important is the right of legislative initiative conferred upon the Commission. When the Council meets to "make regulations, issue directives, take decisions,"[25] it normally does so on the basis of a draft put before it by the Commission and therefore, one might presume, formulated in a way which furthers the Community interest.

If the Council wants to adopt an act constituting an amendment of that proposal, it may only do so acting unanimously. This latitude however does not extend to adopting an act which bears no resemblance to the original proposal. One must apply here, by analogy, the Court's view on the requirement for renewed consultation of Parliament by the Council in case the latter modifies the wording of the proposal in such a way as to affect its substance.[26] This means that when the modifications which the Council unilaterally introduces in a Commission proposal affect its substance, the decision of the Council is annulable on the ground of infringement of an essential procedural requirement.[27] Indeed in such a case it could not be said that the decision was taken "on a proposal from the Commission." The provision granting power to the Council to amend a Commission proposal, being an exception to a geneal rule, must be strictly interpreted.[28]

The Treaty explicitly provides that the Council shall exercise its powers to take decisions "in accordance with the provisions of this Treaty."[29] It thereby restates a basic principle underlying the transfer of sovereign powers from the Member States to the Community institutions. This principle can be found at the very beginning of all the European Treaties[30]: "each institution shall act within the limits of the power conferred upon it by this Treaty." The Council, therefore, is not endowed with a general

---

[25] EEC, Art. 189(1).

[26] Case 41/69 *ACF Chemiefarma* v. *Commission* [1970] E.C.R. 661 at 662(3).

[27] EEC, Art. 173.

[28] Another question is whether the Commission, in order to avoid amendments to its proposal, may withdraw it. Since one may not deny the Council the right to amend those proposals within acceptable limits, withdrawing a proposal under those conditions would empty Art. 149(1) of its content.

[29] EEC, Art. 145.

[30] ECSC, Art. 3; EEC, Art. 4 and Euratom, Art. 3.

regulatory competence, but may only take those decisions which are explicitly provided for by a provision of Community legislation[31]; in other words it only has "conferred powers."

There are, however, cases where action by the Council appears necessary to attain one of the objectives of the Community, while the Treaty has not provided the necessary powers. In such a case, the Council may, acting unanimously on a proposal from the Commission and after consulting Parliament, take the appropriate measures.[32] This must not, however, be considered as opening unlimited opportunity for the institutions to increase the powers of the Council, although it does constitute a way of supplementing the Treaty provisions without going through the cumbersome procedure for amending the Treaty.[33] Indeed, the appropriate measures may only be taken when action is necessary "to attain one of the objectives of the Treaty," which clearly indicates that the powers granted by this provision are purely complementary. Also, the required unanimous vote of the Council should provide the necessary guarantee, since the extension of the Community's powers will, almost inevitably, reduce the powers of the Member States in the same proportion. Furthermore, the Commission's proposal and the opinion of Parliament should ensure that the Community's interests are sufficiently taken into consideration.[34] Finally, there is always the judicial control by the Court of Justice.[35]

Related to the principle of "conferred powers" is the question of "implied powers." In several cases the Court has admitted that "rules established by international agreements or by law are

---

[31] See Rules of procedure of the Council, Art. 11, It provides that a Council regulation must contain the indication of the provision by virtue of which the regulation is enacted. For further details see below, "Community Acts."

[32] EEC, Art. 235.

[33] EEC, Art. 236.

[34] At the Paris Summit meeting in October 1972, it was agreed that for the purpose of carrying out the tasks laid down in the different programmes of action, "it was desirable to make the widest possible use of all the dispositions of the Treaties, including Art. 235"; (Cmn. 5109, para. 15).

[35] See Case 8/73 *Hauptzollamt Bremerhaven* v. *Massey-Fergusson* [1973] E.C.R. 897, where the Court accepted the use of Art. 235 and Case 242/87 *Commission* v. *Council,* judgment of May 30, 1989, (not yet published).

considered to imply those rules without which the first either would have no sense or could not be reasonably or successfully applied."[36] This prudent approach to a very delicate question can certainly not be considered as opening the door to extensive Treaty interpretation in regard to the powers of the Community institutions. The principle of "conferred powers" therefore stands.

The decision-making powers of the Council are provided *inter alia* in the field of legislation, financing Community activities and international relations.

When the Council enacts legislation through regulations, directives and decisions, it in fact continues, as was pointed out, the work of the draftsmen of the Treaty. This is particularly true for the EEC Treaty which, in many aspects, contains no more than general principles to guide the Community law-makers and the necessary rules of procedure.[37]

The budgetary powers have been examined in some detail in the previous section on the European Parliament.[38]

As for the international agreements to be entered into by the Community, the powers to do so are based upon the fact that the Community was given legal personality.[39] The Treaty provides that agreements between the Community and one or more States or international organisations shall be negotiated by the Commission and concluded by the Council.[40]

---

[36] Case 8/55 *Fédération Charbonnière de Belgique* v. *High Authority* [1954–1956] E.C.R. 245 at 299 and Case 22/70 *Commission* v. *Council* [1971] E.C.R. 263 at 280(72), where the Court found that the authority to enter into international agreements may flow implicitly from the Treaty provisions.

[37] See, *e.g.* Agricultural policy: EEC, Art. 39 sets out the "objectives," while Art. 43 provides that "the Council shall, on a proposal from the Commission and after consulting the European Parliament, acting unanimously . . . make regulations, issue directives, or take decisions"; free movement of labour, EEC, Arts. 48, 49; the right of establishment, EEC, Art. 54; transport, EEC, Art. 75; competition, EEC, Art. 87; approximation of laws, EEC, Art. 100. The EEC Treaty is therefore referred to as a "*traité-cadre*," as opposed to the ECSC and Euratom Treaties which constitute "*traités-loi*."

[38] See above under (5) "Participation in the budgetary procedure."

[39] EEC, Art. 210.

[40] EEC, Art. 228; see below, "External Relations."

(2) *Co-ordination of economic policies*

Besides having the power to take decisions in all cases provided for by the Treaty, in order to ensure that the objectives set out therein are attained, the Council is more specifically entrusted with the task to "ensure co-ordination of the general economic policies of the Member States."[41]

This co-ordination of the general economic policies constitutes a necessary complement to the establishment and functioning of the common market. Indeed the latter requires implementation of policies in an increasing number of areas, if the "functioning" is to stay abreast with all-over developments in the economic and monetary fields.

Furthermore, the tasks of the Council in this area are by their very nature a question of policy-making rather than law-making; they are not governed by precise timetables set out in the Treaty (as is the case with the establishment of the common market), because they grow and vary with economic and political circumstances. Those tasks are referred to in the Treaty as "Economic policy," "Conjunctural policy," "Balance of payments" and "Commercial policy"; as was indicated, the SEA added to this "Co-operation in economic and monetary policy (Economic and Monetary Union)," "Social policy," "Economic and social cohesion," "Research and technological development" and "Environment."[42]

It should be noted that with regard to the original fields of activity, the Treaty refers to the "application of procedures" rather than to positive action in the form of legislation.[43] This explains the great variety of acts and the number of bodies involved in defining those policies: Declarations of the Council, Resolutions of the Council and of the Representatives of the Governments of the Member States, Work programmes, etc. Out of this ill-defined situation grew, as was mentioned, the necessity to set up an organ with incontestable political power, *i.e.* the

[41] EEC, Art. 145.
[42] EEC, Part Three, Title II and SEA, Arts. 20 to 25.
[43] EEC, Art. 3(g).

meetings of Heads of State or of Government, which later became the European Council.[44] It will also be noticed that with regard to the above-mentioned policies, the Treaty either provides that the Member States shall regard them "as a matter of common concern"[45] or "pursue the needed economic policies"[46] or "co-ordinate their economic policies [and] . . . shall provide for co-operation between their appropriate administrative departments"[47] or, finally, that Member States shall "proceed by common action."[48] The SEA succeeded in inventing new expressions such as "shall co-operate in accordance with the objectives"[49] or "Member States shall pay particular attention to,"[50] or "the Commission shall endeavour to develop,"[51] although in several instances the SEA also provides for directives.[52]

Clearly, the task of co-odinating economic policies is both essential for the develoment of the Community and ill-defined as regards its means and ultimate objectives.[53]

Nevertheless the system works and consideable progress has been made, such as the setting-up of the European Monetary System for which the Treaty provided neither powers nor procedures. However, this success does not make the actual situation satisfactory, since the absence of procedures means that the delicate checks and balances of the institutional framework do not function. When Council decisions are not taken in the form

---

[44] See previous section (4) "The European Council."
[45] EEC, Arts. 103(1) and 107(1).
[46] EEC, Art. 104.
[47] EEC, Art. 105.
[48] EEC, Art. 116, para. 1.
[49] SEA, Art. 102 A(1).
[50] SEA, Art. 118A.
[51] SEA, Art. 118B.
[52] SEA, Arts. 118A(2) and 130d.
[53] At its November 1976 meeting in The Hague, the European Council sought to define the ultimate objective as "European Union." See Statement published at that occasion, Bull. 11–1976, 93. On June 19, 1983, at Stuttgart, the Heads of State or of Government signed the "Solemn Declaration on European Union" designed to further European integration (Bull. 6–1983, 24). In its Preamble and Art. 1, the SEA refers to this Declaration. Earlier, at their conference of 1972 in Paris, the Heads had approved the objective of progressive realisation of Economic and Monetary Union.

of "regulations," "directives" or "decisions," there is often no Commission proposal, no consultation of Parliament, and the possibility of judicial control by the Court is doubtful. The same is true when decisions, often of vital importance to the Community, are taken by the European Council. One gets the impression that the more important the decisions, the more informal they are!

It seems evident that some solution will have to be found, if one wants to preserve a democratic approach to the exercise of the powers transferred by the Member States to the Community institutions.

(3) *Political co-operation*

In the final communiqué of the Conference of the Heads of State or of Government in December 1969 at The Hague, the Ministers for Foreign Affairs were instructed to study the best way of achieving progress in the matter of political unification within the context of enlargement.[54] At the request of the Ministers for Foreign Affairs, Mr. Davignon submitted a report which was accepted by the Ministers[55] and in 1974, the Heads of State or of Government adopted a second report.[56] Finally, in 1986, the Member States adopted the SEA which contains a Title III: "Provisions on European co-operation in the sphere of foreign policy." The latter thereby formally became part of the Treaty.

As was pointed out before, this part of the SEA is drafted in the form of a formal international agreement wherein the signatories are referred to as "High Contracting Parties" rather than the usual and simpler "Member States."[57]

In pursuance of the SEA, the Member States "endeavour jointly to formulate and implement a European foreign policy." This is to be achieved in the following way:

[54] Third General Report (1969), 489(15).
[55] See Bull. 11–1970, 9.
[56] See Seventh General Report (1973), 502.
[57] As was pointed out above, this text was at first supposed to be a separate agreement between the Member States, besides the European Act; having decided to merge the two, the latter became the "single" act!

1. The Member States inform and consult each other before deciding on a final national position. They shall give due consideration to the desirability of adopting and implementing "common European positions" and shall ensure that "common principles and objectives" are gradually defined while avoiding "any action or position which impairs their effectiveness as a cohesive force in international affairs."[58]

2. The Ministers for Foreign Affairs and a member of the Commission meet at least four times a year, the Commission and Parliament being fully associated.[59]

3. The Member States are ready to co-ordinate their positions more closely on the political and economic aspects of "security."[60]

4. The Member States shall endeavour to adopt common positions in international institutions and at international conferences.[61]

5. They shall organise a political dialogue with third countries and intensify co-operation between their representations accredited to third countries.[62]

6. The Presidency of the Political Co-operation is held by the Member State which holds the Presidency of the Council.[63]

7. A Political Committee is set up, composed of the political Directors; it has the direction of a European Corres-

---

[58] SEA, Art. 30(1) and (2).
[59] SEA, Art. 30(3) and (4).
[60] SEA, Art. 30(6).
[61] SEA, Art. 30(7).
[62] SEA, Art. 30(8) and (9).
[63] SEA, Art. 30(10).

pondent's Group, entrusted with monitoring the implementation of the European Political Co-operation and of
Working Groups.[64]

8. Finally a secretariat is based in Brussels.[65]

This detailed set-up strongly resembles that of an institution
and it is important to note that the Political Co-operation
machinery through which the Member States deal with problems
of international politics, is distinct, and additional to, the
activities of the institutions of the Community. Both are now
based on commitments the Member States have undertaken
under the Treaty, but Political Co-operation takes place outside
the usual institutional procedures which apply for all the other
Community activities; consequently, two parallel systems co-exist
within the Community: one is "communautaire," the other is
"inter-governmental." Since the Community is getting more and
more involved in several areas of political co-operation,[66] this
situation does not seem to be satisfactory from an institutional
point of view, although, as was pointed out, the Commission and
Parliament are now closely involved in this Political Co-
operation.

III. THE COMMISSION

Although the Commission participates, as was seen, in the law-
making process of the Community when it exercises its right of
initiative by submitting the required proposals to the Council, the
latter must be considered the Community legislator. The Commission, on the other hand, is responsible for the functioning and
development of the common market and is the "guardian of the
Treaty," *i.e.* makes sure everybody acts in accordance with the

---

[64] SEA, Art. 30(10)(c), (d), (e), (f).
[65] SEA, Art. 30(9).
[66] See, *e.g.* the mandate given to the Commission by the Group of the seven most
industrialised countries with regard to aid to Poland and Hungary.

rules included therein. The Commission also administers the Community's finances, negotiates the international agreements, represents the Community both inside the Community and in the international field and exercises its own power of decision.[67] In short, it should be seen as the executive branch of the Community. As such, it constitutes the moving power behind the Community's activities, and its uninterrupted presence on the Brussels scene, its competent staff and its world-wide relations, create the necessary conditions for it to play the major role within the institutional system of the Community.

More important, however, is the fact that it embodies and represents the common or Community interest and is responsible for ensuring that this interest prevails when decisions are taken by the Member States, the Council and natural or legal persons alike.

1. The European Commissioners

The present Commission consists of 17 members, which, everybody seems to agree, is too many!

The requirements for designation as a European Commissioner are very broadly defined: a member of the Commission must be a national of one of the Member States,[68] and no more than two may have the same nationality.[69] The Treaty also provides that members "shall be chosen on the grounds of their general competence" and that their "independence" must be "beyond doubt."[70]

This independence, which is the main characteristic of the Commission, is given a concrete meaning by the conditions

---

[67] See, *inter alia*, EEC, Art. 155.

[68] EEC, Art. 157(1) which also provides that the Commission must include at least one national of each Member State.

[69] *Ibid.*; presently Germany, Spain, France, Italy and the United Kingdom each have two Commissioners.

[70] EEC, Art. 157(1).

required for the performance of duties.[71] This is particularly important since the Commission represents the general interest and must be in a position to take a stand against any government which tries to put national interests first. The functions of a Commissioner can only be accomplished when the person in question is totally independent of national governments, especially their own.

It should be remembered that it is in connection with the independence of the members of the executive that the ECSC Treaty used the term "supranational."[72] Although the word did not reappear in the later European Treaties, the substance of the concept remains. With regard to this independence, obligations are imposed both on the members of the Commission and upon the Member States. Members of the Commission are bound, both during their period of office and thereafter, to act with integrity and discretion, especially as regards the acceptance of appointments and benefits. If a commissioner were to breach these obligations he might be dismissed by the Court or, if he were no longer in office, deprived of his pension rights.[73]

Taking all this into account, it may seem odd that the members of the Commission are nominated by the very Governments in relation to which their independence is so strongly stressed. Other methods of designation have been suggested at different times, granting *inter alia* some competence in this matter to Parliament.[74]

Members of the Commission are appointed by common accord of the governments of the Member States, for four years; the appointment is renewable.[75] The President, who is designated six

---

[71] EEC, Art. 157(2): "The members of the Commission shall, in the general interest of the Communities, be completely independent in the performance of their duties."

[72] ECSC, Art. 9: "The members of the High Authority will refrain from any action incompatible with the supranational character of their duties. Each Member State undertakes to respect this supranational character. . . . "

[73] EEC, Arts. 157(2) and 160.

[74] See the Tindemans report on European Union (Bull. Suppl. 1–76, 31) and the draft Treaty establishing a European Union adopted by Parliament in February 1984 (Bull. 2–1984, 7).

[75] EEC, Art. 158.

months before taking office, and the six Vice-Presidents, are appointed in the same way from among the members, but for a period of two years; their appointments may be renewed.[76]

2. The Commission's tasks and powers

The tasks and powers of the Commission are described in various Treaty provisions[77] and can be summarised as follows:

— to enforce the application of Community law;
— to issue recommendations and opinions;
— to exercise its powers of decisions;
— to exercise the powers conferred upon it by the Council;
— to participate in the legislative procedure;
— to negotiate international agreements;
— to implement the budget, and
— to publish an annual report on the activities of the Community.

(1) *Enforcement of Community law*

The European Treaties and the acts of the institutions (the latter being referred to as "secondary legislation") impose obligations on the Member States, the institutions and the natural and legal persons operating within the Community. It is the Commission's task to ensure that all those who come under the jurisdiction of the Community abide by the law. For this purpose the Commission was endowed with certain powers consisting mainly in gathering information and instituting proceedings against those who fail to fulfil their obligations under Community legislation.

The power to gather information is provided for, in a general way, by various Treaty provisions and Community acts.[78] The

[76] EEC, Art. 161(1).
[77] EEC, Arts. 155, 156, 169, 229, etc.
[78] EEC, Arts. 72, 73(2), 93(3), 109(2), 111(5), and 213. As for acts see, *e.g.* Reg. 17, Arts. 4 and 5 (it is the first Reg. implementing Arts. 85 and 86) (O.J. 1959–1962, 87).

Commission must indeed be in a position to collect any information and carry out any checks required for the performance of the tasks entrusted to it. And although the Council has not laid down general implementing provisions, the obligation imposed upon the Member States to "facilitate the achievement of the Community's tasks"[79] should provide the necessary legal ground for the Commission to obtain all the required data.

Based upon the information so obtained, the Commission can then, if necessary, start the following actions.

When the Commission considers that a Member State has not fulfilled an obligation under a Community provision:

(a) it shall[80] remind the government in question of its duties and invite it to take the measures necessary to ensure conformity with Community law or submit its observations, all this within a time-limit set by the Commission, usually two months;

(b) if no action is taken by the Member State or no comments are submitted, or if those comments do not convince the Commission, the latter shall deliver a "reasoned opinion" on the matter which will lay down a time-limit for the Member State to comply;

(c) if the Member State does not comply, the Commission may[81] bring the matter before the Court;

(d) if the Court finds that the Member State has indeed failed to fulfil its obligation, "the State shall be required

---

[79] EEC, Art. 5.

[80] EEC, Art. 169. The terms used in this provision seem to indicate that, once the Commission has determined that a Member State has not fulfilled an obligation (and with regard to this determination the Commission enjoys discretionary powers), there is an obligation for the Commission to act. The existence of this obligation is essential in a system where the plea of *non adimpletus contractus* is not admissible. (See Joined Cases 90 and 91/63 *Commission* v. *Luxembourg and Belgium* [1964] E.C.R. 625 at 631.)

[81] At this point the Commission's powers are entirely discretionary.

to take the necessary steps to comply with the judgment."

Since the Treaty[82] does not provide for coercive measures where Member States are concerned, further compliance is left to them. The only other step the Commission can take in case the Member State does not comply with the judgment of the Court, is to start the procedure all over on the ground that by not complying with the judicial decision, the Member State has failed to fulfil an obligation under the Treaty.[83]

On the other hand, the more advanced the economic and political integration of the Member States, the more difficult it becomes for one of them to break the rules, since each Member State is in some way or other dependent on the goodwill of its partners for the implementation of various, sometimes very profitable, common policies.

The majority of infringements by Member States concern quantitative restrictions on the free movement of goods, and more particularly, measures having equivalent effect. It should be noted, however, that the figures concerning those violations published by the Commission[84] do not provide the whole picture. Failures by Member States to comply with the Treaty are practically always the object of contacts and discussions between the Commission and the government concerned and are often settled out of court.

With regard to the institutions (the only one concerned here is the Council) the Commission can initiate a court action both when it is of the opinion that an action by the Council violates some Community provision[85] and when a failure of the Council to act is considered by the Commission to be an infringement of the

---

[82] The ECSC Treaty provided for some kind of coercive measures (see Art. 88), but they were never applied.

[83] See, *e.g.* Case 48/71 *Commission* v. *Italy* [1972] E.C.R. 527 and Case 232/78 *Commission* v. *France* [1979] E.C.R. 2729.

[84] A list of infringements can be found, since 1968, in the Bulletin published monthly by the Commission; see also the General Reports, *e.g.* the twenty-third General Report (1989), 436.

[85] EEC, Art. 173; see below under "Court of Justice."

Treaty.[86] The Commission has no legal recourse against Parliament since the powers of the latter to take binding decisions are extremely limited.[87]

With regard to undertakings (and natural persons), the Commission has been endowed *inter alia* with the power to impose fines in certain cases, the most important ones being in the field of competition.[88] It should be noted also that decisions of the Commission imposing such fines are enforceable in the Member States.[89]

(2) *Recommendations and opinions*

The Commission formulates recommendations and opinions on matters dealt with in the Treaty, when the latter expressly so provides or when the Commission considers it necessary.[90] It should be remembered that recommendations and opinions have no binding force[91] so that in fulfilling this task, the Commission acts in a purely advisory capacity.

The EEC Treaty provides for several instances where a recommendation or opinion from the Commission is required[92] while in other cases it is mentioned as a possibility.[93] When the Commission makes recommendations or delivers opinions not expressly provided for, it must be "on matters dealt with in this Treaty."

(3) *Exercise of power of decision*

The Treaty does not confer upon the Commission a general power to take decisions; the basic principle of "conferred

---

[86] EEC, Art. 175.

[87] See above under "European Parliament."

[88] See Reg. 17 (implementing Arts. 85 and 86), Art. 15 (O.J. 1959–1962, 87), Reg. 11 (implementing Art. 79(3)), Art. 18, abolition of discrimination in transport rates and conditions (J.O. 1960, 1121) and Reg. 1017/68 (applying rules of competition to transport by rail, road and inland waterways) Art. 22, (J.O. 1968, L 175/1).

[89] EEC, Art. 192; see also below under "Community Acts," enforcement.

[90] EEC, Art. 155.

[91] EEC, Art. 189.

[92] See, *e.g.* EEC, Art. 111(2): recommendation concerning tariff negotiations with third countries and Art. 237: opinion on the accession of a new Member State.

[93] See, *e.g.* EEC, Art. 81.

powers" also applies here,[94] as is made clear by the words "in the manner provided for in this Treaty." Since, as was seen, the Council must be considered as the Community law-maker, the fact that the Commission also has the power of decision might create the impression that the legislative power is shared by the two institutions. This, however, is not quite so; indeed a distinction must be made between "legislative" decision-making, which is the task proper of the Council, and the "executive" power of decision, which befalls the Commission.

Both the Legislator and the Executive have the right to make regulations, issue directives and take decisions[95] but they do not operate on quite the same level although it must be recognised that no clear-cut distinction exists between the two.[96]

The power of decision directly entrusted by the Treaty to the Commission mainly concerns the "functioning and develoment of the common market,"[97] *i.e.* administration of the customs union,[98] the application of the safeguard clauses[99] and of the competition rules,[1] the execution of the Community budget[2] and, to some extent, the external relations.[3] Other, more extensive, powers of decision have been provided for the Commission by the Council through the Community secondary legislation.[4]

---

[94] So does the principle of "implied powers," see above under "Council (1) Decision making."

[95] See EEC, Art. 189(1), which makes no distinction between the Council and the Commission.

[96] See, *e.g.* Commission Dir. 80/723 on the transparency of financial relations between Member States and public enterprises (O.J. 1980, L.195/35) and Joined Cases 188 to 190/80, *France, Italy and U.K.* v. *Commission* [1982] E.C.R. 2545.

[97] EEC, Art. 155.

[98] See EEC, Arts. 10(2), 13(2), 22, and 33(6), (7).

[99] See EEC, Arts. 17(4), 25(2), (3), 26, 37(3), 46, 73(1), (2), 107(2), 108(3), 115 and 226.

[1] See EEC, Arts. 89(2), 90(3), 93(2) and 97(2).

[2] The Commission is responsible for implementing the budget and administering the various Community funds, such as the Social Fund (EEC, Art. 124) and the Regional Development Fund (EEC, Art. 130b).

[3] See below, External Relations.

[4] In accordance with EEC, Art. 155, last indent.

When exercising its right to act, the Commission has, in certain cases, a choice as to the form of the measure,[5] in other instances no form is prescribed[6] and sometimes a given act is required.[7]

Decisions of the Commission are taken by the majority of its members[8] and when at least eight members are present.[9] The Commission may not delegate its power of decision either to one of its members or to its civil servants[10]; nor can the Commission delegate such powers to autonomous bodies.[11]

The Rules of Procedure of the Commission, amended several times, have been published in the Official Journal.[12]

(4) *Exercise of powers conferred by the Council*

Most of the Commission's decisions are based on powers provided for in acts of the Council. Indeed, in accordance with the Treaty,[13] the latter confers on the Commission powers for the implementation of the rules it lays down, but may, in respect of the exercise of these powers, impose certain requirements. The Council may also, in specific cases, reserve the right to exercise directly implementing powers itself.[14]

The principles and rules concerning the above-mentioned requirements are laid down in the so-called "Comitology" deci-

---

[5] See, *e.g.* EEC, Art. 90(3); the Commission shall address "appropriate directives or decisions" (of course the choice is dictated by the content of the act!).

[6] See, *e.g.* EEC, Art. 10(2); the Commission shall "determine" the methods of administrative co-operation.

[7] See, *e.g.* EEC, Art. 45(2); "directives issued by the Commission."

[8] EEC, Art. 163.

[9] Rules of procedure, Art. 6 (O.J. 1974 (2nd) vii).

[10] See however, Dec. 68/183 authorising certain management measures to be taken within the framework of the common organisations of agricultural markets (J.O. 1968, L. 89/13). This decision is based on Art. 27 of the Rules of Procedure of the Commission. See Case 8/72 *Cementhandelaren* v. *Commission* [1972] E.C.R. 977, concerning the legality of a document signed by a Director-General rather than by a member of the Commission.

[11] See Case 9/56 *Meroni* v. *High Authority* [1957 and 1958] E.C.R. 133.

[12] O.J. 1975, L. 199/43.

[13] EEC, Art. 155, last indent, as modified by the SEA. See Case 34/78 *Yoshida* v. *Kamer van Koophandel en Fabrieken voor Friesland* [1979] E.C.R. 115.

[14] See, *e.g.* Dir. 89/107 (O.J. 1990 L.40/27, Art. 2(2)).

sion of the Council[15] which provides that before taking an implementation decision the Commission must consult a committee. There are three kinds of committees:

(i) the *Consultative Committee* which formulates a non-binding opinion, although the Commission is supposed to take it into account and mention it in the minutes;

(ii) the *Management Committee* which is widely used in the implementation of the common agricultural policy. When the Committee, by a majority vote (the same as for the Council), emits a negative opinion, the Commission takes its decision anyway and it becomes applicable. It is, however, referred to the Council. There are then two possibilities, one of which is provided in the Council act on which the Commission decision is based:
— either the Commission may postpone the application of the measure for one month, during which time the Council may, by a majority vote, modify or annul it; or
— the Commission must postpone the application for a maximum of three months during which time the Council may modify or annul the measure.

If no decision is taken by the Council within the given time-limit, the Commission's decision becomes definitive.

(iii) the *Regulatory Committee:* in this case the Commission may only take a decision if the committee agrees; in case of disagreement or absence of opinion, the Commission must make a proposal to the Council which can take a decision by a majority vote, unless the Council wants to modify the proposal, in which case unanimity is required. If no decision is taken there are two possibilities, one of

[15] Dec. 87/373, O.J. 1987, L. 197/33.

which is provided for in the Council act which confers the implementing powers:
— if within a maximum of three months the Council has not decided, the Commission takes the proposed decision; this is known as the "net" (filet) procedure;
— if there is no Council decision within that time-limit, the Commission takes the decision, unless a simple majority of the Council has voted against it; this is the so-called "counter-net" (contre-filet), which, in fact, annuls the conferred competence of the Commission and imposes immobility on the Community!

There are no indications about the choice of those various procedures, they are decided on a case-by-case basis.

(5) *Participation in the legislative procedure*

In most instances the Council may only pass Community legislation when it is based on a proposal from the Commission. By submitting drafts for directives, regulations and decisions, the Commission participates, as the Treaty calls it, "in the shaping of measures taken by the Council."[16] Whenever such proposals are required by the Treaty,[17] the Commission is granted an exclusive right of initiative in the Community law-making process. There are cases however, where the Commission is bound to make proposals within a given time limit[18] and there are others where the Commission must use its own judgement as to the suitability of making a proposal.[19]

The Commission's proposal constitutes the basis for the consultation of Parliament by the Council and the proposal may be altered by the Commission, as long as the Council has not acted.[20] This allows the Commission to take into account the amendments

---

[16] EEC, Art. 155, third indent.
[17] See the list of cases under "Council, (2) voting procedure," above.
[18] See, *e.g.* EEC, Art. 21(2).
[19] See, *e.g.* EEC, Art. 94.
[20] EEC, Art. 149(3).

proposed by Parliament both in the normal and in the co-ordination procedure.[21]

The proposal also constitutes, of course, the basis for the Council's decision, and if the Council wishes to adopt an act diverging from the proposal, it may only do so unanimously[22]; this does not mean, however, that the Council is free to adopt an act which bears no resemblance to the Commission's proposal, since this would deprive the right of initiative of any relevance.

Although the Commission enjoys an exclusive right of legislative initiative,[23] the Council "may request" the Commission "to submit to it any appropriate proposals."[24] As is clear from this wording, the Council cannot force the Commission to submit a proposal, but it will not be possible for the Commission to ignore this request, since both institutions are bound to co-operate very closely in the legislative field.

When required by the Treaty, the Commission consults the Economic and Social Committee.[25] Unlike the consultation of Parliament, which only the Council can do, consultation of the Committee can also be initiated by the Commission.

In preparing its proposals to be submitted to the Council, the Commission usually consults informally with experts from the Member States.[26] The main discussion, however, takes place after the proposal has been received by the Council, either with the Committee of Permanent Representatives (Coreper) or with (working) groups set up by the latter. Following these discussions the Commission can then modify its proposal, but it can also demand that, notwithstanding disagreement in Coreper or the group, the proposal be discussed by the Council itself, in the hope that an acceptable solution might be found at the political

---

[21] EEC, Art. 149(2)(d).

[22] EEC, Art. 149(1).

[23] There have been several proposals to grant a similar right to Parliament. This question might be examined during the negotiations for a Treaty creating the European Monetary Union (EMU) which will take place at the end of 1990, as was decided by the European Council at Strasbourg in December 1989.

[24] EEC, Art. 152.

[25] See, *e.g.* EEC, Art. 43(2); for the Committee see below.

[26] See Luxembourg Arrangement, point 1; Bull. 3–1966, 5.

level. At that point the main question for the Commission is to see whether it can muster enough votes for a qualified majority in favour of its position. This requires, of course, constant contacts and discussions with the national delegations in the Council and with the Presidency, the latter being able to play a pivotal role by trying to formulate a compromise acceptable to everyone. All this shows that the reality of law-making within the Community is much more complex than the few Treaty rules seem to indicate.

Finally, it must be noted that the Commission might be called upon to justify the proposals it has made, not only before Parliament,[27] but also before the Court, since the latter has recognised the right of applicants, in an action concerning the legality of a Council decision, to bring proceedings not only against the Council for having adopted the act in question, but also against the Commission for having proposed it.[28]

The Commission's proposals are usually published in the Official Journal.[29] This allows all interested parties to react to them, either directly with the Commission, or with Parliament or the national Ministers who sit in the Council.

(6) *External relations*

The Commission's tasks extend beyond the Community since it is also responsible for maintaining all appropriate relations with all international organisations, in particular with the organs of the United Nations, of its specialised agencies and of the General Agreement on Tariff and Trade (GATT).[30]

The Commission is also entrusted with the task of negotiating the agreements between the Community and one or more States or an international organisation. Since such agreements are concluded by the Council, the Commission must obtain a man-

---

[27] *e.g.* during the debate on the annual General Report or in answers to parliamentary questions.
[28] Joined Cases 63–69/72 *Werhahn* v. *Council* [1973] E.C.R. 1229 at 1247(8).
[29] Proposals are published in the "C" series or available from the Commission and are known as "COM" documents.
[30] EEC, Art. 229.

date from the Council before opening such negotiations. The Commission may also obtain beforehand the opinion of the Court as to whether the envisaged agreement is compatible with the provisions of the Treaty.[31]

(7) *Implementation of the Community budget*

In the budgetary procedure, the role of the Commission is formally limited to drafting its own budget and consolidating the estimates of the other institutions in a "preliminary draft budget" to be submitted to the Council before the first day of September.[32] The Commission must also declare, after consulting the Economic Policy Committee, what the maximum rate of increase is for the "non-compulsory" expenditures.[33] This rate is determined by the growth of the Community GNP, the average variation in the budgets of the Member States and the trend of the cost of living.

Once the budget is adopted, it falls to the Commission to implement it in accordance with the regulations laid down by the Council,[34] the other institutions giving effect to their own expenditure.[35] Afterwards, the Commission must seek discharge in respect of this implementation. To this end the Commission submits annually to the Council and to Parliament the accounts for the preceding financial year together with a financial statement of the assets and liabilities of the Communities.[36] In exercising their powers of control over the implementation of the budget, the Council and Parliament are assisted by the Court of Auditors, which forwards to them an annual report after the close of each financial year.[37] The Council and Parliament exam-

---

[31] The Council and the Member States also have the right to obtain such an opinion. EEC, Art. 228(1). See, *e.g.* Opinions 1/75 [1975] E.C.R. 1355, 1/76 [1977] E.C.R. 741 and 1/78 [1979] E.C.R. 2871.

[32] EEC, Art. 203(2) and (3); for more details on the budgetary procedure see under "Parliament, (5) Participation in the budgetary procedure," above.

[33] *Ibid.,* at (9).

[34] See, *e.g.* O.J. 1976, L. 362/52.

[35] EEC, Art. 205.

[36] EEC, Art. 205a.

[37] EEC, Art. 206a(4); see "Court of Auditors" below.

ine the accounts, the financial statement and the report, and discharge is given by Parliament on a recommendation from the Council, acting by a qualified majority.[38]

As part of the implementation of the Community budget, the Commission administers the Community Agricultural Guidance and Guarantee Fund, the Social Fund and the European Regional Development Fund. The Commission is also responsible for administering the European Development Fund for the African, Caribbean and Pacific States financed by direct Member State contributions, and for the "banking activities" of the European Coal and Steel Community.[39]

The Commission is also empowered to raise loans in order to finance atomic energy projects[40] and to finance infrastructure and industrial projects.[41] The borrowing itself is done by the Commission but the administration of the resources was delegated to the European Investment Bank.

(8) *Publication of an annual General Report*

In pursuance of the Treaty,[42] the Commission publishes in February each year, one month before the opening of the session of Parliament, a General Report on the activities of the Community. This Report covers the activities of all the institutions and organs of the Community, and as such is an invaluable source of information. Several areas, however, are covered very summarily because they are the object of separate Reports either from the Commission or from other institutions or bodies.[43]

---

[38] EEC, Art. 206b. In 1984, Parliament refused to give a discharge for the 1982 budget implementation; see Bull. 12–1984, 67. In 1987 it deferred the discharge in respect of the implementation of the 1985 budget; see twenty-second General Report (1988), 75.

[39] See ECSC, Arts. 54 and 56.

[40] See Euratom, Art. 172(4) and O.J. 1977, L. 88/9.

[41] Officially referred to as NIC (*Nouvel Instrument Communautaire*). See O.J. 1978, L. 298/9.

[42] EEC, Art. 156.

[43] For a list of those Reports see above "Parliament (4) The General Report."

3. The Commission's Staff

The Treaty provides that the Commission shall adopt its rules of procedure so as to ensure that both it and its departments operate in accordance with the provisions of the Treaties.[44] The services are divided into two dozen large units (Directorates-General, Services or Groups) which more or less correspond to the main chapters of the three European Treaties.[45] In regard to

---

[44] EEC, Art. 162.
[45] At the beginning of 1990, the Commission had the following units:
- — Secretariat-General of the Commission,
- — Legal Service,
- — Spokesman's Service,
- — Joint Interpreting and Conference Service,
- — Statistical Office; there were the following Directorates-General:
- — DG I : External Relations,
- — DG II : Economic and Financial Affairs,
- — DG III : Internal Market and Industrial Affairs,
  Task Force : Small and Medium-sized Enterprises,
- — DG IV : Competition
- — DG V : Employment, Social Affairs and Education,
- — DG VI : Agriculture,
- — DG VII : Transport,
- — DG VIII : Development,
- — DG IX : Personal and Administration,
- — DG X : Information, Communication and Culture,
- — DG XI : Environment and Nuclear Safety,
- — DG XII : Science, Research and Development,
  Joint Research Centre
- — DG XIII : Telecommunications, Information Industry and Innovation,
- — DG XIV : Fisheries,
- — DG XV : Financial Institutions and Company Law,
- — DG XVI : Regional Policy
- — DG XVII : Energy
- — DG XVIII : Credit and Investment,
- — DG XIX : Budgets,
- — DG XX : Financial Control
- — DG XXI : Customs Union and Indirect Taxation,
- — DG XXII : Co-ordination of Structural Instruments,
- — DG XXIII : Enterprise Policy, Tourism and Social Economy,
- — Consumer Protection Service,
- — Euratom Supply Agency,
- — Security Office
- — Office for Official Publications of the Communities.

the Community staff, two texts must be mentioned: the Protocol on the Privileges and Immunities of the European Communities[46] and the Staff Regulations of Officials and the Conditions of Employment of other Servants of the European Community.[47] Officials are recruited directly by the various institutions and organs of the Community; in other words the Community staff is not composed of national civil servants seconded by the administrations of the Member States.[48] The obligations concerning the independence of the members of the Commission, described above, apply *mutatis mutandis* to the officials and servants of the Commission.

IV. THE COURT OF JUSTICE

The three European Treaties contain an identical provision to describe the task of the Court: it "shall ensure that in the interpretation and application of this Treaty the law is observed."[49] This short and sibylline text covers an extremely varied series of activities.

The Court's task is complicated by the fact that Community law is basically economic law which, by definition, is essentially evolutive and in need of constant up-dating, while respecting the

---

To this have to be added the European Foundation for the Improvement of Living and Working Conditions and the European Centre for the Development of Vocational Training.

Practically all those units are headed by a Director-General, which explains why there are many more Directors-General than Directorates-General!

A total of 14,058 permanent and 880 temporary posts.

[46] See Annex 2 to the so-called Merger Treaty. See Case 28/83 *Forcheri* v. *Commission* [1984] E.C.R. 1425.

[47] A consolidated version in English was published as a supplement to O.J. 1973, C. 12.

[48] It goes without saying however, that the nationality of the officials must be taken into account, and although "no post may be reserved for a given nationality" (Staff Reg. Art. 27), a "geographical distribution" must exist, based upon the size of the population of the respective Member States. At the end of 1988, there were about 19,000 officials working for the various institutions and other bodies of the Community.

[49] EEC, Art. 164.

basic general principles. Since it was impossible to try to regulate the economic policies of the Community and of the Member States in a document of no more than 250 articles, the interpretation and implementation of those provisions is in continual evolution, the more so, since only part of the Treaty provisions are drafted with detailed precision.[50]

Consequently, when called upon to state what Community law is in a given field, it is in the first place by reference to the objectives of the Community that the Court interprets the existing rules and formulates new ones, the so-called teleological interpretation. Furthermore, the task of the Court is not only to interpret, but also to state what the law is when the Community provisions do not explicitly provide the answer. This, of course, is not particular to the Court of Justice, since "wherever there are courts, the law grows at the hand of the judges,"[51] but for the reasons just mentioned, this applies particularly in the case of the European Community.

This is the reason why it is so important for the judges to be totally independent,[52] the more so since, as was explained above, the Council tends to act as an inter-governmental conference where every member fights for his country's interests, Parliament does not have all the powers required for exercising an effective democratic control and the Commission, which besides its overwhelming administrative tasks must also fulfil a political function, is bound to accept compromises in the implementation of Community legislation by the Member States.

The Court can only express itelf in judgments[53] and when called upon to do so; nevertheless, over the years it was able to build up a set of rules which were of prime importance in the shaping of the Community. This happened mainly through rulings concerning the interpretation of the Treaties and the secondary Com-

---

[50] The evolutive character of Community law is referred to by the Court with the words "at the present stage in the development of Community law," see, *e.g.* Case 27/80 *Fietje* [1980] E.C.R. 3839 at 3853(8).

[51] Schwarzenberger, *International Law*, 24.

[52] See EEC, Art. 167: the judges "shall be chosen from persons whose independence is beyond doubt."

[53] Exceptionally also in "opinions," see EEC, Art. 228(1).

munity legislation,[54] at the request of national courts confronted with questions of interpretation of the Community rules applicable in cases pending before them.

1. Members of the Court

The Court consists of 13[55] Judges and is assisted by six Advocates-General[56]; the latter, however, are not "members" of the court. The Judges and the Advocates-General "shall be chosen from persons whose independence is beyond doubt and who possess the qualifications required for appointment to the highest judicial offices in their respective countries"[57] or "who are jurisconsults of recognised competence."[58]

The Judges and the Advocates-General are appointed for a term of six years by common accord of the Governments of the Member States[59]; however, every three years a partial replacement of six, alternatively seven, Judges and three Advocates-General takes place in order to ensure continuity on the bench. Retiring Judges and Advocates-General are eligible for re-appointment.

The President of the court is elected by the Judges[60] from among their number for a term of three years; he may be re-elected.

---

[54] See EEC, Art. 177.

[55] It started out in 1952 with seven; this number was gradually increased with each new accession, the last one being that of Portugal and Spain, Act of Accession ESP/PORT., Art. 17. Each Member State designates one judge and the five larger ones, in turn, designate the thirteenth.

[56] Five of them are appointed by the five larger countries, the sixth being "shared," in turn, by the seven other countries.

[57] EEC, Art. 167; this means that qualifications are determined in accordance with national law.

[58] This provision makes it possible to include persons without a law degree, as was the case in the first ECSC Court.

[59] Further provisions concerning the Judges and Advocates-General are to be found in the Protocol on the Statute of the Court of Justice annexed to the Treaty and in the Rules of Procedure.

[60] It goes without saying that the choice is the object of informal discussions with the Governments of the Member States, since some kind of geographical equilibrium is desirable among the Presidents of the various institutions and organs of the Community.

The 13 Judges are grouped in five chambers of three or five Judges each[61]; cases brought before the Court are normally heard by one of these chambers. However, when the Court hears cases brought by a Member State or an institution, or when the Court has to give a preliminary ruling,[62] the Court shall sit in plenary session.[63]

The position of the Advocates-General is a particularly interesting one: their independent position (they do not participate in the discussions that lead to the Court's decision) allows them to carry out their own personal examination of the case and express personal opinions, something the Judges cannot do. They can also examine any related question not brought forward by the parties. Although the reasoned oral submissions they present in open court do not necessarily reflect the Court's views, they often contain precious indications in regard to the reasoning which led to the decision. Those submissions are published, together with the judgments, in the Court's Reports.

2. The Court's Jurisdiction

As was pointed out at the beginning of this section, the Court fulfils many tasks; in the order of the Treaty provisions the Court's jurisdiction consists mainly of the following:

— to find whether or not a Member State has failed to fulfil an obligation under the Treaty; actions can be brought either by the Commission or another Member State[64];
— to exercise unlimited jurisdiction with regard to penalties; actions can be brought by natural and legal persons[65];

---

[61] EEC, Art. 165(2).
[62] See EEC, Art. 177.
[63] EEC, Art. 165(3).
[64] EEC, Arts. 169, 170 and 171.
[65] EEC, Art. 172.

—   to review the legality of an act, or of a failure to act of the Council and the Commission at the request of Member States, the Council or the Commission and under certain conditions, Parliament [66] and natural and legal persons[67];

—   to give a preliminary ruling at the request of a national court or tribunal[68];

—   to grant compensation for damage caused by the institutions; actions can be brought against the Community by Member States and natural or legal persons[69];

—   to decide in disputes between the Community institutions and their servants,[70] and

—   to act as Court of Appeal for the judgments of the Court of First Instance.[71]

(1) *The finding of a failure by a Member State to fulfil its Treaty obligations*

When the Commission or a Member State considers that a Member State has failed to fulfil an obligation under the Treaty, it may bring the matter before the Court. The possibility for the Commission to initiate an action of this kind constitutes the main instrument at its disposal for fulfilling the task of "guardian of the law of the Community." The procedure to be followed by the Commission was explained in some detail above.[72]

As regards the procedure to be initiated by Member States, the Treaty provides for an intermediate phase consisting of bringing the matter first before the Commission which shall deliver a reasoned opinion after having heard the parties.[73]

---

[66] EEC, Art. 175 and above under "European Parliament, (6) Procedures in The Court of Justice."

[67] EEC, Arts. 173–176.

[68] EEC, Art. 177.

[69] EEC, Arts. 178 and 215.

[70] EEC, Art. 179 although only on appeal from the Court of First instance.

[71] SEA, Art. 168a.

[72] See above "The Commission, 2(1) Enforcement of Community law."

[73] EEC, Art. 170; the first time this procedure was used was in 1977, Case 58/77 *Ireland* v. *France* (O.J. 1977, C. 142/8); it was later withdrawn.

The Court's jurisdiction in cases brought against a Member State consists merely in "finding"[74] that the State in question has failed to fulfil an obligation under the Treaty. If such a finding is made, the Member State "shall take the necessary measures to comply with the judgment of the Court."[75]

With regard to cases brought by a Member State against another Member State, attention must be drawn to the obligation undertaken by the Member States[76] "not to submit a dispute concerning the interpretation or application of the Treaty to any method of settlement other than those provided for therein."[77] The principal method provided for being the recourse to the Court, this provision guarantees, together with the preliminary ruling, uniformity in the interpretation of Community law. It should also be noted that the Court shall have jurisdiction in disputes between Member States which relate to the subject matter of the Treaty, if the dispute is submitted to it under a special agreement between the parties.[78]

(2) *Unlimited jurisdiction with regard to penalties*

In order to ensure compliance with the obligations laid down in its regulations, the Council may make provisions for penalties to be imposed in case of infringement, on natural or legal persons.[79] The latter have the right to ask the Court to review the legality of the decision taken[80] and also, under its unlimited jurisdiction, to

---

[74] EEC, Art. 171. This "finding" has no direct legal consequences, contrary to the Court's unlimited jurisdiction in the case, *e.g.* of penalties (EEC, Art. 172) or powers to annul an act of an institution (EEC, Art. 174).

[75] The Court could therefore indicate what the Member State must do in order to comply with its Treaty obligations; but the Court never does and simply concludes that the Member State has indeed not fulfilled its obligations, and nothing more.

[76] EEC, Art. 219.

[77] Another method could have been recourse to the International Court of Justice whose compulsory arbitration is accepted by several Member States.

[78] EEC, Art. 182.

[79] EEC, Arts. 79(3) and 87(2); it is debatable whether or not Art. 172, besides attributing unlimited jurisdiction to the Court, also confers upon the Council a general competence to provide for fines in its regulations.

[80] EEC, Art. 173.

review the amount of the fine fixed under such provisions.[81] When
the Council wants to grant unlimited jurisdiction to the Court, it
must do so explicitly.[82] Under this jurisdiction, the Court may not
only suppress the fine, but it may also decide to increase or
decrease it.[83]

The Court's unlimited jurisdiction also applies in two other
areas: claims for damages resulting from the non-contractual
liability of the Community[84] and disputes between the institutions
and their servants.[85]

(3) *Review of the legality of an act or failure to act of an institution*

(a) Appeal for annulment[86]

In reviewing the legality of Community acts,[87] the Court protects
all those who are subject to Community law against arbitrary
action of the institutions, but it also ensures that Community

---

[81] EEC, Art. 172.

[82] See, *e.g.* Reg. 11, Art. 18 (J.O. 1960, 1121; O.J. 1959–1962, 60) and Reg. 17,
Art. 17 (J.O. 1962, 204; O.J. *ibid.* at 87).

[83] See, *e.g.* Case 27/76 *United Brands* v. *Commission* [1978] E.C.R. 207 where the
fine was reduced from 1 million units of account to 850,000, because part of the
decision was annulled. There are no examples of the Court increasing the fine;
undertakings upon which a fine has been imposed automatically go to the Court
to plead for reduction which they nearly always get, with the consequence that
the Commission systematically imposes very high fines!

[84] EEC, Arts. 178 and 215; see below.

[85] EEC, Art. 179.

[86] EEC, Art. 173. It should be noted that an action for annulment must be lodged
with the Court within two months after publication or notification of the
measure; EEC, Art. 173(3).

[87] The Treaty refers to "acts of the Council and the Commission other than
recommendations or opinions" (EEC, Art. 173(1)); these other acts are mainly
the regulations, directives and decisions provided for in EEC, Art. 189, but are
by no means limited to those. They include also agreements and generally
speaking any measure which binds (some of) those who are subject to
Community law. See Case 22/70 *Commission* v. *Council* [1971] E.C.R. 263 at
277(42): "an action for annulment must therefore be available in the case of all
measures adopted by the institutions, whatever their nature or form, which are
intended to have legal effects," Case 60/81 *IBM* v. *Commission* [1981] E.C.R.
2639 at 2651(9) and Case 108/83 *Luxembourg* v. *Parliament* [1984] E.C.R. 1945,
where the Court annulled a Resolution of the latter.

activities remain within the boundaries laid down by the Treaty and that the institutions respect the balance of powers within the Community.

Who may lodge an appeal for annulment? With regard to the admissibility of court actions, all the Member States apply in their national law a principle well coined in French as "pas d'intérêt, pas d'action." The same principle applies within the Community: the Member States, the Council and the Commission are considered to have an overall interest in the correct implementation of Community law, and have therefore, subject to a two months time-limit, an unlimited right to initiate proceedings aimed at controlling the legality of Community acts.[88] Natural and legal persons, on the other hand, must prove their specific and particular interest in such a control.[89] In this respect it is assumed that acts having a general application concern everybody and nobody in particular. Therefore they cannot, normally, be challenged in Court by individuals, unless it can be shown that these acts contain provisions which in reality have an "individual"[90] rather than a "general" application. This can be the case

---

[88] All Member States have at one time appealed for annulment of an act of the Commission; rarer are appeals by Member States against Council acts: Case 151/73 *Ireland* v. *Council* [1974] E.C.R. 285. Appeals of the Commission against the Council are not uncommon: Case 242/87 *Commission* v. *Council*, May 30, 1989 (not yet published). Lately the Court has also accepted appeals by a Member State for annulment of acts of Parliament, although this is not explicitly provided for under the EEC Treaty: Case 230/81 *Luxembourg* v. *Parliament* [1983] E.C.R. 255, at 281, where the Court found that such an appeal is provided for under the ECSC Treaty, and Case 108/83 *Luxembourg* v. *Parliament* [1984] E.C.R. 1945. See also Case 34/86 *Council* v. *Parliament* [1986] E.C.R. 2155 and Joined Cases 358/85 and 51/86 *France* v. *Parliament*, September 22, 1988 (not yet published).

[89] Case 77/77 *BP* v. *Commission* [1978] E.C.R. 1513 at 1525(13).

[90] The Treaty refers to an act which "is of direct and individual concern" to a person. This, according to the Court, is the case only "if that decision affects them by reason of certain attributes which are peculiar to them or by reason of circumstances in which they are differentiated from all other persons and by virtue of these factors distinguishes them individually just as in the case of the person addressed"; Case 25/62 *Plauman* v. *Commission* [1963] E.C.R. 95 at 107. This would not be the case if the Plaintiff is affected by the act because he belongs to a category designated abstractly and as a whole; Case 42/71 *Nordgetreide* v. *Commission* [1972] E.C.R. 105 at 110(5). See also Case 72/74 *Union Syndicale* v. *Council* [1975] E.C.R. 401 at 410(17).

with an act taken in the form of a general act, *e.g.* a regulation,[91] or with an individual act, *e.g.* a decision, but addressed to another person.[92]

The interpretation of the Treaty provisions is of course essential in determining the extent of the legal protection enjoyed by individuals and undertakings within the Community. Hence the importance of the case law of the Court in this field. Without resorting to "extensive interpretation," the Court has always given the Treaty provisions a meaning which allowed a wide access to the Court, thereby providing ample opportunity for review of the legality of Community acts,[93] although the Court explicitly recognised that the EEC Treaty "lays down more restrictive conditions than the ECSC Treaty for the admissibility of applications for annulment by private individuals."[94]

It follows that the opportunities for natural and legal persons to appeal directly for annulment of Community acts are much more limited than for the Member States and the institutions. However, other means exist whereby persons and enterprises may obtain a Court ruling, if not on the legality, at least on the applicability of Community acts, which, for the plaintiff, has identical consequences if the action is well founded.[95]

[91] See Joined Cases 41–44/70 *International Fruit Company* v. *Commission* [1971] E.C.R. 411 at 422(21) (where the Court held that Art. 1 of Reg. 983/70 "is not a provision with a general application but must be analysed as a bundle of individual decisions"); Case 138/79 *Roquette Frères* v. *Council* [1980] E.C.R. 3333.

[92] Joined Cases 16 and 17/62 *Producteurs de fruits* v. *Council* [1962] E.C.R. 471 at 479 (a measure entitled by its authors a Regulation can contain provisions which are capable not only of direct but also of individual concern to certain natural or legal persons); Case 101/76 [1977] *Koninklijke Scholten Honig* v. *Council and Commission* E.C.R. 797 and Case 169/84, *Cofaz* v. *Commission* [1986] E.C.R. 408.

[93] According to the Court, "another person" in EEC 173(2) can include a Member State since no limitation as to the meaning of those words is to be found in the Treaty. Persons can therefore appeal against acts of the institutions addressed to a Member State when they are directly concerned; Case 730/79 *Phillip Morris* v. *Commission* [1980] E.C.R. 2671 at 2687.

[94] Joined Cases 16 and 17/62 *Producteurs de fruits* at 478 (n. 92 above).

[95] See below "Preliminary Ruling," "Compensation for Damage" and "Exception of Illegality."

Grounds for annulment. The Treaty provides for four grounds for annulment[96] which have their origin in French administrative law.

(i) *Lack of competence*: this is the equivalent, in judicial terms, of the basic principle, mentioned before, according to which the institutions only have those powers which have explicitly been attributed to them by Community law. It also follows from this principle that the choice of the Community provision on which an act is based is of essential importance: if the wrong Article is invoked, the act may be annulled.[97]

(ii) *Infringement of an essential procedural requirement*: as was mentioned before, if the Council were to take a decision without a proposal from the Commission or without consulting Parliament (when these procedures are required for by the Treaty) it would infringe an essential procedural requirement and therefore an appeal for annulment of the decision in question could be lodged. The same would apply if the Commission were to make a proposal to the Council without asking for the opinion of the Social and Economic Committee, when required by Community law to do so.

Failure to mention sufficient reasons in a Community act must also be considered as a ground for annulment under this heading.[98]

(iii) *Infringement of the Treaty or of any rule of law relating to its application*: it could of course be argued that the two grounds just mentioned also constitute infringements of the Treaty and that

---

[96] EEC, Art. 173; the same grounds are provided for in the ECSC and EURATOM Treaties, under Arts. 33 and 146 respectively.

[97] See, *e.g.* judgment of November 16, 1989 in a case *Commission* v. *Council* (not yet published). Since appeals for annulment must be lodged within two months after publication or notification, it can happen that a Community act without legal basis continues to be implemented (see however the Exception of illegality, below). The French Government raised the question whether such an act could be challenged after the time-limit has elapsed: see Joined Cases 6 and 11/69 *Commission* v. *France* [1969] E.C.R. 523 at 539 (11–13).

[98] See below under "Community Acts: 2. Regulations, Directives and Decisions must be reasoned."

mentioned also constitute infringements of the Treaty and that this ground, in fact, covers all possible illegalities. However, the Treaty refers to four grounds and accordingly they must be examined here.

In the expression "infringement of the Treaty," the word "Treaty" must be understood as referring also to the secondary legislation of the Community, *i.e.* the acts of the institutions, whatever their form, as long as they impose obligations, including, *e.g.* the international agreements concluded by the Community.

As for the expression "any rule of law relating to its application," it refers to the general principles of law[99] and to international law.[1] The general principles include, besides the principles universally recognised, those principles which are particular to the Member States and which the Court formulates on

---

[99] See, *e.g.* Case 92/71 *Interfood* v. *Hauptzollamt Hamburg* [1972] E.C.R. 231 at 242(6), confirmed in Case 112/77 *Töpfer* v. *Commission* [1978] E.C.R. 1019 at 1033(19) (the protection of legitimate expectation).
Other principles of law recognised by the Court are:
  — the right to be heard: Case 17/74 *Transocean Marine Paint Association* v. *Commission* [1974] E.C.R. 1063 at 1080(15);
  — respect for fundamental rights: Case 36/75 *Rutili* v. *Minister for the Interior* [1975] E.C.R. 1219 at 1232(32);
  — freedom of trade-union activity: Case 175/73 *Union Syndicale, Massa and Kortner* v. *Council* [1974] E.C.R. 917 at 925 (9 and 14);
  — legal certainty: Case 21/81 *Openbaar Ministerie* v. *Bout* [1982] E.C.R. 381 at 390(13);
  — equality of treatment: Case 148/73 R *Louwage* v. *Commission* [1974] E.C.R. 81 at 89(12);
  — contractual certainty: Case 48/72 *Brasserie de Haecht* v. *Wilkin-Janssen* [1973] E.C.R. 77 at 86(9);
  — protection of legal expectation: Case 97/76 *Merkur* v. *Commission* [1977] E.C.R. 1063 at 1078(7);
  — proportionality (between the means employed and the end in view): Case 122/78 *Buitoni* v. *FORMA* [1979] E.C.R. 677 at 684(16).
[1] See Case 8/55 *Fédération Charbonnière de Belgique* v. *High Authority* [1954–1956] E.C.R. 245 at 299; Joined Cases 21 to 24/72 *International Fruit Company* v. *Produktschap voor Groenten en Fruit* [1972] E.C.R. 1219 at 1226(6); see also Case 41/74 *Van Duyn* v. *Home Office* "it is a principle of international law which the EEC Treaty cannot be assumed to disregard" [1974] E.C.R. 1337 at 1351 (22). However in other cases, the Court did not accept arguments based on international law; see, *e.g.* Joined Cases 90 and 91/63 *Commission* v. *Luxembourg and Belgium* , [1964] E.C.R. 625 at 631.

the basis of the wording, the contents and the system of the Treaty and also on the basis of comparative studies of the twelve legal systems.[2]

(iv) *Misuse of power*[3]: there is misuse of power when a public authority uses its lawful powers to attain an objective for which the powers were not intended. Although this ground has been invoked many times, the Court does not often base an annulment on misuse of power.[4]

Consequences of annulment. When reviewing the legality of a binding Community act, the Court limits itself, where the action is well founded, to declare the act void. After that it is up to the institution which issued the act to "take the necessary measures to comply with the judgment of the Court of Justice."[5]

Since annulment means that the act is to be considered as never having existed (the Court's declaration has effect *ex tunc* and *erga omnes*) the institution must endeavour to recreate the situation which would have existed had the act not been issued. This might be impossible, especially when the nullity affects a regulation; for this reason, the Treaty provides that in the case of annulment of a regulation, the Court may state which of the effects of the regulation shall be considered as definitive,[6] or that the act remains valid until replaced.[7]

It should also be noted that annulment does not mean that the whole act becomes void: if the nullity concerns only certain provisions, the others are not affected as long as they can remain operative independently of those which were annulled.

[2] See EEC, Art. 215 and below, "Community Law: 4. Sources of Community law."
[3] Probably better known by its French equivalent "*détournement de pouvoir.*" For more details concerning its meaning see the comparative study of the law of the original six Member States, made by the Advocate General in his opinion in Case 3/54 *ASSIDER* v. *High Authority* [1954–1956] E.C.R. 63 at 75.
[4] See, *e.g.* Case 92/78 *Simmenthal* v. *Commission* [1979] E.C.R. 777 at 811(106).
[5] EEC, Art. 176. See Case 30/59 *Steenkolenmijnen* v. *High Authority* [1961] E.C.R. 1 at 17.
[6] EEC, Art. 174(2).
[7] See Case 275/87 *Commission* v. *Council*, February 2, 1989 (not yet published).

(b) Appeal against failure to act

In the case of failure to act,[8] the Court may be called upon to
declare that this failure constitutes an infringement of the Treaty;
the term "Treaty" must be interpreted as also including secondary legislation.[9] Although there is a marked difference between
the results of an appeal for annulment and those of an appeal for
failure to act, since in the former case the Court can annul while
in the second the Court can only declare the failure to be an
infringement, "both provisions merely prescribe one and the
same method of recourse."[10]

Another difference between the two appeals is that the Treaty
provides that the action for failure to act can also be brought by
Parliament.[11]

Actions for failure to act are not limited to cases in which the
Council or Commission are supposed to take a binding decision;
the Council, the Commission, Parliament and the Member States
can also bring an action when, *e.g.* the Commission fails to send a
proposal to the Council where this is required by the Treaty.

Natural and legal persons may only bring proceedings for
failure to act when an institution fails to issue[12] a binding act of
which they would have been the addressee.[13]

---

[8] EEC, Art. 175. Such an appeal is admissible only when the plaintiff has first
called upon the institution to act, and the latter has not defined its position
within two months; the plaintiff then has another two months to bring his action.

[9] *I.e.* regulations, directives, decisions, etc. Whether in the absence of the words
"or any rule of law relating to its application," a failure to act in violation of
such rules could be challenged in the Court has not yet been tested. It seems
however that if an act violating such rules can be declared illegal, the same
should apply to failure to act.

[10] Case 15/70 *Chevalley* v. *Commission* [1970] E.C.R. 975 at 979(6).

[11] EEC, Art. 175(1) "the other institutions"; see Case 13/83 *Parliament* v. *Council*
[1985] E.C.R. 1556.

[12] Failure to act must be distinguished from refusal to act; the latter constitutes a
decision which can only be challenged under Art. 173, annulment; see Case
8/71 *Komponistenverband* v. *Commission* [1971] E.C.R. 705 at 710(2). See also
Joined Cases 10 and 18/68 *Eridania* v. *Commission* [1969] E.C.R. 459 at
483(17).

[13] Case 15/71 *Mackprang* v. *Commission* [1971] E.C.R. 797 at 804(4).

(4) *Preliminary ruling*

The preliminary ruling[14] which presupposes direct effect of Community law, (*i.e.* the possibility to invoke Community rules before national courts), constitutes the ideal instrument in the hands of the Court to define and develop Community law and has been widely used to this effect with great success. It is also for the citizens of the Community, together with the action for compensation for damage,[15] the best means of protection against illegal actions of the institutions when they are not in a position to directly challenge their legality in the Court. When the Court interprets[16] a provision of Community law, this interpretation must be accepted and applied by national courts[17] when called

[14] EEC, Art. 177.

[15] EEC, Arts. 178 and 215.

[16] With regard to methods of interpretation, see, *e.g.* Case 75/63 *Hoekstra* v. *Bedrijfsvereniging Detailhandel* [1964] E.C.R. 177 and Case 53/81 *Levin* v. *Staatssecretaris van Justitie* [1982] E.C.R. 1035 at 1048(9).

[17] See 1972 European Communities Act, s.3(1) and Case 33/76 *Rewe* v. *Landwirtschaftskammer Saarland* [1976] E.C.R. 1989 at 1997(5), where the Court based this obligation on EEC, Art. 5. According to the Court, EEC, Art. 177 calls for "judicial co-operation" between the Court and the national Courts; see Joined Cases 110 and 111/78 *Ministère Public and A.S.B.L.* v. *Van Wesemael* [1979] E.C.R. 35 at 51(21). By and large the national Courts are responsible for applying Community law, while the Court has exclusive competence to interpret its provisions. Those respective tasks and powers have been specified over the years in the Court's case law:
(a) the Court has no jurisdiction under Art. 177 to apply the Treaty to a specific national case: Case 6/64 *Costa* v. *ENEL* [1964] E.C.R. 585 at 592. It may nevertheless furnish the national court with the interpretative criteria necessary to enable it to dispose of the dispute: Case 106/79 *Vereniging Boekhandels* v. *Eldi Records* [1980] E.C.R. 1137 at 1147(7);
(b) the considerations which may have led a national court or tribunal to its choice of questions, as well as the relevance which it attributes to such questions in the context of a case before it, are excluded from review by the Court: Case 53/79 *ONPTS* v. *Damiani* [1980] E.C.R. 273 at 281(5);
(c) the Treaty does not prescribe a particular form in which a national court must present its request for a ruling; the Court must derive from the wording of the request the questions which relate exclusively to the interpretation of the Community provisions: Case 5/69 *Völk* v. *Vervaecke* [1969] E.C.R. 295 at 301(2/4);
(d) it is not for the Court to appropriate to itself an assessment of the jurisdiction of the national court to refer the question or of the presence of a

upon to ensure application of the said provision. On the other hand, parties will not contest lightly such an interpretation, although they remain free to do so. In other words, if the Court's interpretation given in a preliminary ruling is *de jure* limited to the case under review, it has, *de facto*, effect *erga omnes*.[18]

legal interest requiring protection on the part of the applicant in the main action: Case 65/81 *Reina* v. *Landeskreditbank Baden-Württemberg* [1982] E.C.R. 33;

(e) the Court may not, on the basis of Art. 177, give judgment on the interpretation of a provision of national law: Case 152/79 *Lee* v. *Minister for Agriculture* [1980] E.C.R. 1495 at 1507(11);

(f) the Court, in applying Art. 177, is not competent to decide on the compatibility of a national provision with Community law: Case 10/71 *Ministère Public Luxembourgeois* v. *Muller* [1971] E.C.R. 723 at 729(7). Nevertheless, the Court has the power to provide a national court with criteria of interpretation coming within Community law enabling that court to determine whether such rules are compatible with the Community rule invoked: Joined Cases 95 and 96/79 *Kefer and Delmelle* [1980] E.C.R. 103 at 112(5);

(g) The preliminary ruling of the Court is binding on the national court as to the interpretation of the Community provision: Case 811/79 *Amministrazione delle Finanze* v. *Ariete* [1980] E.C.R. 2545 at 2553(6);

(h) the jurisdiction of the Court to give rulings on the validity of measures adopted by the institutions extends to all the grounds capable of invalidating those measures, including the fact that they are contrary to a rule of international law: Joined Cases 21–24/72 *International Fruit Company* v. *Produktschap voor Groenten en Fruit* [1972] E.C.R. 1219 at 1226(6);

(i) a question relating to the application of Art. 215(2) (non-contractual liability of the Community) cannot be determined in proceedings for a preliminary ruling: Case 101/78 *Granaria* v. *Hoofdproduktschap voor Akkerbouwprodukten* [1979] E.C.R. 623 at 638(10);

(j) the Court has jurisdiction to give a ruling only when there is a genuine dispute before the national court: Case 104/79 *Foglia* v. *Novello* [1980] E.C.R. 745 at 760(11);

(k) when the Court declares a regulation void under a procedure under Art. 177, it may, by analogy with Art. 174, state which of the effects of the regulation shall be considered as definitive: Case 145/79 *Roquette Frères* v. *French Customs Administration* [1980] E.C.R. 2917 at 2946(52);

(l) it is for the national court, in the framework of close co-operation established by Art. 177 between the national Courts and the Court based on the assignment to each of different functions, to decide at what stage in the proceedings it is appropriate to refer a question to the Court: Case 72/83 *Campus Oil Limited* v. *Minister for Industry and Energy* [1984] E.C.R. 2727 at 2745(10).

[18] See Case 66/80 *International Chemical Corporation* v. *Amministrazione delle Finanze dello Stato* [1981] E.C.R. 1191 at 1215(13); see however Case 61/79 *Amministrazione delle Finanze dello Stato* v. *Denkavit Italiana* [1980] E.C.R. 1205 at 1223(17).

The object of the Court's competence in this field is to ensure uniform interpretation and application, within all the Member States, of the provisions of Community law; such uniformity constitutes an essential requirement for the existence and functioning of the common market.[19]

Requests for a preliminary ruling must emanate from national courts or tribunals.[20] The national court or tribunal may or, when there is no judicial remedy against its decision, must[21] request such a ruling each time it considers that, in order to give judgment in a case pending before it, it needs a decision on the question. This can occur when, having to apply a Community rule, the national judge finds himself confronted with a question concerning the interpretation or legality of this rule. A distinction must be made here between primary Community law, in which case only interpretation can be requested, and secondary law, in

---

[19] See Case 6/64 *Costa* v. *ENEL* [1964] E.C.R. 585 at 594; see also Case 28/67 *Molkerei-Zentrale Westfalen* v. *Hauptzollamt Paderborn* [1968] E.C.R. 143 at 153.

[20] Whether or not a national organ which transmits a question to the Court is a court of law must be determined in accordance with national law. See, *e.g.* Case 61/65 *Vaassen* v. *Beambtenfonds Mijnbedrijf* [1966] E.C.R. 261 at 273. The Court can only be requested to give a ruling by a court which is called upon to give judgment in proceedings intended to lead to a decision of a judicial nature: Case 138/80 *Borker* [1980] E.C.R. 1975 at 1977(4). Arbitrators in disputes between parties to a contract under a clause inserted in that contract cannot be considered as a "court or tribunal": Case 102/81 *Nordsee* v. *Reederei Mond* [1982] E.C.R. 1095 at 1110(13). On the other hand, an appeals committee set up by a professional body and which may affect the exercise of rights granted by Community law is considered a "court"; Case 246/80 *Broekmeulen* v. *Huisarts Registratie Commissie* [1981] E.C.R. 2311 at 2328(17).

[21] EEC, Art. 177(3). The particular purpose of the third paragraph of Art. 177 is to prevent a body of national case-law that is not in accord with the rules of Community law from coming into existence in any Member State; Joined Cases 35 and 36/82 *Morson and Jhanjan* v. *State of the Netherlands* [1982] E.C.R. 3723 at 3734(8). The obligation to refer a question to the Court does not exist however when it is raised in interlocutory proceedings and the decision to be taken is not binding on the court or tribunal which later has to deal with the substance of the case; Joined Cases 35 and 36/82 *Morson*, see above, at 3734(10). There are situations where the obligation does not apply: (1) the question raised is not relevant, (2) the Community measure has already been interpreted or (3) the correct application of Community law is so clear (*acte clair*) that there is no room for any reasonable doubt; Case 283/81 *CILFIT* v. *Ministry of Health* [1982] E.C.R. 3415 at 3428(8–16).

which case the Court also has jurisdiction to give a ruling on the validity.

As to the precise meaning of the words "where such a question is raised," it seems that this condition is fulfilled as soon as a difference of opinion arises concerning the interpretation (and in the case of acts also the validity) of a provision of Community law. According to the Court, questions can be raised by the parties to the dispute, but also by the national court or tribunal itself.[22]

However, the obligation to refer a question only exists when the national judge considers that a decision on the question is necessary to enable him to give judgment; in other words, it is his decision. Furthermore, it is also within the discretionary power of the national judge whether a question is raised in good faith or whether it is a purely procedural move initiated by a party, for instance to delay judgment.[23] There is therefore nothing automatic in the procedure of the preliminary ruling: as was said, it lies entirely within the discretionary powers of the national judge and neither the Court,[24] nor national law[25] nor a Community rule[26] can deprive him of this right.

Once the national judge has decided to refer a question to the Court, he suspends the proceedings in the national court or tribunal, and awaits the answer from the Court before resuming them.

It should be noted also that the "summary and urgent character of a procedure in the national court does not prevent the Court from regarding itself as validly seized" to give a preliminary ruling.[27] However, a national court or tribunal is not required to refer to the Court (even when no judicial remedy is available

---

[22] Case 126/80 *Salonia* v. *Poidomani and Giglio* [1981] E.C.R. 1563 at 1577(7).
[23] See the opinion of the Advocate General in Case 6/64 *Costa* v. *ENEL* [1964] E.C.R. 585 at 607 where mention is made of a "preliminary inquiry of legality" concerning the relevance of the question to the solution of the dispute.
[24] Case 5/77 *Tedeschi* v. *Denkavit* [1977] E.C.R. 1555 at 1574(17).
[25] Case 166/73 *Rheinmühle* v. *Einfuhr-und Vorratsstelle Getreide* [1974] E.C.R. 33 at 38(4).
[26] Case 127/73 *BRT* v. *Sabam* [1974] E.C.R. 51 at 63(23).
[27] Case 107/76 *Hoffmann-La Roche* v. *Centrafarm* [1977] E.C.R. 957 at 973(4).

against its decision) a question raised in interlocutory proceedings for an interim order. However this only applies if each of the parties is entitled to institute proceedings or to require proceedings to be instituted on the substance of the case. Furthermore, it must be possible, during such proceedings, to re-examine the question provisionally decided in the summary proceedings and to refer it to the Court.[28]

It is clear from the abundance of requests for preliminary rulings[29] that here lies an essential function, not only in regard to the development of Community law, but also as an instrument at the disposal of natural and legal persons confronted with Community measures whose legality they cannot directly challenge in the Court. Indeed when, in a preliminary ruling, an act is declared by the Court to be invalid, it becomes inapplicable, which has, practically speaking, the same result for the plaintiff as an annulment.

(5) *Compensation for damage caused by institutions*

In case of non-contractual liability, the Community shall make good, in accordance with the general principles common to the law of the Member States, any damage caused by its institutions or by its servants in the performance of their duties.[30]

In one of its first judgments concerning claims for redress, the Court held that an administrative measure which has not been annulled cannot in itself constitute on the part of the administration a wrongful act inflicting damage upon those whom it affects.[31] In later judgments, however, the Court reversed its

---

[28] *Ibid.*, at 973(5). In a decision in summary proceedings, the President of the Arrondissementsrechtbank at Utrecht gave an interim order which was subject to the proviso that the plaintiff initiate proceedings in the same court within a period of six weeks so as to be able to request the Court to make a preliminary ruling, which indeed was done; Case 36/74 *Walrave* v. *Union Cycliste Internationale* [1974] E.C.R. 1405.

[29] Until December 31, 1989, 1917 cases were filed (Twenty-third Gen. Rep. (1989), 437).

[30] EEC, Arts. 178 and 215.

[31] Case 25/62 *Plauman* v. *Commission* [1963] E.C.R. 95 at 108. See also Joined Cases 35/62 and 16/63 *Leroy* v. *High Authority* [1963] E.C.R. 197 at 207 and Case 93/63 *Minot* v. *Commission* [1964] E.C.R. 489 at 511.

position, indicating that actions for annulment and claims for damage were different proceedings and that the Treaty in providing for an appeal for damage introduced an autonomous form of action, and subject to conditions on its use dictated by its specific nature. Indeed, it differs from an application for annulment in that its end is not the abolition of a particular measure, but compensation for damage caused by an institution in the performance of its duties.[32]

However, the Court indicated that non-contractual liability of the Community pre-supposes at the very least the unlawful nature of the act besides actual damage and causal relationship between act and damage.[33] On the other hand, the unlawful nature does not, in itself, make the Community responsible for compensation in case of damage.[34] Where legislative action involving measures of economic policy is concerned, the Community does not incur non-contractual liability unless a sufficiently flagrant violation of a superior rule of law for the protection of the damaged party has occurred.[35]

The damage for which compensation is sought must of course be certain and have been assessed or be assessable. The Court has, however, accepted the admissibility of an action in which the Court is asked to declare the Community liable for imminent damage foreseeable with sufficient certainty even if the damage cannot yet be precisely assessed.[36]

As follows from the Treaty and as was confirmed by the Court, the latter has exclusive jurisdiction to hear cases based upon the Community's non-contractual liability, but there is now an exception: when such a case is raised in a proceeding before the Court

[32] Case 5/71 *Zuckerfabrik Schöppenstedt* v. *Council* [1971] E.C.R. 975 at 983(3).
[33] Case 51/81 *De Franceschi* v. *Council and Commission* [1982] E.C.R. 117 at 134(9).
[34] Joined Cases 83 and 94/76, etc. *HNL* v. *Council and Commission* [1978] E.C.R. 1209 at 1224(4).
[35] Joined Cases 197 etc./80 *Ludwigshafener Walzmühle* v. *Council and Commission* [1981] E.C.R. 3211 at 3246(19).
[36] Case 256/81 *Pauls Agriculture* v. *Council and Commission* [1983] E.C.R. 1707 at 1721(15) and Case 59/83 *Biovilac* v. *EEC* [1984] E.C.R. 4057 at 4075(9).

of First Instance.[37] The Court also stated that it has no jurisdiction in cases in which the application for compensation is, in fact, directed against measures adopted by the national authorities for the purpose of applying provisions of Community law. But the fact that a claim against the Community was dismissed by the Court does not prevent an undertaking from suing a Member State for faulty implementation of Community law.[38] When the damage caused by the national implementing measures finds its origin in the underlying Community rule, the liability of the Community can only be established by the Court on the basis of Community law.[39] As was indicated,[40] claims for compensation cannot be brought in a proceeding for a preliminary ruling.

Actions for compensation for damage are subject to a five-year period of limitation.[41]

When the Court allocates compensation for damage caused by a Community act, the latter becomes virtually inapplicable with regard to the plaintiff, in the same way as an act declared invalid in a proceeding for a preliminary ruling. The action for compensation for damage, therefore, constitutes another instrument at the disposal of natural and legal persons confronted with Community measures whose legality they cannot directly challenge in the Court.

---

[37] Joined Cases 106 to 120/87 *Asteris* v. *Hellenic Republic and Commission*, September 28, 1988 (not yet published). See the Decision establishing the Court of First Instance, Art. 3(2), O.J. 1988, L. 319/1.

[38] *Ibid.*

[39] Case 126/76 *Dietz* v. *Commission* [1977] E.C.R. 2431. See also Case 101/78 *Granaria* v. *Hoofdproduktschap voor Akkerbouwprodukten* [1979] E.C.R. 623 at 640(3) and Case 310/81 *EISS* v. *Commission* [1984] E.C.R. 1341, where the Court recognised a financial relationship between the Commission and the Member State and between that Member State and the institution receiving Community assistance, and it is incumbent upon the latter to produce evidence of a causal link between the alleged damage and a wrongful Community act.

[40] See under "(4) Preliminary Ruling," above.

[41] Protocol on the Statute of the Court, Art. 43 (this Protocol is annexed to the Treaty). See Joined Cases 256, etc./80 and 5/81 *Birra Wührer* v. *Council and Commission* [1982] E.C.R. 85.

(6) *Other cases within the Court's jurisdiction*

The objection of illegality[42] gives, according to the Court,

> "expression to a general principle conferring upon any party to proceedings the right to challenge, for the purpose of obtaining the annulment of a decision of direct and individual concern to that party, the validity of previous acts of the institutions which form the legal basis of the decision which is being attacked, if that party was not entitled under Article 173 of the Treaty to bring a direct action challenging those acts by which it was thus affected without having been in a position to ask that they be declared void."[43]

Although the Treaty refers to a "regulation," the Court mentions "acts" in general.[44]

For the Court it is clear from the wording and the general scheme of Article 184 that, although this is not specified, a declaration of inapplicability is only possible in proceedings brought before the Court itself under some other provision of the Treaty and that the plea may only be used against a measure which is the basis for the act in dispute. In other words, the objection of illegality does not constitute an independent action and may only be sought incidentally.[45]

The objection of illegality constitutes, with the request for a preliminary ruling and the claim for compensation for damage, the third way for natural and legal persons to challenge a measure whose legality they cannot directly ask the Court to review.

Disputes between the Community and its servants.[46] With some rare exceptions, actions brought by Community servants present

---

[42] EEC, Art. 184; see, *e.g.* Case 258/80 *Rumi* v. *Commission* [1982] E.C.R. 487.
[43] Case 15/57 *Hauts Fournaux de Chasse* v. *High Authority* [1957 and 1958] E.C.R. 211 and Case 9/56 *Meroni* v. *High Authority* [1957 and 1958] E.C.R. 133.
[44] Case 92/78 *Simmenthal* v. *Commission* [1979] E.C.R. 777 at 800(39).
[45] See Joined Cases 275/80 and 24/81 *Krupp* v. *Commission* [1981] E.C.R. 2489.
[46] EEC, Art. 179 and Staff Regs. Art. 91.

little interest for Community law as such.[47] Since the establishment of the Court of First Instance,[48] those cases come first under the jurisdiction of the latter[49] and an appeal to the Court is possible on points of law by the party which has succumbed in its conclusions before the Court of First Instance. In such disputes the four institutions, including the Court itself, appear as defendants; although it is not an institution, the same applies to the Social and Economic Committee[50] and to the Court of Auditors.[51]

Reference must also be made to the possibility provided for in the Treaty of *attributing jurisdiction* to the Court in contracts concluded by or on behalf of the Community, whether those contracts are governed by public or private law.[52] An explicit attribution of jurisdiction is necessary since the Treaty provides that disputes to which the Community is a party shall not on that ground be excluded from the jurisdiction of the courts and tribunals of the Member States.[53]

In this context should be mentioned the attribution of jurisdiction to the Court by the Protocol on the interpretation of the Convention on jurisdiction and the enforcement of judgments in civil and commercial matters[54] concluded between the Member States.[55]

---

[47] See, *e.g.* Joined Cases 7/56 etc., *Algera* v. *Common Assembly* [1957 and 1958] E.C.R. 39 at 55 and Case 6/60 *Humblet* v. *Belgium* [1960] E.C.R. 559, which in fact concerned a dispute between the Community and a Member State.

[48] See Decision of the Council of October 28, 1988, O.J. 1988, L 319/1.

[49] *Ibid.,* Art. 3(1)(a).

[50] Art. 1(2) of the Staff Regs. assimilates the Committee to the institutions; see, *e.g.* Case 277/82 *Papageorgopoulos* v. *Economic and Social Committee* [1983] E.C.R. 2897.

[51] See, *e.g.* Joined Cases 316/82 and 40/83 *Kohler* v. *Court of Auditors* [1984] E.C.R. 641 and Case 257/83 *Williams* v. *Court of Auditors* [1984] E.C.R. 3547.

[52] EEC, Art. 181.

[53] EEC, Art. 183.

[54] See Art. 3 of the Protocol of June 3, 1971 to the Convention of Brussels of September 27, 1968 (O.J. 1978, L. 304). See Joined Cases 9 and 10/77 *Bavaria Fluggesellschaft and Germanair* v. *Eurocontrol* [1977] E.C.R. 1517. See also Protocol of the Convention of February 29, 1968 on the mutual recognition of companies and bodies corporate and Art. 73 of the Convention of December 15, 1975 for the European Patent for the Common Market.

[55] This Protocol does not constitute a special agreement to submit disputes between Member States to the Court, in the sense of EEC, Art. 182, since the Convention does not concern a "subject matter of the Treaty."

The Court, in cases before it, may also prescribe the necessary *interim measures*[56] which can be divided into measures suspending the application of the contested act and of the enforcement measures[57] and other interim measures.[58] With regard to the suspension of the application of measures it must be noted that actions brought before the Court do not have suspensory effect.[59] An application to suspend the operation of any measure adopted by an institution shall be admissible only if the applicant is challenging that measure in proceedings before the Court.[60] The criteria used by the (President of the) Court in determining whether or not to grant suspension, lies in the harm the application of the measure may cause to the applicant.[61]

Other interim measures can be prescribed against persons, institutions and Member States.[62] It should be noted that the Treaty grants the Court wide discretionary powers in the choice of measures it can prescribe, since the only criterion is that they must be "necessary." It should be noted, however, that the (President of the) Court has always been rather reluctant to grant interim measures and that the Court considers that they should only be ordered in exceptional circumstances.[63]

There seems to be no limit as to the kind of interim measures the Court may prescribe: besides the suspension of the application of an act of an institution, the Court has, *e.g.* ordered parties to start negotiations to agree upon an alternative solution,[64] authorised a Member State to take temporary measures with the

---

[56] EEC, Arts. 185, 186 and 192 and Rules of procedure, Title III, Chap. I.
[57] EEC, Art. 185.
[58] EEC, Art. 186.
[59] EEC, Art. 185.
[60] Rules, Art. 83(1).
[61] See, *e.g.* Case 113/77R and 113/77R-/Int. *NTN Toyo* v. *Council* [1977] E.C.R. 1721 at 1725(6).
[62] For persons, see Case 3/75R *Johnson & Firth Brown* v. *Commission* [1975] E.C.R. 1; for institutions, see Case 113/77R *NTN* (n. 61 above) and for Member States, see Joined Cases 31/77R and 53/77R *Commission* v. *U.K.* [1977] E.C.R. 921 at 925.
[63] Case 113/77R *NTN* (n. 61 above).
[64] Case 61/77R *Commission* v. *Ireland* [1977] E.C.R. 937 at 943(34).

consent of the Commission[65] and suspended the application of a measure on condition that a party continues to provide security.[66]

(7) *Court of Appeal*

Since 1989, the Court of Justice also functions as a court of appeal from the decisions of the newly created Court of First Instance.[67]

An appeal may be brought before the Court within two months of the notification of the decision appealed against. This decision may concern a final decision, a decision disposing of the substantial part of the substantive issues only or a decision disposing of procedural issues concerning a plea of lack of competence or inadmissibility.[68]

The appeal may be brought by the unsuccessful party (the interveners when the decision directly affects them), the Member States and the Community institutions.[69]

An appeal to the Court shall be limited to points of law. It shall lie on the grounds of lack of competence of the Court of First Instance, a breach of procedure as well as the infringement of Community law.[70]

If the appeal is well-founded, the Court shall quash the decision and may itself give final judgment or refer the case back to the Court of First Instance.[71]

(8) *Judicial remedies: a summary*

As was pointed out, the Member States, the Council and the Commission have, subject to time-limits, unlimited access to the

---

[65] Case 61/77R *Commission* v. *Ireland* [1977] E.C.R. 1411 at 1415(2).
[66] Case 113/77R and 113/77R-Int *NTN Toyo* (see n. 61 above) at 1726(2).
[67] Council Dec. of October 24, 1988 establishing a Court of First Instance of the European Communities, O.J. 1988, L 319/1.
[68] Protocol on the Statute of the Court of Justice (as modified by the above -mentioned Dec.) Art. 49(1).
[69] *Ibid.*, Art. 49(2).
[70] *Ibid.*, Art. 51.
[71] *Ibid.*, Art. 54.

Court; the access is rather limited for Parliament and for natural and legal persons, although they have several actions at their disposal to obtain from the Court a review of the legality of acts of the institutions.

To summarise, the principal proceedings in the court may be initiated by:

a Member State	— against another Member State for failure to fulfil an obligation under Community law;
	— against the Council and/or the Commission for illegality of an act, failure to act or to obtain compensation;
	— against Parliament for illegality of an act;
the Council	— against the Commission for illegality of an act or failure to act;
	— against Parliament for illegality of an Act;
the Commission	— against a Member State for failure to fulfil an obligation under Community law;
	— against the Council for illegality of an act or failure to act;
	— against Parliament for illegality of an act;
Parliament	— against the Council and/or the Commission for illegality of an act if its prerogatives are at stake and for failure to act;
Persons	— against the Council and/or the Commission for illegality of an act or for failure to act if they are directly and individually concerned;
	— against institutions for compensation for damage.
	— to obtain a preliminary ruling via a national court or tribunal on the interpretation of Community law and the legality of an act;

— to plead inapplicability of an act underlying a measure whose annulment is sought;

Servants   — against the Council, the Commission, Parliament, the Court, the Social and Economic Committee and the Court of Auditors under the court's full jurisdiction.

3. The procedure

The rules concerning the procedure before the Court are laid down in the Protocol on the Statute of the Court annexed to the Treaty and in the Rules of Procedure which the Court adopts after having received the unanimous approval of the Council.[72] The Rules contain, apart from the rules "contemplated" by the Statute, "any other provision necessary for applying and, when necessary, for supplementing it."[73]

The procedure before the Court, for which no fees are charged, consists of two parts: a written and an oral one. The language of the proceedings must be one of the nine official languages of the Community and is determined by the applicant.[74]

(1) *The written procedure*[75]

The procedure starts with the submission to the Court of a written *application* addressed to the Registrar.[76] The Statute and

---

[72] EEC, Art. 188. The Rules are published in O.J. 1974, L. 350, and have been modified several times, lastly in 1989 (O.J. 1989, L. 241/1). See also Annex II to the Rules: Extension of time-limits on account of distance; O.J. 1987, L. 165/3 and the Supplementary Rules, *ibid.,* at 4.

[73] Protocol, Art. 44.

[74] Rules, Art. 29(2); the languages are: Danish, Dutch, German, English, French, Greek, Italian, Portugese and Spanish.

[75] Statute, Arts. 18 *et seq.*, and Rules, Title II, Chap. I.

[76] See Instructions to the Registrar O.J. 1982, C 39/35.

the Rules contain various requirements as to form, content and accompanying documents of the application.[77] The Member States and the institutions are represented by an agent appointed for each case; other parties must be represented by a lawyer entitled to practice before a court of a Member State.[78] It is important to note that the application must state the grounds on which it is based, since parties may not, in the course of the proceedings, raise fresh issues, unless these are based on matters of law or of fact which come to light in the course of the written procedure.[79] The time-limit within which the application must be filed is also essential; appeals for annulment must be instituted within two months of the publication of the measure or of its notification to the plaintiff.[80] This time-limit was extended by Annex II to the Rules of procedure for parties living outside Luxembourg.

The fact that an application is lodged with the Court is published in the Official Journal; besides the names of the parties, the subject-matter of the dispute and the claims of the applicant, "a summary of the contentions and of the main arguments" are also published.[81]

The application is notified to the defendant who then has one month to file a *defence*.[82] The plaintiff's application and the defence may (but not *must*) be supplemented by a *reply* from the applicant and *a rejoinder* from the defendant. The time-limit within which those pleadings have to be lodged is fixed by the President of the Court.

Before formally closing the written part of the procedure, the Court, at the suggestion of the Judge-Rapporteur[83] or the Advo-

---

[77] Statute, Art. 19 and Rules, Arts. 18 *et seq.*

[78] Statute, Art. 17. The application must also state an address for service at the place where the Court has its seat. It shall also give the name of a person who is authorised and has expressed willingness to accept service; Rules, Art. 38(2).

[79] Rules, Art. 42(2); see Case 139/79 *Maizena* v. *Council* [1980] E.C.R. 3393 at 3424(32).

[80] EEC, Art. 173(3). If publication in the Official Journal allows the date to be determined with some precision, (*i.e.* the moment it becomes available), the matter is more delicate with letters, especially when they are not registered, see Case 108/79 *Belfiore* v. *Commission* [1980] E.C.R. 1769 at 1781(7).

[81] Rules, Art. 16(6).

[82] Rules, Art. 40(1).

[83] Rules, Art. 9(2).

cate-General, may decide to prescribe measures of inquiry[84] for the case, *i.e.* interrogation of the parties, request for information, hearing of witnesses,[85] etc.

In the case of a preliminary ruling, the parties, the Member States, the Commission and, where appropriate, the Council, are entitled to submit statements of case or written observations to the Court.[86] Finally, it should be noted that the Member States and the institutions may always intervene in cases before the Court; legal and natural persons have the same right when they establish an interest in the result of a case.[87]

(2) *The oral procedure*

The oral procedure[88] starts with the reading of the report of the Judge-Rapporteur, the hearing by the Court of agents, legal advisers or council and of the Opinion of the Advocate-General, as well as the hearing of witnesses and experts, if any. The Opinion of the Advocate-General is usually read during a separate Court session which indicates the end of the oral part of the procedure.[89] The judgment[90] is, in turn, read in open Court, at a later date.

(3) *Special forms of procedure*

The Statutes and the Rules contain provisions for several special forms of procedure[91] such as a summary procedure (examined

---

[84] For details, see Rules, Arts. 45–54.
[85] The rules contain several provisions concerning witnesses: the Court may impose penalties in case of default (Statute, Art. 24); the Court may have a witness heard by the judicial authorities of the place of his permanent residence (Statute, Art. 26); Member States must treat any violation of an oath by a witness in the same manner as if the offence had been committed before one of their courts with jurisdiction in civil procedure and prosecute the offender before their competent court at the instance of the Court (Statute, Art. 27).
[86] Statute, Art. 20.
[87] Statute, Art. 37.
[88] See Statute, Art. 18(4) and Rules, Arts. 55–62.
[89] Rules, Art. 59.
[90] For the prescribed content of the judgment, see Rules, Art. 63. The judgment always contains a decision on the costs which are normally born by the losing party; Rules, Arts. 69 *et seq.*
[91] See Statute, Arts. 36 *et seq.* and Rules, Arts. 83 *et seq.*

above under "other cases within the Court's jurisdiction"), intervention, judgment by default, third party proceedings,[92] interpretation and revision.

Further Reading

C. Lenz, "The Court of Justice of the European Communities" 127, (1989) E.L.Rev.

T. Kennedy, "The Essential Minimum: The Establishment of the Court of First Instance" 7, (1989) E.L.Rev.

H. Rasmussen, "Between Self-Restraint and Activism": A Judicial policy for the European Court" 28. (1988) E.L.Rev.

K. Borgsmidt, "The Advocate General at the European Court of Justice: A Comparative Study" 106 (1988) E.L.Rev.

K. Bradley, "The European Court and the Legal Basis of Community Legislation" 379, (1988) E.L.Rev.

M. Cappelletti, "Is the European Court of Justice 'Running Wild'?" 1, (1987) E.L.Rev.

V. THE COURT OF FIRST INSTANCE

As provided for in the SEA,[93] the Council attached to the Court of Justice[94] "a court with jurisdiction to hear and determine at first instance, subject to a right of appeal to the Court of Justice on points of law only and in accordance with the conditions laid down by the Statute, certain classes of action or proceedings brought by natural or legal persons."[95] This Court of First Instance started functioning in November 1989.

(1) *Members of the Court of First Instance*

There are twelve members chosen from persons whose independence is beyond doubt and who possess the ability required for

---

[92] See Case 292/84 *T.P. Bolognese* v. *Scharf and Commission* [1987] E.C.R. 3563.
[93] SEA, Art. 11.
[94] Council Decision of October 24, 1988, O.J. 1988, L. 319/1.
[95] EEC, Art. 168A(1).

appointment to judicial office. They are appointed by common accord of the Governments of the Member States for a term of six years. The membership is partially renewed every three years, and retiring members are eligible for re-appointment.[96] They elect their President for three years.

The members of the Court of First Instance may be called upon to perform the task of Advocate-General; contrary to the Court of Justice there are no appointed Advocates-General, but their task is the same[97] and they may make their submissions in writing.[98]

The Court of First Instance only sits in chambers of three or five judges.[99] It establishes its rules of procedure in agreement with the Court of Justice; those rules require unanimous approval of the Council.[1]

(2) *Jurisdiction*

The Court of First Instance exercises at first instance the jurisdiction conferred by the Treaty on the Court in:

(a) disputes between the institutions and their servants[2];

(b) actions brought against the Commission by undertakings concerning ECSC levies, production, prices and agreements and concentrations[3];

---

[96] EEC, Art. 168A(3).

[97] Decision of October 24, 1988, Art. 2(3).

[98] *Ibid.,* Art. 9 (46(3)).

[99] *Ibid.,* Art. 2(4).

[1] EEC, Art. 168A(4). Since the Rules of Procedure have not been adopted yet, the Court of First Instance presently applies the Rules of the Court of Justice.

[2] See above under "Court of Justice, (6) other cases within the Court's jurisdiction" and EEC, Art. 179. The first case is T 159/89 *Vitranyani* v. *Commission.* Another 153 cases were transferred from the Court of Justice; Dec. of October 24, 1988, Art. 14.

Cases before the Court are from now on preceded by the letter C (for Cour) and the cases before the Court of First Instance by the letter T (for Tribunal).

[3] Dec., Art. 3(b) and ECSC, Arts. 50 and 57 to 66.

(c) actions brought against an institution by natural or legal persons relating to the implementation of EEC competition rules applicable to undertakings[4];

(d) actions for compensation for damage caused by an institution through an act or failure to act which is the object of an action for which the Court of First Instance has jurisdiction,[5] and

(e) actions brought against an institution concerning dumping and subsidies, if the Council so decides after two years of operation of the Court of First Instance.[6]

(3) *Procedure before the Court of First Instance*

Most of the rules provided for in the Protocol on the Statute of the Court of Justice apply to the Court of First Instance.[7] Interestingly, the Court of First Instance may dispense with the written procedure.[8]

Where a case is referred back by the Court of Justice, the Court of First Instance shall be bound by the decision of the Court of Justice on points of law.[9]

Further Reading

John Usher, *European Court Practice*, (1983) London, Sweet & Maxwell.
Brown and Jacobs, *The Court of Justice of the European Communities,* (3rd ed., 1989) London, Sweet and Maxwell.

---

[4] *Ibid.,* at (c) and EEC, Arts. 85 *et seq.*
[5] Dec., Art. 3(2).
[6] *Ibid.,* at (3). See EEC, Art. 113.
[7] *Ibid.,* Art. 9 (46 *et seq.*).
[8] Decision, Art. 9(52). The first judgment was given on January 30, 1990, only two weeks after the formal hearing; *York von Wartenburg* v. *Parliament.*
[9] *Ibid.,* Art. 9 (55(2)).

VI. OTHER BODIES OF THE EUROPEAN COMMUNITIES

1. The Court of Auditors[10]

The Court of Auditors was set up by the Treaty amending certain financial provisions of the European Treaties and of the Merger Treaty.[11] The twelve members are appointed by the Council after consulting Parliament. Generally speaking, the provisions concerning the members are similar to those which apply to the members of the Court of Justice.[12]

The Court of Auditors examines the accounts of all revenue and expenditure of the Community and of any body created by the latter,[13] not only to determine whether all revenue has been received and expenditure incurred in a lawful manner, but also whether the financial management has been sound. Since a vast proportion of the Community revenue is collected and made available by the Member States, on-the-spot checks by the Court of Auditors are provided, not only in the institutions, but also in the Member States where it is carried out in liaison with the national audit bodies. It can require them to forward any document or information necessary to carry out its task.

The Court of Auditors draws up an annual report after the close of each financial year and forwards it to all the institutions.[14] This report allows Parliament to exercise its budgetary control.[15]

[10] EEC, Art. 206.
[11] This Treaty was signed at Brussels on July 22, 1975 but entered into force only on June 1, 1977 (O.J. 1977, L. 359/20); see Art. 15 modifying EEC, Art. 206.
[12] See EEC, Art. 206(2–10).
[13] EEC, Art. 206a(1); see, *e.g.* the European Centre for the Development of Vocational Training (O.J. 1975, L. 39/1) and the European Foundation for the Improvement of Living and Working Conditions (O.J. 1975, L. 139/1). An annex to the Treaty provides that the Court of Auditors also has jurisdiction to audit the European Development Fund. It does not audit the European Investment Bank.
[14] See, *e.g.* Report for the 1987 budget, O.J. 1988, C. 316.
[15] See under "European Parliament (5) Participation in the budgetary procedure," above.

It is published in the Official Journal, together with the replies of the institutions to the observations of the Court of Auditors. It may also submit observations on specific questions on its own initiative and deliver opinions at the request of the institutions.[16]

At the beginning of 1990, the Court of Auditors employed 372 people.

2. The Economic and Social Committee

The Economic and Social Committee[17] plays a consultative role mainly within the decision-making process of the Community: it is generally consulted by the Council, together with Parliament before final decisions are taken. If the Council fails to consult it when it is provided for by the Treaty, the final act can be annulled by the Court for infringement of an essential procedural requirement[18]; the required consultation must also be referred to in the relevant Community act.[19]

The Committee may also be consulted, either by the Council or the Commission, in all cases in which they consider it appropriate. At the 1972 Paris Summit meeting, the Heads of State or Government decided to invite "the Community institutions to recognise the right of the Economic and Social Committee in future to advise on its own initiative on all questions affecting the Community."[20]

The Committee is composed of 189 members appointed for four years by the Council in their personal capacity[21]; they may not be bound by mandatory instructions. The members are

[16] See, *e.g.* O.J. 1988, C. 188, on regional co-operation financed by the EDF under the Lomé Convention; O.J. 1988, C. 274, on management and control of public storage.
[17] EEC, Arts. 193–198.
[18] See above "Court of Justice, Grounds for annulment."
[19] See below "Community Acts: Regulations, etc., must be reasoned."
[20] See the own-initiative opinions in O.J. 1988, C.95, C.134 and C.318.
[21] See Case 297/86 *CIDA* v. *Council*, June 30, 1988 (not yet published) asking for annulment of the Council's decision nominating the members.

representatives of various categories of economic and social activities, in particular: producers, farmers, carriers, workers, tradesmen, craftsmen, members of the professions and the general public.[22]

3. The Consultative Committee of the ECSC

The ECSC Treaty provides for the creation of a Consultative Committee[23] attached to the High Authority, now the Commission. It consists of between 72 and 96 members made up of an equal number of producers, workers, consumers and dealers. They are appointed for two years in their personal capacity by the Council from a list drawn up by representative organisations also designated by the Council. The functions of the Consultative Committee are comparable in every respect to those of the Economic and Social Committee.

4. The Scientific and Technical Committee of Euratom

This Committee, set up by the Euratom Treaty, is attached to the Commission[24]; it consists of 33 members appointed for five years in their personal capacity by the Council after consultation with the Commission. It has an advisory status. The Commission must consult it *inter alia* before setting up the Joint Nuclear Research Centre or before working out the basic standards for the protection of the health of workers and the general public against dangers arising from ionizing radiations.

5. The European Investment Bank (EIB)

The task of the EIB[25] is to facilitate the economic expansion of the Community by opening fresh resources.[26]

[22] For further information on the Committee's composition and activities, see its annual report and the accounts published in the Bulletin of the European Communities.
[23] ECSC, Arts. 18 and 19.
[24] Euratom, Art. 134.
[25] EEC, Arts. 129–130 and Protocol annexed to the Treaty.
[26] EEC, Art. 3(j).

(1) *Internal structure*

The Bank is directed and managed by a Board of Governors, a Board of Directors and a Management Committee.

The Board of Governors consists of the Ministers of Finance of the Member States. It lays down general directives for the credit policy of the Bank; it also decides on possible increases in the subscribed capital,[27] on grants of special interest-bearing loans to the Bank to finance specific projects by Member States and on the granting of loans for investment projects to be carried out entirely or partially outside the European territory of the Member States.

The Board of Directors consists of 22 directors and 12 alternates nominated by each Member State and the Commission and appointed by the Board of Governors for five years.[28]

The Management Committee consists of a President and six vice-Presidents appointed for six years by the Board of Governors. The Management Committee is responsible for the current business of the Bank under the authority of the President and the supervision of the Board of Directors.

The officials and other employees of the Bank are not servants of the Community, but under contract to the Bank.

A Committee of three members verifies annually that the operations of the Bank have been conducted and its books kept in a proper manner.

The Bank has legal personality and its members are the Member States.[29] Its Statute is laid down in a Protocol annexed to the Treaty.

(2) *Activities of the Bank*

The EIB operates on a non-profit making basis; it grants loans to its members or to private and public undertakings for investment projects to be carried out in the European territories of the

---

[27] The capital of the Bank is presently 28 billion ECU.
[28] Statute, Art. 11(2).
[29] EEC, Art. 129.

Member States.[30] Loans are granted only on condition that other sources of financing are also used. When granting a loan to a body other than a Member State, it is conditional on an adequate guarantee, *e.g.* from the Member State concerned. The necessary funds are borrowed[31] on the international capital markets or those of the Member States.

(3) *Procedure for granting loans*

Requests for loans are sent either directly or through the Commission or the Member State concerned. Decisions regarding applications for loans or guarantees[32] are taken by the Board of Directors on proposals from othe Management Committee. Before deciding on the financing of a project[33] the Bank must secure the opinion of the interested Member State and the Commission. If the latter delivers an unfavourable opinion, the Board of Directors may not grant the loan (or guarantee) unless its decision is unanimous, the director nominated by the Commission abstaining.

Originally the bank was mainly intended to provide financial resources for the economic development of Southern Italy, the Mezzogiorno. This is still the case today, but other regions have been added, first by the successive enlargements of the Community and secondly by the economic crisis of the 1970's. About two-thirds of the Bank's loans go to the development regions of the Community[34] as a means of increasing economic and social cohesion.[35]

---

[30] This excludes only the French overseas departments: to go outside this area a derogation authorised by the Board of Governors is needed; Statute, Art. 18.

[31] In 1989, the Bank borrowed more than 9 billion ECU.

[32] The Bank may also guarantee loans contracted by public or private undertakings or other bodies; Statute, Art. 18(4).

[33] EEC, Art. 130 provides that the Bank shall finance in all sectors of the economy projects which are: (a) for developing less-developed regions; (b) for modernising or converting undertakings or for developing fresh activities; and (c) of common interest to several Member States.

[34] In 1989, out of 11,634 billion ECU lent in the Community, 64 per cent. went in loans for regional development.

[35] EEC, Title V.

The EIB also administers the so-called "NIC"[36] with which the Commission can finance the same kind of projects within the Community.

The Bank also provides loans for projects situated outside the Community, either from its own resources[37] or, under mandate for the account and at the risk of individual Member States, the EEC or Euratom. Generally speaking, these loans consist of financial aid provided for under various agreements, financial protocols and decisions concerning mainly Turkey, the African Carribean and Pacific States, the Overseas Countries and Territories (French), Yugoslavia, Lebanon, Maghreb and Machreck, etc.[38]

Through its sound financial operations both inside and outside the Community, the EIB has acquired a world-wide reputation as one of the major financial institutions for economic development.

VII. FINANCING COMMUNITY ACTIVITIES

1. Financial contributions of the Member States and the Community's own resources

The Decision on the Replacement of Financial Contributions from Member States by the Community's own Resources[39] inaugurated a new era in the history of the Communities. On the one hand, it made them, in a certain way, financially independent, with all the economic and political consequences this entails. On

---

[36] Nouvel Instrument Communautaire, *i.e.* new borrowing and loan facilities of the Community. It was set up in 1978 by Dec. 78/870 (O.J. 1978, L.298/9; see also Bull. 1978–10, 21). In 1989, the NIC lent 78·3 million ECU.

[37] In 1989, the Bank lent 612 million ECU outside the Community, of which 486 million came from its own resources.

[38] The loans granted in those countries amounted in 1988 to nearly 1 billion ECU.

[39] Dec. 70/243 of April 21, 1970, J.O. 1970, L. 94/19; O.J. Dec. 1970 (I), 224; it became effective on January 1, 1971 after ratification by the six national Parliaments.

the other hand, the Treaty amending Certain Budgetary Provisions of the ECSC, EEC and Euratom Treaties and of the Merger Treaty, conferred at the same time certain budgetary powers upon Parliament, as a necessary complement to the transfer of resources to the Community.[40]

In 1975 the budgetary provisions were again modified and complemented by the creation of the Court of Auditors.[41]

(1) *The Decision of April 21, 1970*

The main features of this decision can be summarised as follows:

(a) Both the agricultural levies and the Common Customs Tariff duties constitute own resources to be entered in the budget of the Community;

(b) The transfer of revenue from customs duties takes place progressively over a period of four years. From then on the budget of the Community is, save other revenue,[42] entirely financed from own resources.

(c) Since revenue accruing from the duties and levies does not suffice to cover the expenditures of the Community, revenue from the Value Added Tax is also allocated.[43]

---

[40] This Treaty became effective on January 1, 1971. The budgetary powers of Parliament are analysed above under "The European Parliament, (5) Participation in the budgetary procedure."

[41] Treaty amending Certain Financial Provisions of the Treaties establishing the European Communities and the Merger Treaty of July 22, 1975, O.J. 1977, L. 359/1.

[42] Other revenues are, *e.g.* the fines imposed upon enterprises for violation of the competition rules and the income-tax levied on the salaries of the officials.

[43] Dir. 77/388 (O.J. 1977, L. 145/1). The revenue results from the application of a rate not exceeding 1·4 per cent. of the basis used for assessing VAT, determined in a uniform manner for the Member States. The decision to increase the rate from 1 per cent. to 1·4 per cent. from January 1, 1986 and to 1·6 per cent. on January 1, 1988 was taken by the European Council at Fontainebleu in June 1984; see Bull. 6–1984, 11. The Dec. of April 21, 1970 was implemented by Reg. 2892/77 (O.J. 1977, L.336), see the Commission's report on the implementation of this Regulation: Com(88) 99 final.

As from January 1, 1980, the Community's expenditures were entirely financed by the revenue accruing from the agricultural levies, the customs duties and a percentage of the VAT collected in the Member States.

A decision on the system of the Community's own resources adopted in June 1988,[44] introduced the changes adopted by the European Council at Brussels, in February 1988:

   (i) the overall ceiling on own resources is set at 1.20 per cent. of total Community GNP for payments (1.30 per cent. for commitments);

   (ii) customs duties on ECSC products are to be paid to the Community;

   (iii) the costs of collecting traditional own resources will be deduced from the Member States' payments;

   (iv) the third source (VAT) will be collected at a rate of 1.4 per cent. applied to a VAT base limited to 55 per cent. of GNP to take account of the situation of Member States where consumption accounts for a high proportion of GNP;

   (v) a fourth resource, based on a GNP scale, is introduced.[45]

The Brussels European Council resolved a long standing feud about the Community's own resources which had become insufficient to cover the expenditures. This "liberated" the Community and allowed it to go ahead with the completion of the internal market by the end of 1992.

It should also be noted that the "budget correcting mechanism" introduced in 1976 to enable payments to be made to

[44] O.J. 1988, C. 102 and Bull. 3–1988, 105.
[45] For details see, *e.g.* Bull. 2–1988, 13 *et seq*.

Member States which, due to special economic conditions, are considered to bear a disproportionate burden in financing the budget,[46] will remain applicable. Furthermore, an adjustment was made to offset the effect of the introduction of the fourth resource. Compensation to the United Kingdom[47] is financed on the basis of a GNP scale, Germany's contribution is reduced by a third, and for Spain and Portugal abatement arrangements are applied in accordance with their Act of Accession.[48]

2. The Community budget, revenue and expenditure

As the Commission remarked about the budgetary procedure of 1988: "Thanks to the new instruments governing Community finances the problems which have beset the budgetary procedure in the past were very largely avoided."[49] The Commission was referring to the Interinstitutional Agreement on budgetary discipline and improvement of the budgetary procedure[50] and the Regulation amending the implementing regulation of the Decision of April 21, 1970 creating the Community's own resources.[51]

All items of revenue and expenditure of the three Communities must be included in estimates to be drawn up for each

---

[46] *I.e.* the U.K. Fourteenth General Report (1980), 59; Bull. 5–1980, 7 and Reg. 2744/80 (O.J. 1980, L. 284/4).

[47] In 1980 agreement was reached on the United Kingdom's contribution to the budget: the financial correcting mechanism was modified to allow a reduction for the U.K. and supplementary Community expenditures were provided for to help reduce certain regional disparities in the U.K. This compensated 66 per cent. of the difference between the U.K. VAT transfers and its receipts from the Community. The correction for 1990 was 2,430 million ECU.

[48] Act of accession, Arts. 187 and 374.

[49] Twenty-second General Report (1988), 66.

[50] This agreement came into force on July 1, 1988; O.J. 1988, C. 142. A novelty is the Financial Perspective 1988–1992; another important aspect of the agreement is the mutual obligation to comply with the financing objectives set by the European Council for certain priority policy areas (structural funds, integrated Mediterranean programmes, framework research programme). See Bull. 6–1988, 112.

[51] O.J. 1988, L. 176/1. The own resources for 1990 were estimated at 47·7 billion ECU; levies: 2,283, customs duties: 11,350, VAT: 28,218, GNP-based: 1,964, balance from previous year: 2,598, other: 304.

financial year and be shown in the budget.[52] The revenue and expenditure shown in the budget must be in balance.[53] The financial year runs from January 1 to December 31.[54] The structure of the general budget and the form in which it is to be presented are determined by Financial Regulations.[55] The budget consists of separate sections dealing with the revenue and expenditure of each institution. The section dealing with the Commission provides for expenditure in the following fields: agriculture, regional development, social fund, transport, environment, information and culture, fisheries, energy, research, innovation, development and administration. Total commitments for 1990 stood at 47.7 billion ECU.

(1) *Commitment and payment appropriations*

The Community budget contains "non-differentiated" and "differentiated" appropriations. Under the former, commitments can be made during the financial year and the corresponding payments can be made practically at the same time, *i.e.* during that financial year and the next. The differentiated appropriations consist of both commitments, *i.e.* the maximum that may be committed during that financial year, and the corresponding payments which may be disbursed either during that same year or at any time thereafter. This system is particularly suited for medium and long term operations such as research projects and infrastructure investments. The advantage of this method is that the total amount of the Community's financial participation can be committed at the start of the project but the payments only have to be made as the work progresses over the years.[56]

---

[52] One important item not covered by the Community budget is the European Development Fund (resources destined to finance aid to developing countries; the activities of the European Investment Bank do not appear on the budget either.

[53] EEC, Art. 199 and Merger Treaty, Art. 20.

[54] EEC, Art. 203(1).

[55] See O.J. 1977, L. 356/1, Arts. 15 and 16. This Regulation was amended in June 1988; see O.J. 1988, L. 185/3.

[56] The commitment and payment appropriations are mainly used for Euratom research and investment projects and for the regional fund expenditures.

(2) *Compulsory and non-compulsory expenditure*

The Treaty of July 22, 1975 amending certain financial provisions of the existing Treaties introduced the concept of "expenditure necessarily resulting from this Treaty or from acts adopted in accordance therewith,"[57] otherwise referred to as "compulsory" expenditures. A budgetary item is considered compulsory when the principle and the amount of the expenditure (either a figure or a precise mechanism for arriving at it) are statutorily prescribed in the Treaties, secondary legislation, international conventions or private contracts.[58]

A typical example of compulsory expenditures are those of the agricultural fund. Non-compulsory expenditures are practically speaking all the others: regional, social, research and staff appropriations. In practice however the expenditures are classified in one or the other category in a rather pragmatic way, by agreement between the Council and Parliament. One now even finds "non-privileged" non-compulsory expenditure.[59]

As was pointed out before, the distinction is important with regard to the budgetary powers of Parliament. The final decision concerning non-compulsory expenditure belongs to Parliament, although the possible increase is limited by the maximum annual rate which is established by the Commission on the basis of objective criteria,[60] while the recent Interinstitutional Agreement has imposed a discipline on all the institutions.

(3) *The European Currency Unit (ECU)*

Introduced by the European Monetary System (EMS), the ECU is now used in all areas of Community activity. The value of the

---

[57] EEC, Art. 203(4).
[58] D. Strasser, *The Finances of Europe* (New York, 1977), 33. Another definition given by the Council reads: "expenditure in respect of which, by virtue of existing enactments, no budgetary authority, be it the Council or the European Parliament, has the right freely to determine the appropriations." See also the Joint Declaration of Parliament, Council and Commission of June 1982, Bull. 6–1982, 7.
[59] Twenty-second General Report (1988), 69.
[60] EEC, Art. 203(9).

ECU in the Member States' currencies is determined each day by the Commission on the basis of the official exchange rates notified to it by the Member States' central banks. The rates are published daily in the Official Journal.

CHAPTER 4

COMMUNITY ACTS

The main lines of the decision-making process within the Community were outlined in respect of the role played therein by Parliament, the Council and the Commission. Reference was made also to the various forms which the Community acts can take. As was pointed out, the actual practice does differ from what the Treaty provides. The tendency is to multiply the forms of the decisions, the procedures leading up to them and the bodies issuing them. Besides the "Communiqués," "Declarations" and "Conclusions" of the European Council, there are "Programmes"[1] and "Resolutions." These are issued not only by the Council, but also by the Representatives of the Governments of the Member States in Council or by the Council and the Representatives of the Governments. Since, generally speaking, these acts do not directly create rights and obligations, none of the above-mentioned measures constitutes an act whose legality the Court can review. Neither are they issued on the basis of a Commission proposal, although often there will be one. Nor is Parliament or the Social and Economic Committee consulted. Nonetheless those acts shape essential Community policies and consequently, the development of the Community itself. It sometimes appears that the more important the decision, politically speaking, the less formal the procedures and the forms.

[1] Some programmes, however, are provided for in the Treaty, see, *e.g.* EEC, Art. 54.

Nevertheless, the acts expressly provided for by the Treaty still play an essential role and the conditions laid down for the decision-making process and for the contents of those acts must be seen as so many guarantees for lawfulness and judicial control and protection.

The above-mentioned developments seem to run counter to the Treaty provisions which invest the Council and the Commission with the responsibility for implementing the objectives of the Community. To carry out this task they were empowered to make regulations, issue directives, take decisions, conclude international agreements, make recommendations and deliver opinions. It may only be done, however, "in accordance with the provisions of the Treaty."[2] Furthermore, each one of those acts fulfils a specific function in the development of Community law and the Treaty therefore explicitly provides in several cases which kind of act must be adopted. Different procedural rules apply to various categories and, more important, the extent of the legal protection afforded legal and natural persons varies widely from one category to another.[3]

1. Acts provided for in Article 189

A *regulation* has general application; it is binding in its entirety and is directly applicable in all the Member States. The criterion for the distinction between a regulation and other acts, especially decisions, must be sought in the "general application." Being essentially of a "legislative nature, a regulation is applicable not to a limited number of persons, defined or identifiable,[4] but to categories of persons viewed abstractly and in their entirety."[5]

---

[2] EEC, Art. 189(1).

[3] It should be noted that it is not the name given to an act which classifies it in one of the above-mentioned categories, but rather the contents and objectives of its provisions. See Case 15/70 *Chevalley* v. *Commission* [1970] E.C.R. 975 at 980(10). The Court has also admitted that the same act can contain provisions pertaining to different categories. See Joined Cases 16–17/62 *Producteurs de fruits* v. *Council* [1962] E.C.R. 471 at 479.

[4] Joined Cases 789–790/79 *Calpak* v. *Commission* [1980] E.C.R. 1949 at 1961(9).

[5] Joined Cases 16–17/62 *Producteurs de fruits* (n. 3 above).

Secondly, a regulation is, as was mentioned, "binding in its entirety." This distinguishes it from a directive which only imposes on the Member States to which it is addressed the obligation to achieve specific results. The Court has considered that, since the regulation is binding in its entirety, it cannot be accepted that a Member State should apply in an incomplete and selective manner provisions of a Community regulation so as to "render abortive certain aspects of Community legislation."[6]

Finally, a regulation is "directly applicable" in all the Member States. This means that it does not require a national measure to become binding upon institutions, States, undertakings and natural persons. It also means that the national authorities and national legal or administrative measures, even those posterior to the Community act, cannot prevent its application.[7] By this is meant the precedence of Community law over national law.[8]

Direct applicability must not be confused with "direct effect." A Community measure has direct effect when it creates rights for those who are subject to Community law. This is the case every time a Community rule imposes an obligation upon a Member State, an Institution or a natural or legal person.[9] The beneficiaries of those obligations can invoke them in the national courts and tribunals and the latter are under Treaty obligation to uphold them. This applies even when these obligations conflict with national measures, whether anterior or posterior.

Not all Community provisions have direct effect, but the Court considers that a regulation, by reason of its very nature and its function in the system of sources of Community law, has direct

---

[6] Case 128/78 *Commission* v. *U.K.* [1979] E.C.R. 419 at 428(9).
[7] See Case 230/78 *Eridania* v. *Ministry of Agriculture* [1979] E.C.R. 2749 at 2772(35). Certain provisions contained in a regulation might need national implementing measures to become applicable, but the regulation itself does not have to be transformed into national law by a national measure.
[8] The French Conseil d'Etat only recognised this basic principle in 1989, 37 years after the first Community was established!
[9] For a more extended analysis of direct effect, see Chapter 8, "Community Law, 2. Direct effect."

effect, *i.e.* it is capable of creating individual rights which national courts must protect.[10]

Directives can be issued by the Council and by the Commission. They constitute the appropriate measure when existing national legislation must be modified or national provisions must be enacted. The Member States are free to decide, *e.g.* whether those measures will be legislative or administrative in nature.

Although directives are not directly applicable, since they normally require implementing measures, their provisions can nevertheless have direct effect. This must be ascertained on a case by case basis, taking into account their nature, background and wording. According to the Court those provisions are capable of producing direct effect in the legal relationship between the addressee of the act, *i.e.* the Member State and third parties.[11] This is what is referred to as "vertical direct effect of a directive" as opposed to "horizontal direct effect." The latter would occur if two third parties could claim rights, under a directive, in their bilateral relationship. This effect was rejected by the Court.[12] In other cases, however, where a question concerning the interpretation of a directive was raised in a case between a natural and a legal person, pending in a national court, the Court did not hesitate to give the requested interpretation. By doing so, the Court seems to admit that the directive could be relied upon in the relationship between two "third parties."[13]

---

[10] It is for the national legal system to determine which court or tribunal has jurisdiction to give this protection and, for this purpose, to decide how the individual position thus protected is to be classified. Case 43/71 *Politi* v. *Italy* [1971] E.C.R. 1039 at 1048(9). See also Case 93/71 *Leonesio* v. *Italian Ministry of Agriculture and Forestry* [1972] E.C.R. 287 at 295 (22–23).

[11] Case 9/70 *Grad* v. *Finanzamt Traunstein* [1970] E.C.R. 825 at 839(5). The Court used as an argument the fact that Art. 177 empowers the national courts to refer to the Court of Justice all questions regarding the validity and interpretation of all acts of the institutions without distinction, which implies that individuals may invoke such acts before the national courts. See also Case 51/76 *Nederlandse Ondernemingen* v. *Inspecteur der Invoerrechten en Accijnzen* [1977] E.C.R. 113 at 127(23). This last decision is referred to in many subsequent judgments.

[12] Case 152/84 *Marshall* v. *Southampton and South-West Hampshire Area Health Authority* [1986] E.C.R. 723(48).

[13] Case 262/84 *Beets-Proper* v. *Van Lanschot Bankiers* [1986] E.C.R. 773.

As for a *decision,* it is binding in its entirety upon those to whom it is addressed. The addressee can be a Member State or a legal or natural person. A decision can be taken by the Council and by the Commission. Decisions are normally of an administrative nature, implementing other Community rules, *e.g.* granting of an exception or authorisation or imposing fines.[14]

There are no requirements as to the form of a decision, so that it can be doubtful whether a given act constitutes a binding decision or not. Obviously, the institutions must ensure that a decision is recognisable as a binding act by its very form.[15] Being binding in its entirety, a decision can have direct effect.[16]

Finally the Treaty provides for *recommendations* and *opinions* which have no binding force. However, according to recent case law, recommendations should not be dismissed as having no legal effect whatsoever. They do not, it is true, create rights which can be invoked in the courts, but the national judges must take recommendations into consideration when solving cases submitted to them. This is especially so if the recommendations can help with the interpretation of other national or Community legal measures.[17]

Generally speaking, recommendations aim at obtaining a given action or behaviour from the addressee. An opinion, on the other hand, expresses a point of view, often at the request of a third party. Having no binding effect, the legality of recommendations and opinions cannot be reviewed by the Court. Neither can they be submitted to the Court for a preliminary ruling concerning their validity or interpretation. The Court has nevertheless agreed to examine whether recommendations had legal effects when a Member State failed to take the recommended action.[18]

---

[14] In Case 226/87 *Commission* v. *Greece*, where the Court rejected the Greek Government's contention that the Commission decision adopted pursuant to Art. 90(3) should merely be considered a non-binding opinion.

[15] Case 28/63 *Hoogovens* v. *High Authority* [1963] E.C.R. 231 at 235.

[16] Case 9/70 *Grad* (n. 11 above) at 837(5).

[17] Case 322/88 *Grimaldi* v. *Fonds des maladies professionnelles*, judgment of December 13, 1989 (not yet published).

[18] *Ibid.*

2. Regulations, directives and decisions must be reasoned

Regulations, directives and decisions must state the reasons on which they are based and must refer to the proposals and opinions which were required to be obtained pursuant to the Treaty.[19]

"Reasons" should be understood as referring both to the legal provision which entitles the institution to take the measure and the reasons which motivated the institution to act. The mention of the provision is particularly important since, as was mentioned, the Community institutions may only exercise those powers which are explicitly provided for by the Treaty.

As for the motives which prompted the institution to act, they must be mentioned in order to make it possible for the interested parties and for the Court to reconstruct the essential elements of the institution's reasoning[20], thereby permitting the parties to defend their rights, the Court to exercise its control, and the Member States, and in the same way all the interested citizens, to know the conditions under which the institution has applied the Treaty.[21]

To attain those objectives, it is sufficient for the act to set out, in a concise but clear and relevant manner, the principal issues of law and fact upon which it is based and which are necessary in order that the reasoning which has led the institution to its decision may be understood.[22] The extent of this requirement depends on the nature of the measure in question. The condition can also be considered as fulfilled when reference[23] is made to the reasons developed in an earlier act.[24]

If an act is not sufficiently "reasoned," this constitutes a ground for annulment: infringement of an essential procedural

---

[19] EEC, Art. 190.
[20] Case 14/61 *Hoogovens* v. *High Authority* [1962] E.C.R. 253 at 275.
[21] Case 24/62 *Germany* v. *Commission* [1963] E.C.R. 63 at 69.
[22] *Ibid.* See also joined Cases 36, 37, 38 and 40/59 *Geitling* v. *High Authority* [1960] E.C.R. 423 at 439.
[23] Case 75/77 *Mollet* v. *Commission* [1978] E.C.R. 897 at 906(12).
[24] Case 1/69 *Italy* v. *Commission* [1969] E.C.R. 277 at 285(9). See, however, Case 73/74 *Papiers peints* v. *Commission* [1975] E.C.R. 1491 at 1514 (31).

requirement which can be invoked in an action for review of the legality of the act concerned by the Court of Justice. The Court can and must of its own motion take exception to any deficiencies in the reasons which would make such review more difficult.[25]

As for the reference to the required proposals and opinions, a simple mention is considered sufficient; the institutions are not required to indicate whether or not the option was favourable[26] still less to refute dissenting opinions expressed by the consultative bodies.[27]

3. Publication and entry into force[28]

Since regulations are of a legislative nature and therefore concern an unidentifiable group to whom they apply, they must be published in the *Official Journal* which is published in the nine official languages[29] of the Community. They enter into force on the day specified in the act or, in the absence thereof, on the twentieth day following their publication.[30]

Directives and decisions on the other hand concern only a limited number of persons—Member States or natural or legal persons—and must therefore be notified directly to those to whom they are addressed. However, since the Court may review

[25] EEC, Art. 173, Case 18/57 *Nold* v. *High Authority* [1959] E.C.R. 41 at 52 and Case 158/80, *Rewe* v. *Hauptzollamt Kiel* [1981] E.C.R. 1805 at 1834 (27) where Reg. 3023/77 was declared void for not containing a statement of the reasons on which it is based.

[26] This, however, is no secret since both the Commission's proposals and the Parliament's opinions are published in the *Official Journal*.

[27] Case 4/54 *I.S.A.* v. *High Authority* [1954–1956] E.C.R. 91 at 100 (6).

[28] EEC, Art. 191.

[29] The official languages of the institutions of the Community are Danish, German, English, French, Greek, Italian, Dutch, Spanish and Portuguese.

[30] A typical example is Reg. 17 giving effect to the principles of competition: the regulation was adopted by the Council on February 6, 1962, published in the *Official Journal* on February 21, 1962 and, since it did not mention the date of entry into force, it became effective on March 13, 1962. See also Case 98/78 *Racke* v. *Hauptzollamt Mainz* [1979] E.C.R. 69 at 84 (15) and Case 99/78 *Decker* v. *Hauptzollamt Landau* [1979] E.C.R. 101 at 109 (3).

the legality of decisions at the request of parties which are not addressees of such acts, when the latter are of "direct and individual concern"[31] to them, it is important that they be informed of the contents of all such decisions. The same applies to directives; as was seen, citizens may invoke them in the national courts and request the latter to ask the Court of Justice for a preliminary ruling on their validity or interpretation. Consequently directives are always published in the *Official Journal* as are decisions which may affect the rights of third parties.[32]

4. Enforcement[33]

Decisions of the Council and the Commission which impose a pecuniary obligation[34] on persons other than Member States and judgments of the Court of Justice[35] are enforceable.

Enforcement of Community acts is governed by the rules of civil procedure in force within the Member State where it is carried out. The following steps must be taken. The institution which wants to enforce a decision presents it for verification of authenticity to the national authority which the Government of each Member State has designated for this purpose[36] and made

---

[31] EEC, Art. 173(2).

[32] See in this respect Joined Cases 73–74/63 *Handelsvereniging Rotterdam* v. *Minister van Landbouw* [1964] E.C.R. 1 at 14 and Case 130/78 *Salumificio* v. *Amministrazione delle Finanze* [1979] E.C.R. 867.

[33] EEC, Art. 192.

[34] For instance decisions of the Commission imposing fines pursuant to Art. 15 of Reg. 17, for violation of the competition rules (J.O. 1959–1962, 87).

[35] EEC, Art. 187.

[36] *The Netherlands*: Law of February 24, 1955, Stb 73, modified by Law of January 13, 1960, Stb 15: Minister of Justice is addressee of request; Griffier of Hoge Raad implements. *Belgium*: Law of August 6, 1967: Greffier en Chef of the Court of Appeal at Brussels. *France*: Décret No. 57/321 of March 13, 1957, *Journal Officiel*, March 19, 1957, 2885, designates (1) persons who have received delegation from the Prime Minister and (2) Secrétariat Général du Comité Interministériel. *Germany*: Bundesgesetzblatt, February 3, 1961, II, 50:

known to the Commission and the Court of Justice. This authority then appends to the decision an order for its enforcement.[37] The institution can then proceed to enforcement in accordance with national law, by bringing the matter directly before the competent national authorities. From that moment on, the national rules of civil procedure apply with the exception that suspension of the enforcement may only be decided by the Court.

An action brought before the Court against the decision which is being enforced has no suspensory effect.[38]

5. Binding acts not provided for under Article 189

Community acts are not limited to regulations, directives and decisions. As was pointed out, judgments of the Court are also binding upon the parties and can be enforced. The same applies

Minister of Justice. *Italy*: Decree of December 2, 1960, *Gazzetta Officiale*, February 21, 1961, No. 46, 738: Minister of Foreign Affairs. *Luxembourg*: Reg. of October 17, 1962, Memorial of October 31, 1962, No. 58, 1028: verification by Minister of Foreign Affairs, and order for enforcement appended by Minister of Justice. *United Kingdom*: European Communities (Enforcement of Community Judgments) Order 1972, S.I. 1972, No. 1590, which provides for the registration in the High Court of England and Northern Ireland and the Court of Session in Scotland of Community judgments and orders to which the Secretary of State has duly appended an order for enforcement. *Ireland*: S.I. 1972, No. 331: enforcement order appended by the Master of High Court. *Denmark*: by the Minister of Justice; *Greece*: the head of the tribunal of first instance at Athens. *Spain:* B.O.E. no. 160, July 5, 1986, 17843 Minister of Justice. *Portugal:* Diano da Republica, Law no. 104/88 of August 31, 1988 verification of authenticity: Minister of Foreign Affairs; apposition of formula: through Minister of Justice, competent tribunal.

[37] In the United Kingdom "order for enforcement" means an order by or under the authority of the Secretary of State that the Community judgment to which it is appended is to be registered for enforcement in the United Kingdom (S.I. 1972, No. 1590).

[38] When the Commission takes a decision imposing fines on a person, it usually does not seek enforcement in case an appeal has been lodged against the decision. The Court has approved this practice but only on condition that interest is paid in respect of the period of suspension and that a bank guarantee is lodged covering the amount of the fine; see Case 86/82 R *Hasselblad* v. *Commission* [1982] E.C.R. 1555.

to agreements concluded by the Community with third countries or international organisations; they are binding upon the institutions of the Community and on the Member States.[39]

The same applies to agreements concluded by the Member States among themselves regarding matters connected with the Treaty.[40] Somewhat different is the position of international agreements concluded by the Member States with third countries: in so far as, under the Treaty, the Community has assumed the powers previously exercised by Member States in the area governed by such international agreement, the provisions of that agreement have the effect of binding the Community.[41] These agreements can be submitted to the control of legality exercised by the Court when the Community is a party[42] to them and they constitute rules of law relating to the application of the Treaty[43]; the result being that regulations, directives and decisions can be annulled in case of infringement of these rules.

Finally, there are the decisions of the Representatives of the Governments of the Member States in Council; these cannot be submitted to the Court, since they do not emanate from the Council or the Commission, but they can be binding within the whole Community.[44] However it will have to be established on a case by case basis whether those decisions are binding only for the Member States or also for the institutions of the Community and even for natural or legal persons. Although those "decisions," not provided for under the Treaty, constitute a flexible instrument to solve a number of questions within the scope of the treaties, they are not without danger for the institutional equi-

[39] EEC, Art. 228(2).
[40] See, *e.g.* EEC, Arts. 50 and 220.
[41] Joined Cases 21 to 24/72 *International Fruit Company* v. *Produktschap voor Groenten en Fruit* [1972] E.C.R. 1219 at 1227 (18).
[42] See, *e.g.* Case 22/70 *Commission* v. *Council* [1971] E.C.R. 263.
[43] EEC, Art. 173.
[44] See, *e.g.* the "acceleration" decisions by which the Member States agreed to establish the customs union within a shorter time-limit than provided for under the Treaty (J.O. 1960, 1217 and 1962, 1284). These decisions are not to be confused with decisions of the Member States such as the appointment of the Members of the Commission (Merger Treaty, Art. 11) or of the Judges of the Court of Justice (EEC, Art. 167).

librium provided by the Treaty. Besides immunity from the Court's control, these acts do not require a Commission proposal or an opinion of Parliament. Of course, nothing can prevent the latter from trying to exercise its political control over these acts anyway.

Binding acts not provided for under Article 189 can have "direct effect"; this applies in the first place to international agreements.[45]

6. Other forms of Community measures

A form often used is the *resolution*, either of the Council,[46] or of the Council and of the Representatives of the Governments of the Member States.[47] These resolutions are not to be confused with the decisions of the Representatives of the Governments of the Member States in Council; in the first place the decisions of the Representatives of the Member States are legally binding upon the latter, while resolutions sometimes only constitute a political commitment; secondly, the fact that the Member States act within the institutional framework is intended to indicate that the matter directly concerns the implementation of the Treaty. Resolutions, generally speaking, concern matters directly connected with the Community, but not explicitly provided for under Community law.

There is also the *programme* or programmes of action, which intend to lay down general principles for future action both by

---

[45] See Joined Cases 21–24/72 *International Fruit Company* and Joined Cases 290 and 291/81, *Singer and Geigy* v. *Amministrazione delle Finanze* [1983] E.C.R. 847 concerning direct effect of GATT rules.

[46] See, *e.g.* Council Resolution of February 6, 1979 concerning the guidelines for Community Regional Policy (O.J. 1979, C. 36/10) and the conclusions of the Council of December 4, 1984, concerning measures necessary to guarantee the implementation of the conclusions of the European Council concerning budgetary discipline. Bull. 12–1984, 24. In one case, the Court was asked to interpret a Council resolution in a request for a preliminary ruling: Case 9/73 *Schlüter* v. *Hauptzollamt Lörrach* [1973] E.C.R. 1135 at 1162.

[47] See, *e.g.* J.O. 1972, C.38/3.

the Member States and by the institutions of the Community. Such programmes are generally adopted by the Council and by the Representatives of the Governments of the Member States meeting in Council, either by a decision,[48] a *declaration*[49] or a resolution.[50]

Other matters are decided upon by *decisions* which are not formal binding acts[51] in the sense of EEC, Article 189, since they are not provided for under the Treaty; they are used to settle questions related to Community affairs but do not impose rights or obligations upon the institutions of the Community nor on natural or legal persons.[52] Once again, these "decisions" are not to be confused with the decisions taken by the Governments of the Member States in pursuance of the Treaty provisions such as the appointment of the Judges and Advocates-General of the Court of Justice and the members of the Commission. The latter are Community acts, but do not constitute acts of the institutions of the Community and do not therefore come under the jurisdiction of the Court of Justice.

Further Reading

K. C. Wellens and G. M. Borchardt, "Soft Law in European Community Law" (1989) 14 E.L.Rev. 267.

John Bridge, "Procedural aspects of the enforcement of European Community Law through the legal systems of the member states" (1984) 9 E.L.Rev. 28.

---

[48] See, *e.g.* O.J. 1982, L.236/10.
[49] See, *e.g.* O.J. 1973, C.112/1.
[50] See, *e.g.* O.J. 1977, C.139/1.
[51] Other languages such as Dutch and German use a word ("Besluit; Beschluß") which clearly distinguishes this act from an Art. 189 decision ("Beschikking; Entscheidung").
[52] See, *e.g.* O.J. 1973, L.207/46.

CHAPTER 5

THE COMMON MARKET

1. INTRODUCTION

While the Treaties establishing the Coal and Steel Community and Euratom have remained unchanged as to their scope, the range of activities of the EEC has been continuously extended either informally or through formal treaty revisions, the latest of which was the Single European Act (SEA). This is the consequence of the built-in dynamism of the Treaty establishing the European Economic Community; and indeed, the full implementation of its objectives requires, besides policies common to the Member States, Community policies in fields which were not explicitly mentioned in the provisions of the Treaty itself. This is the case for instance for regional policy, economic and monetary union, protection of the environment and of the consumer, industrial and intellectual property rights, research and development and energy policy. In each one of these fields the Community has developed activities over the past years, and consequently the institutions of the Community and the Member States had to develop new means and procedures, such as the European Council. This body now takes the necessary political decisions, leaving it to the Community institutions to enact the corresponding legal measures. This is possible under Article 235 of the Treaty, according to which the Community may, under given conditions, take measures required to attain the objectives of the Community, although the Treaty has not provided the necessary powers.

Objectives are to be found, in the first place, in the Preamble to the Treaty where they are very broadly formulated and do not therefore constitute practical guidelines for Community action. More specific aims are set out in Articles 2 and 3. Article 2 summarises, in a few words, not only the basic objectives, but also the means by which these objectives are to be attained. The objectives are to promote throughout the Community

— harmonious development of economic activities,
— continuous and balanced expansion,
— increased stability,
— accelerated raising of the standards of living, and
— closer relations between the Member States.

To achieve those objectives the Community institutions have been provided with two comprehensive means, *i.e.* the establishment of the common market and the progressive approximation of the economic policies of the Member States. These two means are of a rather different nature but essentially complementary.

The first corresponds to the abolition of all obstacles to the free movement of goods, persons, services, establishment, capital and payments, together with the development of an agriculture, transport and competition policy. The rules provided in the Treaty in those areas are of a rather legal-technical nature: they constitute a set of more or less specific provisions with time limits. Unfortunately the latter were not respected, mainly with regard to the so-called basic freedoms, which made it necessary to give this action new impetus, with more specific rules and dates; this was, briefly speaking, the purpose of the SEA which will be discussed below.

The second instrument, *i.e.* the progressive convergence of national economic policies, corresponds to a more constructive phase: less legal, more political and therefore much less defined and also dependent upon economic and political circumstances, and consequently probably more exciting and interesting. It is this phase indeed which arouses passions and provokes strong political statements such as the Bruges speech of the British Prime Minister.

The economic policies referred to in the Treaty were until recently rather limited: conjunctural policy and balance of payments. The SEA has remedied this situation by adding to Title II a new chapter entitled, "Co–operation in economic and monetary policy (Economic and monetary union)" and a new Title V, "Economic and social cohesion" which formalises the existing regional policy. However, other existing "policies" such as the European Monetary System are not even mentioned in the Treaty.

After the broad formulation of the objectives of the Community in the Preamble and in Article 2, a more concrete description of the main activities of the EEC is to be found in Article 3. To each activity mentioned therein correspond several provisions in Parts Two, Three, Four and Five of the Treaty, defining in more detail the actions required and the procedures to be followed. Those provisions of Article 3 should not be considered as merely containing a general programme devoid of legal effect; this view was rejected by the Court "because it ignores that the pursuit of the objectives laid down by Article 3 is indispensable for the achievement of the Community's tasks."[1]

The various activities of the Community, including those not mentioned in the Treaty, will be examined below, together with the corresponding EEC law. They will be grouped in three Parts: the Common Market, the Community Policies, and the External Relations, with emphasis on those with developing countries.

2. The Common (Internal) Market

As was pointed out above, the "common market" constitutes, with the "approximation of the economic policies of the Member States," the means to achieve the objectives of the Community. However, the Treaty does not define the term common market, but the modifications introduced by the SEA now indicate what is

---

[1] Case 6/72 *Europemballage and Continental Can* v. *Commission* [1973] E.C.R. 215 at 244 (23, 24).

to be understood by "internal market," *i.e.* "an area without internal frontiers in which the free movement of goods, persons, services and capital is ensured in accordance with the provisions of this Treaty."[2] What then is the meaning of "common" market? According to Part Two of the Treaty, "Foundations of the Community," it comprises the same basic freedoms[3] plus agriculture and transport. In other words "common" market is a wider concept than "internal" market, the latter being included in the former.

But more important is the fact that in order to allow for the proper functioning and development of this market, much more is needed in the form of accompanying policies such as competition, taxation, environment protection, regional development, approximation of laws, industrial and commercial policy, consumer protection, etc. Provisions concerning such policies are to be found mainly in Part Three of the Treaty, "Policy of the Community" and in measures decided by the Council in pursuance of EEC Article 235.[4]

The most important of the above-mentioned freedoms is, without doubt, the free movement of goods; practically all other Community activities referred to in the Treaty can be connected in some way with the accomplishment of that single goal.

I. The Free Movement of Goods

Free movement of goods within the Community[5] is made possible by:

---

[2] EEC, Art. 8a, 2nd para., added by the SEA.
[3] These are often understood (see, *e.g.* EEC, Art. 8a) as referring to goods, persons, services and capital; in fact the Treaty divides "persons" into "workers" and "self employed persons," the latter enjoying both the right (freedom) of establishment and the freedom to provide services, while, on the other hand, free movement of capital must be distinguished from free movement of payments (EEC, Art. 106). The Treaty therefore provides for six basic freedoms: they concern goods, workers, establishment, services, capital and payments.
[4] See above under "Council, (1) Decision making."
[5] For a geographical description of the EEC see EEC, Art. 227.

— the establishment of a customs union, and
— the elimination of quantitative restrictions and measures having equivalent effect on imports and exports, the so-called "technical" or "non-tariff trade barriers."

1. The Customs Union

Article 9 of the EEC Treaty provides that "the Community shall be based upon a customs union which shall cover all trade in goods" and then goes on to define what such union consists of:

    (i) the prohibition between Member States of "customs duties and measures having equivalent effect" on imports and exports, and, as a necessary complement,[6]

    (ii) the adoption of a common customs tariff in the relations with third countries.

The "goods" referred to in Article 9 are both industrial and agricultural products whether originating in the Member States or imported from third countries.[7] For the latter, import formalities must have been complied with in any one Member State and all payable duties and charges must have been levied and not reimbursed.[8] When those conditions are fulfilled these imported products are considered to be "in free circulation in Member States,"[9] *i.e.* assimilated to products originating within the Com-

---

[6] It is a necessary complement since, without it, products from third countries would all enter the Community through the country with the lowest tariffs thereby depriving the others of external trade.
[7] EEC, Art. 9(2). The inclusion of imported products differentiates a customs union from a free trade area: the latter, having no common customs tariff, only covers products originating within the Member States; see, *e.g.* EFTA Treaty, Art. 4.
[8] EEC, Art. 10(1).
[9] EEC, Art. 10(2).

munity. The customs union among the original six Member States was established progressively over a period of ten and a half years (January 1, 1958 to June 30, 1968), shorter than the 12 years originally estimated.[10] The customs union was similarly extended to Denmark, Ireland and the United Kingdom over a period of a little more than four years (April 1, 1973 to July 1, 1977) and to Greece on January 1, 1986. It is presently in the process of being applied to Portugal and Spain until January 1, 1993.

(1) *Elimination of customs duties between Member States*[11]

Since the elimination was achieved gradually over a period of several years, it was important to prevent, during that period, the introduction of new customs duties. Consequently, the Treaty provides for a ban on the introduction of new duties and on the increase of existing ones.[12] This ban applies both to imports and exports within the Community[13] and to duties of a fiscal nature.[14] The Treaty refers not only to "customs duties," but also to "charges having equivalent effect"; this addition is of the utmost importance since without it the ban and the elimination would have been much less effective. Those charges have been defined by the Court as any levy imposed by a Member State on a product at the occasion of it crossing a border and which, although not formally designated as a customs duty (*i.e.* appearing on a tariff list), does nevertheless have the same impeding effect on imports or exports.[15] The concept of "charges having

---

[10] See EEC, Art. 8 which provides for a transitional period of 12 years in three stages and Arts. 13, 14 and 32. Twice the Representatives of the Member States in Council decided to accelerate the establishment of the customs union: Dec. of May 12, 1960 (J.O. 1960, 1217) and Dec. of May 15, 1962 (J.O. 1962, 1284); a final decision abolished all duties on industrial goods as of July 1, 1966 (J.O. 1966, 2971).

[11] EEC, Arts. 12 to 17.

[12] EEC, Art. 12.

[13] EEC, Arts. 13 and 16. See Case 89/76 *Commission* v. *Netherlands* [1977] E.C.R. 1355.

[14] EEC, Art. 17.

[15] Unless the charge is a consideration for a benefit provided for the importer or exporter; see however Case 89/76 *Commission* (n. 13 above) where a fee levied upon products intended for export was considered not to constitute a charge with equivalent effect.

equivalent effect" gave rise to an abundant case law of the Court[16] which, in one of its first judgments, stated that EEC, Art. 12 also creates for the citizens of the Community individual rights which the national courts must protect.[17]

(2) *The Common Customs Tariff (CCT)*

As was pointed out, the elimination of the customs duties and other charges between the Member States had to coincide with the setting up of the CCT which determines the duties to be levied on goods entering the Community from third countries. It was gradually introduced over the same period as the one that was needed for the elimination of the internal tariffs. The CCT was adopted by a Council Regulation[18]; it replaced the existing customs tariffs of the Benelux, Germany, France and Italy. The tariffs of the CCT were established, as a general rule, at a level corresponding to the mathematical average of the duties applied by the four above-mentioned customs territories, on January 1, 1957.[19]

As a consequence of the introduction of the CCT, individual Member States no longer have jurisdiction over the duties which are levied on goods entering their territory from third countries: they can neither modify them nor interpret them.[20] Furthermore, since the entry into force of the Council decision concerning the

---

[16] See, *e.g.* Case 222/78 *ICAP* v. *Beneventi* [1979] E.C.R. 1163 (duty falling within a general system of internal taxation can constitute a charge having equivalent effect); Case 132/80 *United Foods and Van den Abeele* v. *Belgium* [1981] E.C.R. 995 (duties and charges for health inspection on imported goods incompatible with Arts. 9, 12 and 13); Case 132/82 *Commission* v. *Belgium* [1983] E.C.R. 1649 (storage fee for imported goods contrary to Art. 12).

[17] See Case 26/62, *Van Gend & Loos* v. *Dutch Fiscal Administration* [1963] E.C.R. 1 at 12.

[18] Reg. 950/68 (J.O. 1968, L.172/1). The customs tariff is regularly updated: see O.J. 1989, L.4/19.

[19] EEC, Art. 19. Exceptions to this rule are the products of the lists B, C, D and E for which the Treaty provides a maximum and those of list F for which the duties are fixed therein. These lists constitute Annex I to the EEC Treaty and form part of it.

[20] See Case 38/75 *Nederlandse Spoorwegen* v. *Inspecteur der invoerrechten en accijnzen* [1975] E.C.R. 1439 at 1449(14).

Communities' own resources, the revenue accruing from the duties they levy belong to the Community.[21] Modification or suspension of CCT duties is an exclusive Community matter and is introduced either autonomously by the Council[22] or as a measure of common commercial policy towards third countries.[23] Within the framework of this policy important reductions were introduced following multilateral trade negotiations pursuant to the General Agreement on Tariffs and Trade (GATT), the so-called Kennedy Round (1964–1967) and the Tokyo Round (1973–1979). The consequence of the latter was that the level of industrial tariffs was reduced world-wide by about one third. A similar reduction will undoubtedly result from the Uruguay Round which started in 1988 and should end in 1990.

It should be noted, however, that from a commercial point of view a reduction of customs tariffs is much less important than the elimination of non-tariff trade barriers which are often much more difficult to detect.

In terms of commerce, the creation of the customs union has resulted in shifts in the trade patterns, since, generally speaking goods become less expensive for Community consumers when imported from other Member States rather than from outside the EEC. Also trade within the EEC tends to increase much faster than trade with third countries.[24] In relation to the latter the Community uses the customs union as an instrument to guarantee the effectiveness of its commercial policy.[25] It must be noted that establishing identical levels for each external tariff is only a first step towards setting up the CCT. Indeed, the customs union also calls for uniform interpretation, continuing administration, har-

---

[21] Dec. of April 21, 1970, J.O. 1970, 224. See EEC, Art. 201.
[22] EEC, Art. 28; see Case 158/80 *Rewe* v. *Hauptzollamt Kiel* [1981] E.C.R. 1805.
[23] See EEC. Arts. 111 and 113 which provide for agreements with third countries.
[24] Between 1959 and 1970, trade within the Community increased by 16 per cent. while exports to third countries grew on average by 9 per cent.
[25] Both for the voluntary restraint agreements concluded with textile exporting countries (Eleventh General Report (1977), 88, 220) and for the policy to deal with the steel crisis, the Community used the technical machinery of the customs union to ensure their implementation: Tweelfth General Report (1978), 110.

monisation of customs rules, simplification of checks and formalities and, generally speaking, the reinforcement of the structure of the customs union.[26]

2. Elimination of quantitative restrictions between Member States

As was pointed out above, the elimination of customs duties and charges having equivalent effect is not sufficient to guarantee the free circulation of goods, since there are many other ways of hindering imports and exports. The EEC Treaty therefore provides for the "elimination of quantitative restrictions on imports, and all measures having equivalent effect."[27] Since the elimination is carried out gradually over several years,[28] as for the customs duties, the Treaty prohibits here also the introduction of new quantitative restrictions and measures[29] or making the existing ones more restrictive.[30] The words "measures having equivalent effect" are, in this case also, of particular importance for the functioning of the common market. They cover, as the Court ruled, "all trading rules[31] enacted by Member States which are capable of hindering, directly or indirectly, actually or potentially, intra-Community trade."[32] It was not the first time the Court used this formula: similar words can be found in various other judgments[33] interpreting the Treaty provisions concerning

---

[26] See Sixteenth General Report (1982), 97 *et seq.*

[27] EEC, Art. 30. The situation is different for exports: Case 15/79 *Groenveld* v. *Produktschap voor vee en vlees* [1979] E.C.R. 3409.

[28] EEC, Art. 32(2).

[29] EEC, Art. 31(1).

[30] EEC, Art. 32(1).

[31] This includes rules of a temporary nature. See Case 82/77 *Openbaar Ministerie of The Netherlands* v. *van Tiggele* [1978] E.C.R. 25 at 40(20).

[32] Case 8/74 *Procureur du Roi* v. *Dassonville* [1974] E.C.R. 837 at 852(5). The extreme form of hindrance is of course prohibition of imports; therefore the term "restriction" in EEC, Art. 30 must be understood as equivalent to the expression "prohibitions or restrictions on imports" occurring in Art. 36; see Case 34/79 *Regina* v. *Henn and Darby* [1979] E.C.R. 3795 at 3812(12) and Case 124/81 *Commission* v. *U.K.* [1983] E.C.R. 203: by prohibiting the import of sterilized milk the U.K. infringed Art. 30.

[33] See, *e.g.* Joined Cases 56 and 58/64 *Consten and Grundig* v. *Commission* [1966] E.C.R. 299 at 341.

the rules of competition and more specifically the words of
Article 85 "which may affect trade between Member States."
This similarity is not surprising since the objective pursued by
Articles 12 to 36 (the customs union) and Articles 85 to 94
(competition rules) is the same, *i.e.* to guarantee the free
movement of goods throughout the Community.

The formula means in the first place that the prohibition of
Article 30 applies not only in case of actual refusal to admit a
product but also when an import is merely made difficult and, in
the second place, that actual hindrance does not have to be
proven: the mere existence of a possibility suffices. More simply
stated, the prohibition of Article 30 applies when the import of a
product from one Member State into another is, or can be made,
unnecessarily[34] difficult.

However, in order to benefit from this free movement certain
conditions must be met: indeed, according to the Court, the basic
rule of Article 30 is that all products which have been produced
and commercialised in one Member State, in accordance with the
legal provisions of that country, must be admitted into all the
other Member States, each one recognising the legal provisions
of the first Member State; this is what is referred to as "mutual
recognition."[35] This concept plays a very important role in the
completion of the internal market.

In its "White Paper" of June 14, 1985 on completing the
internal market,[36] the Commission recognised that a genuine
common market could not be achieved by 1992 if the Community
relied exclusively on traditional methods of harmonisation. It
therefore recommended a new strategy combining the principles
of the mutual recognition of national regulations and standards
based on Articles 30 to 36 of the EEC Treaty, together with a

---

[34] This means that there are cases where imports are hindered out of necessity;
see below: "Exceptions to the free movement of goods" (EEC, Art. 36) and
see, *e.g.* Case 6/81 *Industrie Diensten Groep* v. *Beele* [1982] E.C.R. 707.
[35] Case 8/74 *Procureur du Roi* v. *Dassonville* [1974] E.C.R. 837 at 852(5) and
Case 120/78 *Rewe* v. *Bundesmonopolverwaltung für Branntwein* (*Cassis de
Dijon*) [1979] E.C.R. 649. See also the Commission's Communication concerning the consequences of this judgment (O.J. 1980, C.256/2).
[36] Com(85)510 final.

more efficient mechanism for the harmonisation of laws based, in particular, on Article 100 of the Treaty.[37]

On the other hand, according to the Court, the basic principle of Article 30 cannot yet be fully applied under all circumstances, since "in the absence of common rules relating to the production and marketing of [a given product], it is for the Member States to regulate all matters relating to the production and the marketing of [the said product] on their own territory."[38] Consequently, "obstacles to movement [of goods] within the Community resulting from disparities between the national laws relating to the marketing of the products in question, must be accepted in so far as those provisions may be recognised as being necessary in order to satisfy mandatory requirements"[39] of the public interest.

These mandatory requirements are to be carefully distinguished from the exceptions provided for in Article 36 of the Treaty; the latter render the provisions of Articles 30 to 35 inapplicable as soon as the conditions provided for are fulfilled and those exceptions will always exist, being embodied in the Treaty itself.

The mandatory requirements, on the other hand, can be relied upon by the Member States only in so far as there is "absence of common rules"; they do not constitute exceptions to the principle of the free movement of goods. They justify a temporary suspension of the total and strict applicability of the rules embodied in the EEC Treaty. They will cease to be applicable when all the matters relating to the free movement of goods, which cannot be solved by the principle of mutual recognition, will have been regulated by Community rules. This should, in

---

[37] *Ibid.,* p. 1.
[38] Case 120/78 *Cassis de Dijon* (n. 35 above at 662(8)).
[39] *Ibid.* Mandatory requirements are, *e.g.* the effectiveness of fiscal supervision, the protection of public health, the fairness of commercial transactions, the defence of the consumer (see Case 120/78 *Cassis de Dijon*, n. 35 above), legitimate elements of economic and social policy (Case 155/80 *Oebel* [1981] E.C.R. 1983 at 2008(12)), the fight against inflation (Case 181/82, *Roussel Laboratoria* v. *Netherlands* [1983] E.C.R. 3849 at 3870(24)), the protection of the environment (Case 302/86 *Commission* v. *Denmark* [1988] (not yet published)).

theory, be the case by the end of 1992 when according to Article 8a, introduced by the SEA, all the measures necessary for establishing the internal market will have been adopted.

What is the rationale behind the introduction, by the Court, of those "mandatory requirements"? The provisions of Article 30, like those of other Treaty provisions, impose obligations on the Member States. Consequently, they confer rights upon the direct beneficiaries of those obligations, *i.e.* the natural and legal persons within the Community. They acquire *inter alia* the right to trade freely between all the Member States. But, on the other hand, this right is not unlimited (no right is) and its limitations result from the necessity to protect the public interest. Since the Member States are the guardians of this public interest they may impose measures "required" to protect it; such measures can, in the absence of Community rules, constitute obstacles to the free movement of goods and must, temporarily, be accepted.

On the other hand, the obstacles to the free movement of goods resulting from measures imposed under those conditions by the Member States "must only be accepted in so far as those provisions may be recognised as being necessary."[40] They must be proved to serve a purpose which is in the general interest and such as to take precedence over the requirement of the free movement of goods, which constitutes one of the fundamental rules of the Community.

In certain judgments the Court simply stated that such laws and regulations should be "reasonable"[41]; from there comes the expression "the rule of reason." The latter is often identified with the *Cassis de Dijon* judgment, but wrongly so. The basic rule of that judgment is that all goods legally produced and commercialised in one Member State must be admitted in all the others. The rule of reason temporarily mitigates this basic rule for as long as Community legislation has not yet been enacted. In all

---

[40] See Case 58/80 *Dansk Supermarked* v. *Imerco* [1981] E.C.R. 181 and Case 6/81 *Industrie Diensten Groep* (n. 34 above at 718(13)): unfair competition comes under "protection of consumers and fairness of commercial transactions."
[41] Case 8/74 *Dassonville* (n. 32 above at 852(6)) and Case 104/75 *De Peijper* [1976] E.C.R. 613 at 636(18).

other cases, restrictions on inter-state trade resulting from the implementation of national rules are caught by the prohibition of Article 30.[42] Such restrictions exist, generally speaking, in the case of measures which do not apply equally to domestic and imported products, but even measures which do apply equally can have restrictive effects[43]; in such a case the possible influence on trade is "indirect." It is also important to note that "a measure caught by the prohibition provided for by Article 30 of the Treaty does not escape this prohibition simply because the competent authority is empowered to grant exemptions, even if this power is freely applied to imported products."[44] Finally, mention must be made here of restrictions resulting from discrimination in awarding public supply contracts; in this area also specific Community legislation was enacted to prevent the use of public supply contracts to limit the free movement of goods.[45]

3. Exceptions to the free movement of goods

Every rule has its exceptions and they can be found either in the provisions of the law laying down the rule or in the interpretation

---

[42] Case 27/80 *Fietje* [1980] E.C.R. 3839 at 3854(14).

[43] See Case 7/80 *Fietje* (n. 42 above) and Case 53/80 *Officier van Justitie* v. *Kaasfabriek Eyssen* [1981] E.C.R. 409, where the national measures only applied to products destined for the domestic market.

[44] In numerous cases the Court was called upon to rule on the compatibility with the common market of national rules concerning, *e.g.* fees charged for veterinary inspection (Case 46/76 *Bauhuis* v. *Netherlands* [1977] E.C.R. 5 at 20(51)); pricing (Joined Cases 16 to 20/79 *Joseph Danis* [1979] E.C.R. 3327); import certificates (Case 251/78 *Denkavit* [1979] E.C.R. 3369); description of origin (Case 27/80 *Fietje* (n. 42 above at 3839)); licences (Case 82/77 *Openbaar Ministerie* v. *van Tiggele* [1978] E.C.R. 25); regulating the content of a product (Case 130/80 *Kelderman* [1981] E.C.R. 527); requiring indication of origin (Case 207/83 *Commission* v. *U.K.* [1985] E.C.R. 1207); use of specific shape of bottle (Case 16/83 *Prantl* [1984] E.C.R. 1299); health checks of animal feeding-stuffs Case 73/84 *Denkavit Futtermittel* v. *Land Nordrhein-Westfalen* [1985] E.C.R. 1013).

[45] Dir. 77/62 (O.J. 1977, L.13/1), Dir. 80/767 (O.J. 1980, L.215/1) and Dir. 88/295 modifying Dirs. 77/62 and 80/767 (O.J. 1988, L.127/1).

of the rule as given by the judges.[46] From the previous paragraphs it follows that the free movement of goods within the Community is the result of three activities: the elimination of customs duties and similar charges, the setting up of the common customs tariff and the prohibition and removal of all quantitative restrictions and measures having a similar effect; all three combine to ensure free intra-Community trade.

But, on the other hand, Title I of Part Two of the Treaty provides for so-called "escape clauses" from the rules concerning the application of the common customs tariff and the quantitative restrictions.[47] As regards the Common Customs Tariff, Article 25 allows exemptions under specific conditions[48] and where quantitative restrictions are concerned, Art. 36 provides for several exceptions. In pursuance of the latter, prohibitions or restrictions on imports and exports may be justified[49] on the ground of: public morality[50], public policy or public security[51], the protection of health and the life of humans, animals or plants[52], the protection of national treasures possessing artistic, historic and archaeologi-

---

[46] Exceptions to the basic freedoms are provided in Art. 36 for the free movement of goods, in Art. 48(3) for the free movement of workers; in Arts. 56 and 66 for the freedom to provide services and in Art. 73 for the free movement of capital.

[47] There are therefore no exceptions whatsoever to the rule prohibiting and eliminating customs tariffs and charges with equivalent effect; it is the only absolute rule in the EEC Treaty, unless one considers EEC, Art. 115 as an exception to this rule rather than a temporary measure of commercial policy.

[48] Art. 25(1): when demand for a particular product cannot be satisfied from within the Community, the Council shall grant a Member State tariff quotas at reduced rate or duty free; Art. 25(2): *idem* by the Commission, when the shortage entails harmful consequences for the processing industry and Art. 25(3): the Commission enjoys wide discretionary powers to grant Member States authorisation to suspend collection of duties on agricultural products.

[49] According to the Court "justified" means "necessary for the effective protection of the grounds mentioned in Art. 36"; Case 104/75 *De Peijper* (n.41 above at 636(16)).

[50] See Case 34/79 *Regina* v. *Henn and Darby* [1979] E.C.R. 3795 (prohibition on imports of pornographic articles).

[51] See Case 7/78 *Regina* v. *Thompson* [1978] E.C.R. 2247 (export ban on silver alloy coins).

[52] The Court considers that "health and the life of humans ranks first among the interests protected by Art. 36" (Case 104/75 *De Piejper* (n. 41 above, at 635(15)). This ground has given rise to numerous rulings by the Court; see, *e.g.* Case 32/80 *Officier van Justitie* v. *Kortmann* [1981] E.C.R. 251.

cal value[53], and, finally, the protection of industrial and commercial property.[54] Mention must also be made of Article 115 under which Member States may be authorised to take the necessary protective steps in order to ensure the execution of measures of commercial policy taken in accordance with the Treaty.

Attention must be drawn to the second sentence of Article 36 which is designed to prevent restrictions on trade justified under the first sentence from being diverted from their proper purpose and used in such a way as to create discrimination against imported goods or indirectly protect national products.[55]

A final remark concerns the role of the Community institutions in defining the scope of the derogations provided for in Article 36. The Court considered[56] that this article is not designed to reserve certain matters to the exclusive jurisdiction of the Member States, but permits national laws to derogate from the principle of the free movement of goods to the extent to which such derogation is and continues to be justified for the attainment of the objectives referred to in this provision. Where, in application of Articles 100 or 100a[57] Community directives[58] provide for the harmonisation of the national measures necessary to protect the interests mentioned in Article 36, recourse to that article will be much more limited. In the same way, as was pointed out, recourse to mandatory requirements will tend to disappear as more and more Community legislation is enacted; it must indeed be noted that when the Court introduced the so-called rule of reason, it made it clear that this could only be invoked "in the absence of common rules."[59]

---

[53] See Case 7/68 *Commission* v. *Italy* [1968] E.C.R. 423.
[54] See below "Industrial and Intellectual Property Rights" and Case 144/81 *Keurkoop* v. *Nancy Kean Gifts* [1982] E.C.R. 2853.
[55] See, *e.g.* Case 40/80 *Commission* v. *United Kingdom* [1982] E.C.R. 2793.
[56] Case 5/77 *Tedeschi* v. *Denkavit* [1977] E.C.R. 1555.
[57] This provision was introduced in the Treaty by the SEA.
[58] *e.g.* Dir. 70/54 (J.O. 1970, L.270/1; O.J. 1970(III), 840) and Dir. 74/63 (O.J. 1974, L.38/31).
[59] Case 8/74 *Dassonville* (n. 32 above, at 852(6)).

4. Theory and reality of free movement of goods—The Single European Act

The elimination of all customs duties, quantitative restrictions and measures having equivalent effect, as provided for in the EEC Treaty, does not seem to have completely liberalised inter-state trade within the Community. There still are, twenty years after the common market was supposed to have been established,[60] controls at all the borders and long queues of cars and trucks can still be seen waiting to be cleared to pass the frontier.[61] It is undoubtedly a disconcerting experience for the European citizen.

What explains this state of affairs? Is everything that was outlined in the previous paragraphs pure theory or are there other reasons? The answer is not, of course, a simple one. If custom duties and quantitative restrictions have indeed been abolished, this is not the case with all the measures having equivalent effect, the so-called "non-tariff or technical trade barriers" which continue to impede imports in many cases. Furthermore, there have always existed in all the Member States perfectly legal national measures whose implementation constitutes obstacles to the free flow of goods across national borders[62]; and secondly, it has not been possible to eliminate all the differences in certain important fields.[63] The national fiscal policies are a case in point: the Treaty does not provide for the

---

[60] *i.e.* 1969. See EEC Treaty, Art. 8, paras. 1 and 7.

[61] The European Parliament once calculated that the total yearly costs of all these borders crossings represented some 12,000 million ECU (COM(83)80 final, para. 18).

[62] According to the Commission the most tangible obstalces have been created by the public authorities, *e.g.* at the micro-economic level: customs procedures, technical barriers, taxation, company law, national preference arrangements and state aids; and on the other hand currency regulations, diverging inflation and interest rates and energy costs, all dictated by macro-economic policies (COM(83)80 final, para. 33).

[63] Notwithstanding the fact that several hundred directives were issued by the Council to harmonise the laws, regulations and administrative provisions of the Member States in pursuance of EEC, Art. 100.

harmonisation of the national tax systems; it only prohibits, generally speaking, discriminatory taxation between national products and those imported from other Member States.[64] Although the Treaty provides that the Council shall "issue directives for the approximation of such provisions laid down by law, regulation or administrative action in Member States as directly affect the functioning of the common market,"[65] not much has been done in the field of taxation. Worse, the SEA, which inserts an Article 100a in the Treaty providing for Council decisions by a qualified majority for all measures destined to progressively establish the internal market, excludes from this procedure "fiscal provisions." Consequently decisions in this field still have to be taken unanimously and it is far from certain that tax rates will have been approximated by the end of 1992. And since there exist wide differences, *e.g.* in the rates of VAT, products from other Member States will probably still have to be checked at the borders to determine whether or not VAT was paid and if so, whether the rate applied was the same as in the country of import, precisely in order to avoid discrimination.

A few years ago the Commission noted that "the Community has not yet—to any satisfactory extent—achieved its goals with regard to its internal market"[66] and went on to examine why, notwithstanding considerable achievements, the Customs Union has not yet become a reality. Among the causes mentioned were: bureaucratic inertia; short-term considerations taking precedence over medium-term advantages and resulting in open or disguised protectionist measures; and the differences in administrative and legislative traditions.

It is precisely to put an end to this unsatisfactory situation that the Commission launched its programme for the completion of the internal market by issuing its well-known "White Paper" in April 1985.[67] This programme was endorsed by the European

---

[64] See below Tax Provisions and VAT.
[65] EEC, Art. 100.
[66] COM(83)80 final; see also Bull. 2–1983, 15.
[67] Completing the internal market, White Paper from the Commission to the European Council (COM(85)310 final).

Council in June of the same year and became the point of departure for the negotiations leading up to the signature in February 1986 of the SEA.[68] This Act will not be examined in this book as a separate Community instrument since most of its provisions modify or complement the existing Treaties; it will be analysed as part of the Treaties in the following chapters. However, suffice it to point out here that the main features of the Act concern:

— the achievement of a completely free market, and in order to achieve this;
— the strengthening of the Community's decision making power, by extending qualified majority voting;
— reference in the Treaty to Economic and Monetary Union;
— inclusion in the Treaty of the Regional Development Fund as one of the structural instruments for economic and social cohesion;
— closer involvement of the European Parliament in the legislative procedures;
— the setting up of a legal framework for Community activities in the area of science and technology;
— the protection of the environment, and
— co–operation in the sphere of foreign policy.

In pursuance of the White Paper, the Commission submitted to the Council 279 draft directives based upon the new Article 100a; about 60 per cent of those had been adopted by the Council by the end of 1989, but most of them still had to be transposed into national legislation by the Member States.[69]

Further Reading

Commission communication concerning the free movement of foodstuffs, O.J. 1989 C.271.

---

[68] Bull. Suppl. 2/86. The Act entered into force on July 1, 1987 (O.J. 1987 L.169/1–28).
[69] In its fourth progress report to the Council on the implementation of the programme leading to the achievement of the internal market, the Commission ascertained that only half a dozen had been adopted by the 12 Member States in their national legislation! (COM(89)311).

A. Mattera, *Le Marché Unique Européen, ses règles, son fonctionnement*, (1988) Jupiter, Paris.

F. Burrows, *Free Movement in European Community Law*, (1987) Oxford.

P. Oliver, *Free Movement of Goods in the EEC*, (2nd ed., 1988) E.L.C., London.

M. Quinn and N. MacGowan, "Could Article 30 Impose Obligations on Individuals?" 163, (1987) E.L.Rev.

II. THE FREE MOVEMENT OF PERSONS

The Court of Justice emphasized over and over again that free movement of persons is one of the fundamental freedoms guaranteed by the Treaty, that the provisions in this field may not be interpreted restrictively[70] and that they have direct effect.[71] The Treaty distinguishes between wage earners ("workers"),[72] *i.e.* anyone who pursues an activity as an employed person, and non-wage earners, *i.e.* professional people, tradesmen, etc. (simply referred to as "nationals of the Member States"),[73] which includes both natural and legal persons.

The free movement of workers is mainly based on the principle of non-discrimination on the ground of nationality while the right of non-wage earners to operate freely within the Community is, generally speaking, expressed by the right of establishment[74] and the right to provide services.[75]

In order to facilitate the free circulation of their nationals throughout the whole Community the Member States now issue their passports as a "European Passport" with a uniform format.

---

[70] See, *e.g.* Case 53/81 *Levin* v. *Staatssecretaris van Justitie* [1982] E.C.R. 1035 at 1049(13).
[71] See, *e.g.* Case 48/75 *Royer* [1976] E.C.R. 497 at 512 (31).
[72] See EEC Arts. 52 and 59.
[73] Chapters 2 and 3 of Title III.
[74] EEC Arts. 52 to 58.
[75] EEC Arts. 59 to 66.

As for the Commission, under the title "A People's Europe," it sent to the Council a Communication and a Report on the removal of intra-Community border controls on persons.[76] It also initiated no less than 65 infringement procedures against Member States for failure to apply Community law. With respect to freedom of movement mention must be made of the Schengen Agreement of June 14, 1985 between the Benelux countries, Germany and France to abolish all border controls on persons; it was first opposed by some frightened Parliaments but it was signed in May 1990 and will enter into force on January 1, 1993.

The Commission also sent the Council a proposal for a Directive on voting rights for Community nationals in local elections in their Member State of residence.[77]

1. Free movement of workers[78]

The free movement of workers within the Community can be jeopardised by discriminatory conditions of work and employment, by obstacles resulting from laws, regulations or administrative practice and by the lack of harmonisation of the social security systems of the Member States. The Treaty provides remedies for all those cases. Discrimination based on the nationality of the worker has been abolished,[79] as have administrative procedures and practices which formed an obstacle to the free movement of workers,[80] and the necessary measures were

---

[76] Bull. 12–1988, 39.

[77] O.J. 1988, C.246; twenty-second General Report (1988), 142.

[78] EEC, Arts. 48 to 51. For the definition of worker see Art. 1 of Reg. 1408/71 (J.O. 1971, L.149; O.J. 1971(II), 416). In Case 53/81 *Levin*, n.70 above, at 1050(17) the Court indicated that the activity pursued by the worker must be an economic one and that the concept "worker" may not be defined by reference to the national law of the Member States, but has a Community meaning (*ibid.,* at 1049(11).

[79] EEC, Art. 48(2). See also EEC, Art. 7. In its judgment of February 2, 1989, (not yet published) in the Case 186/87 *Cowan* v. *France*, the Court, basing itelf on EEC, Art. 7, found against the latter for having refused compensation for assault invoking the fact that the victim was not domiciled in France.

[80] EEC, Art. 49(b).

adopted in the field of social security.[81] Consequently, any employed person who exercises an economic activity[82] and is a national of one of the Member States[83] has the right:

(a) without being discriminated against[84] on the ground of nationality to accept offers of employment actually made in other Member States. This does not mean that the free entry into a Community country could be denied to a worker from another Member State who does not have a duly executed employment contract: freedom of movement also extends to persons who "seriously wish to pursue activities as an employed person."[85] Furthermore, the employment must not necessarily be full-employment: the freedom also applies to persons who pursue an activity on a part-time basis and who by virtue of that fact obtain a remuneration lower than the minimum guaranteed wage in the sector under consideration.[86] The Court also determined that the motives which may have prompted a worker to seek employment are of no account and must not be taken into consideration.[87] Finally, it should be noted that the EEC rules in this field only apply to workers from other Member States and not to a worker who is a national of the State concerned and in a wholly national situation[88];

---

[81] EEC, Art. 51. See Case C–114/88 *Delbar* v. *Caisse d'allocations familiales*, December 5, 1989 (not yet published) concerning family allowances when the dependants do not live in the same Member State.

[82] Case 36/74 *Walrave* v. *Union Cycliste Internationale* [1974] E.C.R. 1405, at 1417(5).

[83] Reg. 1612/68, J.O. 1968, L.257/2; O.J. 1968(II), 475.

[84] A typical example: Case 13/76 *Donà* v. *Mantero* [1976] E.C.R. 1333.

[85] Case 53/81 *Levin* (n. 70 above, at 1052(21)).

[86] *Ibid.*, at 1050(16); if part-time employment is covered, it does not however include activities on such a small scale as to be regarded as purely marginal and ancillary, *ibid.* (17). See also Case 96/80 *Jenkins* v. *Kingsgate* [1981] E.C.R. 911 at 925(11).

[87] Case 53/81 *Levin* (n. 70 above, at 1052(22)).

[88] Case 175/78 *Regina* v. *Saunders* [1979] E.C.R. 1129 at 1135(10), where the Court held that Art. 48 does not restrict the power of Member States to lay down restrictions, within their own territory. See also Case 180/83 *Moser* v. *Land Baden-Württemberg* [1984] E.C.R. 2539.

(b) to move freely within the territories of the Member States for this purpose; the necessary directives were enacted by the Council on a proposal from the Commission and after consulting the Social and Economic Committee[89];

(c) to stay in a Member State for the purpose of employment in accordance with the provisions governing the employment of nationals of that State as laid down by law, regulation or administrative action.[90] The right to reside in a Member State is not limited to the worker himself, but extends to his direct family.[91] Furthermore, this extended right is not limited to residence alone, but encompasses the whole treatment afforded national dependents[92];

(d) to remain in the territory of a Member State after having been employed in that State subject to conditions

[89] Reg. 1612/68 (n. 83 above), Dir. 68/360 (J.O. 1968, L.257/13; O.J. 1968(II), 485) and Reg. 1251/70 (J.O. 1970, L.142/24; O.J. 1970(II), 402).

[90] See Case 8/77 *Sagulo, Branca and Bakhouche* [1977] E.C.R. 1495 at 1504(8): the issue of a special residence document provided for in Art. 4 of Dir. 68/360 (n. 88 above) has only a declaratory effect and cannot be assimilated to a residence permit such as prescribed for aliens in general. See however Case 17/75 *Watson and Belmann* [1976] E.C.R. 1185 at 1199(23); the Court upheld the right of a Member State to require foreign nationals to report to the police; however on December 12, 1989 in Case C–265/88 *Messner* v. *Volterra Police Commissioner* (not yet published) the Court held that the time-limit for reporting and the possible sanction had to be reasonable.

[91] Art. 10 of Reg. 1612/68 (n. 83 above) defines the worker's family as follows: (1) his spouse and children under 21 or who are dependants and (2) dependant relatives in ascending line of the worker and his spouse; see also Dir. 68/360 (n. 88 above).

[92] See Case 9/74 *Casagrande* v. *Landeshauptstadt München* [1974] E.C.R. 773 at 779(8) concerning education and training facilities available to nationals: must be extended to children of deceased worker who was employed in Germany and Case 152/82 *Forcheri* v. *Belgium* [1983] E.C.R. 2323 at 2336(18). Those rules however only apply to vocational training and there no discrimination is accepted: Case 42/87 *Commission* v. *Belgium*, September 27, 1988 (not yet published); the obligation to pay tuition for ordinary schools is acceptable, even if not required from nationals: Case 263/86 *Belgium* v. *Humbel*, September 27, 1988 (not yet published); on the other hand, scholarships may not be refused: Case 235/87 *Mattencci* v. *Communauté Française of Belgium*, September 27, 1988 (not yet published).

embodied in implementing regulations drawn up by the Commission.[93] This right must be seen as a corollary to the freedom of movement; it applies both to the worker himself and to his family.

Notwithstanding all the provisions and measures mentioned above, the freedom of movement of workers could nonetheless be illusory if, by moving from one country to another, the worker would lose the rights acquired under social security regulations; this applies particularly to pension rights both for the worker and his family. The Treaty has therefore provided for a system ensuring that:

(a) all periods taken into account under the laws of the several countries where the beneficiary has worked will be added together for the calculation of the amount of his benefits;

(b) those benefits will be paid to the beneficiary in whichever Member State he resides.[94]

Those provisions were worked out in two basic Council Regulations[95] which gave rise to numerous judgments in which the Court gave an interpretation which reflects the objective of

---

[93] Reg. 121/70 (n. 89 above).

[94] EEC, Art. 51.

[95] Reg. 1408/71 (J.O. 1971, L.149/2; O.J. 1971(II), 416), amended by Reg. 1390/81 (O.J. 1981, L.143/1) on the application of Social Security Schemes to employed persons, to self-employed persons and to their families moving within the Community, amended by Reg. 2793/81 (O.J. 1981, L.275/1); a consolidated text is to be found in Annex 1 to Reg. 2001/83, O.J. 1983, L.230/6. The main provisions concern the persons covered (Arts. 1 and 2): it includes, *e.g.* employed and self-employed persons, stateless persons or refugees residing within the EEC, members of their families and their survivors. The Regulation covers the following branches of social security: sickness and maternity (see, *e.g.* Case 41/77 *Regina* v. *Warry* [1977] E.C.R. 2085 (sickness) and Case 69/79 *Jordens-Vosters* v. *Bedrijfsvereniging* [1980] E.C.R. 75 (maternity); invalidity (see Case 2/72 *Murru* v. *Caisse Régionale d'Assurance Maladie de Paris* [1972] E.C.R. 333); old age (see Case 1/72 *Frilli* v. *Belgium* [1972] E.C.R. 457);

freedom of movement for workers.[96] As explained by the Court, Community law did not provide for a common system of social security, but allowed separate systems to exist and "creating separate claims against separate institutions against which the beneficiary has direct rights," either under national law alone, or national law supplemented by Article 51 of the Treaty.[97]

The Administrative Commission and the Advisory Committee on Social Security for Migrant Workers[98] were set up to help the Commission and the Member States with the implementation of the regulations adopted within the framework of social security.[99]

Exceptions to the free movement of workers

While providing for the basic principles determining the free movement of workers, the Treaty at the same time introduces limitations "justified on grounds of public policy, public security or public health."[1] National authorities may therefore invoke those grounds to refuse entry into[2] or residence within their

---

survivors (see family benefits); unemployment (see Case 76/76 *Di Paolo* v. *Office National de l'Emploi* [1977] E.C.R. 315); family benefits (see Case 65/81 *Reina* v. *Landeskreditbank Baden-Württemberg* [1982] E.C.R. 33); benefits in respect of accidents at work and occupational diseases (see Case 268/78 *Pennartz* v. *Caisse Primaire d'Assurance Maladie des Alpes-Maritimes* [1979] E.C.R. 2411) and death grants (see Case 22/81 *Regina* v. *Social Security Commissioner (Browning)* [1981] E.C.R. 3357)).

[96] Between 1953 and December 31, 1980, 461 cases concerning social security and freedom of movement of workers were filed with the Court, which took decisions in 357 of them: twenty third General Report (1989), 436.

[97] Case 2/67 *De Moor* v. *Caisse de Pension* [1967] E.C.R. 197.

[98] Reg. 1408/71, (n. 95 above).

[99] EEC, Art. 51.

[1] EEC, Art. 43(3).

[2] See, *e.g.* Case 41/74 *Van Duyn* v. *Home Office* [1974] E.C.R. 1337 where the Court upheld the right of the Home Office to refuse leave to enter the U.K. and Case 157/79 *Regina* v. *Pieck* [1980] E.C.R. 2171 at 2185(9): those exceptions do not constitute a condition precedent to the acquisition of the right of entry.

territory or to expel[3] workers who are nationals of other Member States. A first attempt to define the scope of these grounds was made by the Council[4] and further clarification resulted from the abundant case law of the Court.[5]

Furthermore, the Treaty provides that the principle of non-discrimination on the ground of nationality towards workers of other Member States does not apply to employment in public service, *i.e.* Member States may restrict "admission" to certain activities; discriminatory measures against a worker, once he has been admitted, cannot be justified on the basis of this provision.[5]

2. Freedom of movement of non-wage earners

As pointed out above, the provisions concerning the free movement of non-wage earners are to be found under the headings "Right of establishment"[6] and "Services."[7] The right of establishment, in so far as it concerns natural persons, includes the right to take up and pursue activities as a self-employed person in another country; it implies that this person moves to that other Member State. The right to provide services, on the other hand,

---

[3] See Case 98/80 *Romano* v. *Inami* [1981] E.C.R. 1241. In Case 98/79 *Pecastaing* v. *Belgian State* [1980] E.C.R. 691, the Court declared however that a person against whom an expulsion order has been issued may exercise all the remedies available to nationals in respect of acts of the administration. The remedies can have suspensory effect. See also Case 131/79 *Regina* v. *Secretary of State for Home Affairs* [1980] E.C.R. 1585 (a recommendation for deportation made under British legislation by a criminal court at the time of conviction may constitute an opinion under Art. 9 of Dir. 64/221 (J.O. 1964, 850; O.J. 1963–1964, 117) on the co-ordination of special measures concerning the movement and residence of foreign nationals which are justified on grounds of public policy, public security and public health).
[4] Concerning the direct effect of this Dir. see Case 41/74 *Van Duyn* (n. 2 above).
[5] EEC, Art. 48(4). See Case 152/73 *Sotgiu* v. *Deutsche Bundespost* [1974] E.C.R. 153 and Case 149/79 *Commission* v. *Belgium* [1980] E.C.R. 3881 and [1982] E.C.R. 1845.
[6] EEC, Part Two "Foundations of the Community," Title III "Free movement of persons, services and capital," Chap. 2, Arts. 52–58.
[7] *Ibid.*, Chapter 3, Arts. 59–66.

concerns nationals of Member States who are established in a State other than the one of the person for whom the services are intended. There is great similarity between the two freedoms: as in the case of free movement of workers, the Treaty only provides that persons from Member States establishing themselves in another Member State to pursue an economic activity and those providing services in another Member State, shall be treated, within that other Member State, like nationals of that country:[8] in other words, nothing more, but nothing less, than the application of the principle of non-discrimination on the ground of nationality.[9]

Both freedoms also apply to undertakings, companies and firms, although special rules are provided for services in the field of transport, banking and insurance.[10] Also, for both freedoms, the Treaty provides for the Council, acting on a proposal from the Commission and after consulting the Economic and Social Committee and Parliament, to draw up a general programme for the abolition of existing restrictions.[11]

The liberal professions present a particular problem because of the required diplomas, certificates and other evidence of formal qualification. The Treaty therefore provides that, before the end of the transitional period, the Council, on a proposal from

---

[8] EEC, Arts. 52(2) and 60. It is interesting to note that in Case 115/78 *Knoors* v. *Secretary of State for Economic Affairs* [1979] E.C.R. 399, at 410(24), the Court determined that the reference to "nationals of Member States" in Art. 52 cannot be interpreted in such a way as to exclude from the benefit of Community law own nationals who want to "establish" themselves in their own country after having resided in another Member State and acquired there trade qualifications which are recognised by Community law; see also Case 246/80 *Broekmeulen* v. *Huisarts Registratie Commissie* [1981] E.C.R. 2311. The reverse also applies, as was seen in respect to the free movement of workers; Case 175/78 *Saunders* (n. 88 above). With regard to journalists, pharmacists, etc. see Case 168/85, *Commission* v. *Italy*, [1986] E.C.R. 2956, where Italy was condemned for requiring Italian nationality!

[9] EEC, Art. 7.

[10] EEC, Art. 61. See below: Freedom of Establishment and Freedom to provide Services.

[11] EEC, Arts. 54(1) and 63(1); the two programmes were adopted in 1962: for establishment J.O. 36/62; O.J. (2nd)IX, 7 and for services J.O. 32/62; O.J. *ibid.* at 3.

the Commission and after consulting Parliament, must issue directives for the mutual recognition of such evidence of qualification and for the co-ordination of the provisions laid down by law, regulation or administrative action in the Member States concerning the taking up and pursuit of activities as self-employed persons.[12] The implementation of the Treaty provisions and the above-mentioned directives was, over the past years, the object of numerous requests for interpretation by the Court which considers that, even in the absence of implementing directives, Articles 52 and 59 have, since the end of the transitional period, had direct effect. Consequently, the prohibition of discrimination based on nationality which is provided therein can

---

[12] Both kinds of Directives (mutual recognition and co-ordination) are grouped below for the main professions; it should be noted that those Directives were amended following the accessions of Greece, Portugal and Spain.
Doctors: Dirs. 75/362 and 75/363 (O.J. 1975 L.167/1 and 14), both were amended in 1982 by Dir. 82/76 (O.J. 1982 L.43/21) and supplemented in 1986 by a Dir. on specific training in general medical practice (O.J. 1986, L.267/26). See Case 246/80 *Broekmeulen* (n. 8 above).
Nurses (responsible for general care): Dirs. 77/452 and 77/453 (O.J. 1977, L.176/1 and 8).
Dental practitioners: Dirs. 78/686 and 78/687 (O.J. 1978, L.233/1 and 10).
Veterinary surgeons: Dirs. 78/1026 and 78/1027 (O.J. 1978, L.362/1 and 7). See Cases 271/82 *Auer* v. *Ministère Public* [1983] E.C.R. 2727 and 5/83 *Rienks* [1983] E.C.R. 4233.
For doctors, nurses, dental practitioners and veterinary surgeons, see Dir. 81/1057 (O.J. 1981, L.282/25) on the acquired rights of holders of diplomas.
See also the Commission's Action Programme against Cancer calling for intensified training for doctors, nurses and dental practitioners (O.J. 1987, L.50).
Midwives: Dirs. 80/154 and 155 (O.J. 1980, L.33/1 and 8).
Architects: O.J. 1985, L.223/15, 372/42 and L.376/1; also O.J. 1986, L.27/71. See Case 11/77 *Patrick* v. *Ministère des Affaires Culturelles* [1977] E.C.R. 1199.
Pharmacists: O.J. 1985, L. 253/34, 37, 43, 47 and L.372/42.
Lawyers: Dir. 77/249 (O.J. 1977, L.78/17), limited however to the right to provide services, but the Court has also recognised the right of establishment. See Case 2/74 *Reyners* v. *Belgian State* [1974] E.C.R. 631; Case 71/76 *Thieffry* v. *Conseil de l'Ordre des Avocats à la Cour de Paris* [1977] E.C.R. 765 and Case 107/83 *Ordre des Avocats au Barreau de Paris* v. *Klopp* [1984] E.C.R. 2971.

be invoked by nationals of the Member States in any national court or tribunal.[13]

Mention must be made of a Directive of 1988 concerning the general recognition of higher-education diplomas[14]; this directive was called for by the Fontainebleau European Council of June 1984, and is a good example of the time required to implement the requests of the European Council.

Other activities present similar problems to those encountered by the liberal professions since the exercise of most of them is also conditioned by the possession of evidence of formal qualifications. Both for "establishment" and for "services," the Treaty provides for the Council to draw up general programmes for the abolition of existing restrictions. Those programmes[15] set out the general conditions under which the two freedoms are to be attained in the case of each type of activity; they have been implemented over the years by dozens of directives laying down detailed provisions in respect of activities of self-employed persons.[16]

The above-mentioned directives concerning both the liberal professions and the other activities provide for measures ensuring freedom in respect of the right of establishment and the right to provide services; these fundamental rights will be examined hereafter.

Further Reading

D. Lassock, *The Professions and Services in the European Economic Community*, (1986) Deventer, Kluwer

---

[13] The most important cases are mentioned in the previous note, but see also Case 33/74 *van Binsbergen* v. *Bedrijfsvereniging Metaalnijverheid* [1974] E.C.R. 1299: requirement of permanent residence in Member State where services are rendered not always incompatible with Arts. 59 and 60.

[14] O.J. 1989, L.19/16. EEC, Art. 57 modified by SEA, Art. 6(6).

[15] J.O. 1962, 32 and 36. Those programmes provided for the liberalisation of 123 groups of activities, mostly in the industry and craft sectors.

[16] A complete list can be found in *Encyclopedia of European Community Law*, Sweet & Maxwell, Part C 13. Concerning conditions for access to and exercise of such activities, see Case 115/78 *Knoors* v. *Secretary of State for Economic Affairs* [1979] E.C.R. 399.

J. Handoll, *Article 48(4) EEC and Non-National Access to Public Employment,* 223 (1988) 13 E.L.Rev.

III. FREEDOM OF ESTABLISHMENT

The right of establishment[17] was briefly examined in the previous section in so far as its exercise is required for the freedom of self-employed persons to move within the Community. As was pointed out this freedom also applies to companies and firms formed in accordance with the law of a Member State and having their registered office, central administration or principal place of business within the Community.[18]

The freedom of establishment includes the right to take up and pursue activities as self-employed persons and to set up and manage undertakings, agencies, branches or subsidiaries "under the conditions laid down for its own nationals by the law of the country where such establishment is effected."[19] In other words, the "freedom" of establishment is not unlimited, but means that the nationals of Member States who wish to pursue economic activities in another member country must be treated in the same way as the natural and legal persons who are nationals of that host-country.[20] As was pointed out above, Article 52 has had direct effect since the end of the transitional period, notwith-standing the fact that the Council failed to issue the necessary directives to implement the general programme for the abolition of existing restrictions[21] and for the co-ordination of the provisions laid down by law, regulation or administrative action in Member States concerning the taking up and pursuit of activities as self-employed persons.[22]

---

[17] EEC, Arts. 52 to 58. It should be noted that in pursuance of Art. 66, Arts. 55 to 58 also apply to the matters covered by the Treaty provisions concerning services, *i.e.* Arts. 59 to 65.

[18] See EEC, Art. 58(1) and 58(2) for a definition of "company or firm."

[19] EEC, Art. 52(2).

[20] Of interest in this respect is Case 115/78 *Knoors* (n. 16 above).

[21] EEC, Art. 54(1).

[22] EEC, Art. 57(2).

[22] EEC, Arts. 54(2) and 57(1).

The Treaty provisions concerning the right of establishment and the right to provide services are very similar.[23] There are, however, differences resulting from the fact that, although the actual economic activity carried out by a person or company under each one of those rights might be the same, "establishment" requires a more or less permanent residence in another Member State. In other words, it implies the setting-up in the host State of a base from which services or other activities are provided inside that same State. "Services," on the other hand, are normally provided directly from the home-country and might require only occasional, temporary entry into the other Member State.[24]

Restrictions the freedom of establishment often result from differences in the laws of the Member States concerning undertakings. The Treaty[25] therefore provides for the co-ordination of the safeguards which are required by Member States of companies and firms for the protection of the interests of "members and others." This provision was, from the beginning, widely interpreted by the Commission which embarked, back in 1968, on an ambitious programme aiming at harmonising the law applying to undertakings, the so-called "company law directives."[26] In this context, the Commission made proposals for a

---

[23] See, *e.g.* n. 17 above.

[24] See, *e.g.* Case 33/74 *van Binsbergen* (n. 13 above).

[25] EEC, Art. 54(g).

[26] The *first* Dir. 68/151 (J.O. 1968, L. 65/8; O.J. 1968(I), 41) on the co-ordination of safeguards concerns *inter alia* disclosure of particulars, validity of obligations entered into on behalf of the company and nullity of companies with limited liability.

The *second* Dir. 77/91 (O.J. 1977, L. 26/1) deals with the formation of public liability companies and the maintenance and alteration of their capital.

The *third* Dir. 78/885 (O.J. 1978, L. 295/36) concerns mergers between companies and requires publication to the shareholders of the merger plan, accounts and reports.

The *fourth* Dir. 78/660 (O.J. 1978, L. 222/11) provides for similar legal requirements concerning the financial information that must be made public; *e.g.* annual accounts. Extended to banks and other financial institutions in 1986 (O.J. 1986, L. 372/1); see also Dirs. 89/117 and 89/299 (O.J. 1989, L. 44/40 and 124/16).

The draft *fifth* Dir. (Commission proposal O.J. 1983, C. 240/2) concerns the

European Company Statute and although 20 years have elapsed since, the Commission hopes to be able to revive the idea with new proposals.[27] On July 1, 1989 a Regulation on the structure of a European Economic Interest Grouping entered into force[28] which provides Community firms with an instrument of co-operation based on Community law; these EEIGs are registered in a given Member State, but operate throughout the whole Community and have legal personality, if provided by national law.

Exceptions to the freedom of establishment

Although it constitutes one of the fundamental freedoms of the Community, the Member States may invoke certain exceptions in

structure of public limited companies and the powers and obligations of their organs. The latest amendments of the proposal concern the board structure: Member States have a choice between requiring a two-tier structure with a supervisory and a management board, or giving the companies a choice between a two-tier structure and a one-tier structure (*i.e.* a single administrative board). As for employees' participation, it is to be regulated by the Member States in accordance with one of four alternative models. (Not to be confused with the so-called "Vredeling" directive on procedures for informing and consulting employees; see below).

The *sixth* Dir. 82/891 (O.J. 1982, L. 378/47) is about divisions of public liability companies. Dir. 79/279 (O.J. 1979, L. 66/21), Dir. 80/390 (O.J. 1980, L. 100/1) and Dir. 82/121 (O.J. 1982, L. 48/26) concern various requirements for companies quoted on an official stock exchange.

The *seventh* Dir. 83/349 (O.J. 1983, L. 193/1) concerns group accounts and was extended to Banks and other financial institutions in 1986 (O.J. 1986, L. 372/1).

The *eighth* Dir. (O.J. 1984, L. 126/20) on approval of persons responsible for carrying out statutory audits of accounting documents.

Draft *tenth* Dir. (O.J. 1985, C. 23), concerns cross-frontier mergers of public limited liability companies.

Draft *eleventh* Dir. (O.J. 1986, C. 203) limiting the list of particulars and documents to be disclosed, but providing an obligation concerning the disclosure of accounting documents of branches of financial and credit institutions.

Draft *twelfth* Dir. (twenty-second General Report 1988, 132) provides for single-member companies to establish anywhere in the Community.

See also Dir. 77/187 (O.J. 1977, L. 61/26) on the safeguarding of employer's rights and advantages in case of mergers, take-overs and amalgamations.

For the draft of the so-called "Vredeling" Dir. see O.J. 1980, C. 297/3; the draft provides for procdures for informing and consulting employees of transnational companies.

[27] See twenty-second General Report (1988), 133.

[28] Reg. 2137/85 (O.J. 1985, L. 199).

order to restrict its implementation. In the first place, the Community rules do not apply to activities which in given Member States are connected, even occasionally, with the exercise of official authority.[29] This exception must, however, be restricted to those activities which in themselves involve a direct and specific connection with the exercise of official authority.[30]

Secondly, Member States may, under certain conditions, apply the provisions laid down by law, regulation or administrative action providing for special treatment of foreign nationals, on grounds of public policy, public security or public health.[31]

As will be seen, the same exceptions apply to the freedom to provide services which is examined hereafter.[32]

Further Reading

Janet Dine, "The Community Company Law Harmonisation Programme", 322, (1989) E.L.Rev.

D. Edward, "Establishment and Services: An Analysis of the Insurance Cases" 231, (1987) E.L.Rev.

IV. FREEDOM TO PROVIDE SERVICES

As was mentioned, the freedom to provide services[33] constitutes, together with the freedom of establishment, the concrete expression of the freedom of movement of non-wage earners or

---

[29] EEC, Art. 55(1). See Dirs. 78/1026 and 78/1027 (O.J. 1978, L. 362/1 and 7) concerning veterinary surgeons: for the first time the Member States declared not to prevail themselves of the possibility to invoke the exception. Under Art. 51(2), the Council may declare the provisions of freedom of establishment non applicable to certain activities: no such declaration exists.

[30] Case 2/74 *Reyners* (see above n. 12). See also Case 152/73 *Sotgiu* (n. 5 above), Case 149/79 *Commission* v. *Belgium* (n. 5 above) concerning the interpretation of similar provisions of Art. 48(4), Case 66/85 *Lawrie-Blum* v. *Land Baden-Württemberg* [1986] E.C.R. 2139.

[31] EEC, Art. 56(1). See Dir. 64/221 (O.J. 1963–1964, 117). Also Dirs. 72/194 (O.J. 1972(II), 474) and 75/35 (O.J. 1975, L. 14/14).

[32] EEC, Art. 66.

[33] EEC, Arts. 59–66.

self-employed persons. Furthermore, there are great similarities between "establishment" and "services" to the point that they have certain Treaty provisions in common.[34] Common to both of them is also the fact that the respective provisions apply both to natural and to legal persons.[35]

The freedom to provide services concerns in particular activities of an industrial or commercial character and activities of craftsmen and the professions.[36] It includes the right for the person who provides the service temporarily to pursue his activity in the State where the service is provided, under the same conditions as are imposed by that State on its own nationals.[37] Once again one finds here the principle of non-discrimination on the basis of nationality which was pointed out in regard to free movement of workers and freedom of establishment. Furthermore this freedom also implies the right, for the beneficiary of the service, to receive it. In other words freedom to "provide" services implies the right to "receive" services.[38]

According to the Court, the essential requirements of Article 59 became directly and unconditionally applicable at the end of the transitional period[39] and have direct effect.[40]

The freedom to provide services does not prevent a Member State from imposing upon a person providing services from another Member State specific requirements, because of the particular nature of the service to be provided, where they have

---

[34] EEC, Art. 66 provides that Arts. 55 to 58 (in Chap. 2 on the right of establishment) shall apply to the matters covered by the Chapter on "services."

[35] EEC, Art. 58.

[36] EEC, Art. 50(2).

[37] EEC, Art. 60(3).

[38] The beneficiary has, *e.g.* the right to enter another Member State to receive the service without being restricted by limitations imposed on the transfer of payments; see Joined Cases 286/82 and 26/83 *Luisi and Carbone* v. *Ministero del Tesoro* [1984] E.C.R. 377.

[39] See Case 33/74 *van Binsbergen* (n. 13 above) and Joined Cases 110–111/78 *Minstère Public and A.S.B.L.* v. *van Wesemael* [1979] E.C.R. 35 at 52(26).

[40] *I.e.* they must be upheld by national courts and tribunals; see Case 13/76 *Donà* v. *Mantero* [1976] E.C.R. 1333.

as their purpose the application of professional rules justified by the general good; it concerns in particular rules relating to organisation, qualification, professional ethics, supervision and liability, which are binding upon any person providing that kind of service.[41] It is interesting to note that the Court refers to a "single market for services" and that the refusal to provide services on a non-discriminatory basis to all nationals of Member States constitutes a violation of Treaty rules.[42]

Of particular importance in the service sector are the "financial services," namely the free circulation of the "financial product," made ever easier by the development of technology, as was pointed out by the Commission in its 1985 White Paper on completing the Internal Market.[43] This free circulation needs a minimal co-ordination on such matters as authorisation, financial supervision and reorganisation, winding up, etc. as the basis for mutual recognition by Member States of what each does to safeguard the interests of the public. Such harmonisation must be guided by the principle of "home country control." This means attributing the primary task of supervising the financial institution to the competent authorities of its Member State of origin, to which would have to be communicated all the necessary information. The authorities of the Member State which is the destination of the service would have a complementary role.[44]

The first Directive on the abolition of restrictions on the freedom of establishment and freedom to provide services in respect of self-employed activities of banks and other financial institutions was published in 1973.[45]

In 1977 the Council adopted the first Directive on the co-ordination of laws, regulations and administrative provisions relating to the taking up and pursuit of the business of credit

---

[41] Case 33/74 *van Binsbergen* (n. 13 above).
[42] Case 7/82 *G.V.L.* v. *Commission* [1983] E.C.R. 483 at 505(37), where the Court held that such refusal affects trade between Member States which is prohibited by Art. 86(1).
[43] White Paper, points 101 *et seq.* (COM(83)310).
[44] *Ibid.*, 103.
[45] O.J. 1973, L. 194/1.

institutions.[46] In 1988, the Commission sent the Council a proposal for a second directive completing the first one and providing *inter alia* for the issue of a single banking licence recognised throughout the whole Community.[47]

It was pointed out above, with respect to the free movement of goods, that not only open, direct limitations in the form of customs duties or quantitative restrictions, but also less transparent measures with equivalent effect are prohibited. Similarly, not only overt discrimination based on the nationality of the person providing the service is prohibited,[48] but also "all forms of covert discrimination which, although based on criteria which appear neutral, in practice, lead to the same result."[49]

Another parallel can be drawn here, this time with the free movement of persons where, according to the Court, the rights provided for in the Treaty apply only to nationals of other Member States. Similarly, the provisions of the Treaty on freedom to provide services cannot apply to activities whose relevant elements are confined within a single Member State.[50]

As to the kind of activities which come within the rules of the right to provide services, there are no clear indications in the Treaty. As the Court pointed out, at a very early stage, the rules

---

[46] O.J. 1977, L. 322/30, last modified O.J. 1985, L. 309/15. The Directive stipulates that banks must comply with an authorisation procedure, with minimum requirements. Furthermore, Member States may no longer require the application for authorisation to be examined in terms of economic needs of the market. It also lays down a common procedure for the permanent supervision of credit institutions: the authorities must establish solvency and liquidity ratios of a kind allowing of uniform monitoring of the work of credit institutions in all the Member States. Finally, the Directive provides for the setting up of an Advisory Committee permitting co-operation between the national authorities responsible for supervising banking activities (Eleventh General Report (1977), 113).

[47] Twenty-second General Report (1988), 126. See also the proposal for a directive on the own funds of credit institutions, O.J. 1989, C. 243.

[48] As contrary to Arts. 59 and 60(3).

[49] Joined Cases 62–63/81 *Seco* v. *Evi* [1982] E.C.R. 223 at 235(8).

[50] Case 52/79 *Procureur du Roi* v. *Debauve* [1980] E.C.R. 833 at 857(15). See also Case 62/79 *Coditel* v. *Ciné Vog Films* [1980] E.C.R. 881.

of the EEC Treaty only apply to economic activities.[51] This, however, does not exclude *per se* any activity.[52]

It is also important to note that the main provisions concerning the free movement of persons have direct effect in the legal orders of the Member States which means that they confer on natural and legal persons rights which national courts and tribunals must protect.[53]

Finally, mention must be made of possible restrictions on the freedom of establishment and the right to provide services resulting from national procedures regarding public works and public procurement contracts. Directives were therefore issued by the Council concerning the abolition of restrictions on freedom to provide services in respect of public works contracts and on the award of public works contracts to contractors acting through agencies or branches.[54]

Several other directives still have to be adopted by the Council to arrive at the opening of all the national procedures to tenderers from all over the Community without discrimination, but Community law is nonetheless being developed in this field.[55]

Exceptions to the freedom to provide services

The same exceptions apply as those provided for the freedom of establishment,[56] *i.e.* activities which in given Member States are

---

[51] See Case 7/78 *Regina* v. *Thompson* [1978] E.C.R. 2247 (export ban on silver alloy coins).

[52] *e.g.* rules or national practices, even adopted by a sporting organisation, can be incompatible with Art. 7 and, as the case may be, with Arts. 48 to 51 (free movement of workers) or Arts. 59 to 66 (freedom to provide services).

[53] EEC, Arts. 48, 59(1) and 66(3). See Case 13/76 *Donà* v. *Mantero* [1976] E.C.R. 1333.

[54] Dir. 71/304 (O.J. 1971(II), 678), based on Arts. 54(2) and 63(20) and Dir. 71/305, (*ibid.*, at 682), based on Arts. 57(2), 66 and 100. With respect to the latter see Case 76/81 *Transporoute* v. *Minister of Public Works* [1982] E.C.R. 417; see also the Dir. on co-ordination of provisions for the award of public supply contracts (O.J. 1977, L. 13/1) modified (O.J. 1988, L. 127/1), incorporating provisions of the Agreement on Government Procurement concluded under the Tokyo Round (Bull. 7/8–1980, 28), work contracts (O.J. 1978, L. 225/41).

[55] See twenty-second General Report (1988), 100.

[56] EEC, Art. 66.

connected, even occasionally, with the exercise of official author-ity[57] and limitations resulting from provisions laid down by law, regulation or administrative action providing special treatment for foreign nationals on grounds of public policy, public security or public health.[58]

Further Reading

Derrick Wyatt and Allan Dashwood, *The substantive law of the EEC* (2nd ed. 1987) London.
Weiss, "Public Procurement in the EEC—Public Supply Con-tracts", 318, (1988) E.L.Rev.

V. Free Movement of Capital

All restrictions on the movement of capital belonging to persons resident in Member States and any discrimination based on the nationality or the place of residence of the parties or on the place where such capital is invested shall, according to the Treaty,[59] be progressively abolished. This elimination is, however, only required "to the extent necessary to ensure the proper function-ing of the common market."

According to the Court, the scope of that restriction, which remained in force after the expiry of the transitional period, varies in time and depends on an assessment of the requirements of the common market and on an appraisal of both the advan-tages and risks which liberalisation might entail for the latter, having regard to the stage it has reached and, in particular, to the level of integration attained in matters in respect of which capital movements are particularly significant.[60]

The provisions concerning the abolition of restrictions were first implemented by a Council Directive requiring Member

[57] EEC, Art. 55; see above under "Freedom of Establishment."
[58] EEC, Art. 56; see, *ibid.*
[59] EEC, Arts. 67–73.
[60] Case 203/80 *Casati* [1981] E.C.R. 2595.

States to grant foreign exchange authorisation in respect of various categories of capital movement.[61] Then, for many years nothing much happened in this area due to the economic difficulties of the 1970s and the ensuing restriction on foreign exchange. But the Commission's efforts to get the liberalisation of capital movements under way again, through a 1983 Communication on financial integration[62] and the 1986 Two-stage Programme,[63] bore fruit.[64]

In 1988 the Council adopted a Directive and a Regulation that form part of the drive to create a European Financial Area. The Directive concerns complete liberalisation of capital movements[65] while the Regulation establishes a single facility providing medium-term financial assistance for Member States' balances of payments.[66]

Under the Directive all monetary and quasi-monetary transactions such as financial loans and credits, current and deposit account operations, transactions in securities and other instruments normally dealt in on the money market will be liberalised.[67] An interesting feature is the provisions on movement of capital to and from non-Community countries: they establish the principle of liberalisation *erga omnes*.

Free movement of capital must be distinguished from the free movement of payments, the latter being closely connected with the other basic freedoms in such a way that the latter would become inoperative if the connected payments were not liberalised.[68]

---

[61] First Dir. as amended by the Second Dir. both enacted pursuant to EEC, Art. 69. (J.O. 1960, 926 and 1963, 62; O.J. 1959–1962, 49 and O.J. 1963–1964, 5) and again in 1986 (O.J. 1986, L. 332). See twentieth General Report (1986), 94.

[62] See seventeenth General Report (1983), 75.

[63] Bull. 5–1986, 13.

[64] See twenty-second General Report (1988), 104.

[65] O.J. 1988, L. 178.

[66] See twenty-second General Report (1988), 88.

[67] *Ibid.*, 105.

[68] See below: Free movement of payments.

Exceptions to the free movement of capital

As for most rules, the Treaty provides here also for exceptions[69]: if movements of capital lead to disturbances in the functioning of the capital market in a Member State, the Commission must authorise it to take protective measures.[70] In case of secrecy or urgency, the Member State may take such measures on its own initiative.[71]

The above-mentioned Directive on complete liberalisation of capital movement allows the Community to take concerted action to deal with external monetary or financial shocks; in such cases measures can be taken in consultation with the Monetary Committee and the Committee of Governors of the Central Banks.[72]

VI. FREE MOVEMENT OF PAYMENTS

Under the free movement of payments,[73] Member States must authorise payments from a debtor in one Member State to a creditor or beneficiary residing in another, but only in so far as they are connected with the free movement of goods, services and capital. The freedom to make payments must therefore be distinguished from the freedom to move capital or current payments connected with the movement of capital between the Member States.[74]

On the other hand, means of payment as such, *e.g.* silver or gold coins, when they are legal tender in a Member State are covered neither by the provisions concerning payments nor by those concerning free movement of goods.[75]

---

[69] EEC, Art. 73. See in this respect Dir. 72/156 (J.O. 1972, L. 91/13; O.J. 1972(I) 296).

[70] See, *e.g.* O.J. 1976, L. 268/59 authorising Italy to maintain certain restrictions. For the U.K. see O.J. 1978, L.45/30.

[71] See Case 203/80 *Casati* (n. 60 above) about the right of Member States to impose control measures in the absence of Community Rules.

[72] Twenty-second General Report (1988), 105.

[73] EEC, Art. 106.

[74] EEC, Art. 67(2).

[75] Case 7/78 *Regina* v. *Thompson* [1978] E.C.R. 2247 and Case 203/80 *Casati* (n. 60 above).

The connection between free movement of payments and the other basic freedoms[76] is obvious. Indeed, the other freedoms would be quite useless if the financial results from their application could not be "repatriated." It follows from this close connection that the freedom of movement of payments also has, like the provisions concerning the other freedoms, direct effect, *i.e.* confers on the nationals of the Member States rights which the national courts and tribunals must uphold.

In respect of payments for goods, services and capital, the national provisions concerning foreign currencies have been progressively abolished.[77] As for obstacles to payments in conjunction with invisible transactions, *i.e.* tourism, transport of goods and persons, publicity, subscriptions, etc. their progressive elimination is done in accordance with the provisions governing the abolition of existing restrictions on freedom to provide services.[78]

Further Reading

EEC Financial Services Cases, ed. Neville March Hunnings, European Law Centre at Sweet and Maxwell, London.

---

[76] EEC, Art. 106(1). Freedom of establishment is not mentioned because it normally goes together with capital movements.

[77] Dir. 63/340 (O.J. 1963–1964, 31). The General Programme for the removal of restrictions on the freedom to supply services, referred to above, contains a timetable for the removal of restrictions upon the transfer of funds and payments.

[78] EEC, Art. 106(3). See Annex III to the EEC Treaty and Dir. 63/474 (O.J. 1963–1964, 45). See Joined Cases 286/82 and 26/83 *Luisi and Carbone* v. *Ministero del Tesoro* [1984] E.C.R. 377.

Chapter 6

THE COMMON POLICIES

The provisions concerning agriculture and transport are, in the Treaty, classified in Part Two, "Foundations of the Community"; competition policy, economic policy, social policy and now[1] also Economic and Social Cohesion, Research and Technological Development and Environment are to be found in Part Three, "Policy of the Community." However, since the proper functioning and development of the common market require common action in all fields of the economy, this split seems artificial. Therefore, the main policies will be grouped together and examined in this chapter.

I. AGRICULTURE

Although the Treaty specifies[2] that the common market shall extend to agriculture and trade in agricultural products[3] and that, save as otherwise provided, the rules laid down for the establish-

---

[1] Those policies were introduced into the Treaty by the SEA, although they have been implemented for years on the basis of Community acts establishing them, *e.g.* regional policy and environment.

[2] EEC, Art. 38(1).

[3] Those products are "products of the soil, of stockfarming and of fisheries and products of first-stage processing directly related to these products" (EEC, Art. 38(1)). Those products are listed in Annex II to the Treaty (EEC, Art. 38(3)). In 1960, a number of products were added to this list, see Third General Report EEC (1960), 209 and Reg. 7a (O.J. 1959–1962, 68).

ment of the common market apply to agricultural products,[4] it also provides that the operation and development of the common market for agricultural products must be accompanied by the establishment of a common agricultural policy.[5] The apparent contradiction between the inclusion of agriculture in the common market, on the one hand, and the requirement of a special policy in order to achieve this, on the other, is symptomatic of the particular place agriculture occupies within the Community. It is also indicative of the problems faced by the drafters of the Treaty, since, in theory at least, one could have established a common market without agriculture.

First, some Member States produce more than they consume, and were very much interested in a system allowing them to dispose of their surpluses, and therefore needed a common policy; others depend heavily on imports and were interested in free imports and low prices and therefore minimal market regulation. The latter would undoubtedly have preferred to continue to import from third countries at low world prices while the first wanted to protect their markets from those very imports. In other words there existed from the beginning, even before the accession of the United Kingdom, a fundamental conflict of interests.

Secondly, agriculture was, long before the establishment of the Community, a particular problem in each Member State and elaborate and costly national measures to aid agriculture existed practically everywhere.

Thirdly, agriculture presents some very particular problems which clearly differentiate it from industrial production.[6]

On the other hand however, agriculture constitutes in all the Member States a sector closely linked with the economy as a whole. Needless to say, the most important industrial sector in the Community is the food and drink industry, which processes

---

[4] EEC, Art. 38(2).

[5] EEC, Art. 38(4).

[6] EEC, Art. 39(2)(a) refers to the "particular nature of agricultural activity which results from the social structure of agriculture and from structural and natural disparities between the various agricultural regions."

more than three quarters of the agricultural products of the Community. It is mainly because of that close link that the inclusion of agriculture in the common market was agreed upon. But, in order to take into account this particular status, the inclusion took place on special terms: the operation and development of the common market for agricultural products was to be accompanied, as pointed out above, by the establishment of a common agricultural policy among the Member States[7] and the necessary adjustments were to be carried out by degrees.[8] In other words, the general rules governing the establishment of the common market are to be applied "save as otherwise provided in the Treaty"[9]. This means *inter alia* that the provisions of the Treaty relating to the common agricultural policy have precedence, in case of conflict, over the rules relating to the establishment of the common market.[10] But it also means that in the absence of specific provisions the general rules of the Treaty have been fully effective for agricultural products since the end of the transitional period.[11] As for the existing national measures, they were replaced by a "common organisation of agricultural markets"[12] which took the form of various common market organisations.

THE COMMON AGRICULTURAL POLICY (CAP)

Immediately after the Treaty came into force, a conference of the Member States was convened[13] by the Commission with a view to

---

[7] EEC, Art. 39(2)(c).

[8] EEC, Art. 38(4).

[9] See, *e.g.* EEC, Art. 42. See also Reg. 26 concerning the application of Arts. 85 and 86 to agriculture (O.J. 1959–1962, 129).

[10] Case 83/78 *Pigs Marketing Board* v. *Redmond* [1978] E.C.R. 2347.

[11] Case 48/74 *Charmasson* v. *Minister for Economic Affairs and Finance* [1974] E.C.R. 1383.

[12] EEC, Art. 40(2).

[13] EEC, Art. 43(1). The conference was held at Stresa, Italy, in July 1958. See Resolution of the Conference in J.O. 281/58 and First General Report EEC (1958), 87.

making a comparison of their agricultural policies, in particular by producing a statement of their resources and needs. On the basis of those findings, the Commission submitted to the Council proposals for a Community policy in the field of agriculture.[14]

As a first step, the Council adopted a number of basic principles which were to determine the future orientation of the CAP: free movement of agricultural products within the Community, establishment of a commercial policy jointly with the CAP and a common price level for all agricultural products throughout the Community. The anticipated results were an economic balance between supply and demand (for which read self-sufficiency) and fair earnings for those employed in agriculture,[15] *i.e.* price support.

With regard to third countries, a uniform system of levies was to be introduced and, finally, the national measures for structural reforms were to be coordinated.[16] It is obvious that all these objectives are not necessarily compatible.[17] After some 30 years of operation with outstanding positive results, the problems created by appalling overproduction in some sectors made a revision of the CAP mandatory.[18] The so-called "reform" of the CAP got under way in 1983 with a Communication of the Commission to the Council[19] proposing practical adaptations to the CAP, so that the Community can work effectively towards the objectives in the changed circumstances. The rationalisation programme had five points:

    (i) retention and extension of the co-responsibility principle and the guarantee thresholds, with, for milk, a delivery quota system;

---

[14] See Third General Report EEC (1960), 186.

[15] See in this respect the objectives listed in Art. 39(1).

[16] See Third General Report EEC (1960), 186.

[17] See Case 5/73 *Balkan-Import-Export* v. *Hauptzollamt Berlin-Packhof* [1973] E.C.R. 1091, where the Court found that the various objectives of the common agricultural policy taken separately appear to conflict with one another and that the Community institutions must, where necessary, allow temporary priority to one of them.

[18] See the Communiqué of the European Council held at Stuttgart in June 1983, Bull 6–1983, 19.

[19] Suppl. Bull. 4–83.

(ii) a prudent and, in certain cases, restrictive price policy including for cereals a reduction in the gap between Community and world prices;

(iii) existing aids and premiums to be discontinued;

(iv) promotion of the Community's agricultural exports;

(v) more rigorous and automatic dismantlement of the monetary compensatory amounts.[20]

Most of those proposals were endorsed by the Council in 1984[21]; the decisions of the Council were considered by the Commission as a "milestone in the development of the [agricultural] policy."[22] In 1985, the Commission presented the Council with a policy document entitled "A future for Community agriculture"[23]; during 1986 and 1987, the Community institutions, faced with the urgent situation posed by a combination of accumulating surplus stocks and acute budgetary difficulties, implemented measures with regard to price restraint, adjustments to certain market organisations and socio-structural policy. Under the first one, nearly all the institutional prices were frozen in ECU terms and under the second, the Commission proposed to introduce expenditure stabilisation mechanisms in all the market organisations.[24] Most of those measures were implemented and further developed thanks to the successful outcome of the meeting of the European Council in Brussels in February 1988; by approving a Commission Communication entitled "The Single Act: A new frontier for Europe," the Community endowed itself with the political and financial resources it needs to achieve the internal market.[25]

---

[20] Seventeenth General Report (1983), 172.
[21] Eighteenth General Report (1984), 164.
[22] *Ibid.*, at 165.
[23] Nineteenth General Report (1985), 208.
[24] Twenty-first General Report (1987), 225.
[25] Twenty-second General Report (1988), 26.

Back in 1960, however, the task of the Community was of a totally different nature and it was decided to act in two domains: a market and price policy through the establishment of common organisations for agricultural products, and a structural policy. Both policies will be examined hereafter.

1. Common organisations for agricultural products

The Treaty provides for the establishment of a common organisation of agricultural markets without specifying what form such organisation should take.[26] The first step was therefore to agree on the basic principles:

(1) unity of the market, *i.e.* free movement of agricultural products throughout the Community;

(2) Community preference, *i.e.* protection of the common market against low-priced imports from third countries thereby encouraging consumers to prefer Community products;

(3) financial solidarity: the CAP must be totally financed out of Community funds; for this purpose the European Agricultural Guidance and Guarantee Fund[27] was set up.

A single market for agricultural products therefore began to function at the end of the sixties; but the beginning of the seventies was marked, as a consequence of the oil crisis, by severe monetary crises which resulted in the formation within the Community of several agricultural markets interlinked by a system of monetary compensatory amounts (MCAs) applied to

---

[26] EEC, Art. 40(2).
[27] Better known as FEOGA: Fonds Européen d'Orientation et de Garantie Agricole.

"imports" and "exports" within the Community.[28] Those MCAs constituted a flagrant violation of the basic principles of the common market[29] and they only maintained the unhealthy situation of the agricultural sector. Competition, on the other hand, as in the other sectors of the economy, would have imposed a restructuring of agriculture through the market mechanism rather than via measures imposed by the Community under the pressure of internal budgetary problems and external demands for reform of the world agricultural market in the framework of the GATT negotiations, as is now the case.

Several times the Commission pleaded for their gradual phasing out, but without much success. However, the setting-up of the European Monetary System (EMS) in 1979[30] was accompanied by an agreement on the so-called "agri-monetary package." This included the policy which was to be followed with regard to the dismantling of existing MCAs and the conditions for the creation of new ones following changes in the central rates.[31] It was not until 1987 that firm arrangements were introduced for dismantling existing positive MCAs and future negative ones.[32]

According to the Treaty, the common organisation of agricultural markets must be limited to the pursuit of the objectives set out therein,[33] but may include all measures to attain them, such as regulation of prices, aids for the production and market-

---

[28] MCAs are applied by Member States in the form of levies on imports, or refunds for exports, of agricultural products within the Community, in order to offset the reduction or increase in prices of those products due to changes in the exchange rates, *e.g.* the re-evaluation of the DM makes German products non-competitive on the French market, hence refunds (*i.e.* export subsidies) are paid to the German farmers; French products, on the other hand, become cheaper on the German market and hence levies are imposed on these products entering Germany to protect the national production and the income of the German farmers.

[29] The system was nevertheless upheld by the Court; Case 9/73 *Schlüter* v. *Hauptzollamt Lörrach* [1973] E.C.R. 1135 at 1158(33).

[30] O.J. 1979, L. 37. See below: Economic and Monetary Policy.

[31] Thirteenth General Report (1979), 150.

[32] O.J. 1987, L. 13. See Twenty-first General Report (1987), 237.

[33] EEC, Art. 39.

ing of various products, storage and carry-over arrangements and
common machinery for stabilising imports or exports.[34]

The form chosen by the Community for the common organisa
tion was the European Market Organisation.[35] Such organisation
are based on the concept of the open market to which every
producer has access and which is regulated solely by the instru
ments provided for by the organisations.[36] Over the years, marke
organisations were set up for practically all the agricultura
products.[37] It is important to note that once a market organisation
has been set up for a given sector, the Member States are under
the obligation to refrain from taking any measure which might
undermine it, or create exceptions to it.[38] Similarly, from the end
of the transitional period, existing national market organisations
became subject to the general Treaty rules, even in the absence
of a Community market organisation.[39]

The first proposal for a market organisation, the one for
cereals, was submitted to the Council in 1961 and the first

[34] EEC, Art. 40(3); an example of special measures is Dir. 75/268 on mountain
and hill-farming and farming in less-favoured areas (O.J. 1975, L. 128/1).
Obviously these organisations present a problem in regard to the Community
competition rules. The Council therefore enacted Reg. 26 (O.J. 1959–1962,
129) applying certain rules of competition to production of and trade in
agricultural products. This Reg. practically excludes the application of Arts. 85
and 86 to agriculture.
[35] EEC, Art. 40(2)(c).
[36] Case 83/78 *Pigs Marketing Board* (n. 10 above) at 2371(57).
[37] Market organisations were set up for the following products, (in chronological
order): cereals (Reg. 120/67, O.J. 1967, 33, replaced by Reg. 2777/75, O.J.
1975, L. 281/10), oils and fats (Reg. 136/66, O.J. 1965–1966, 221), trees, plants,
flowers, etc. (Reg. 234/68, O.J. 1968(I), 26), milk (Reg. 804/68, O.J. 1968(I),
167), beef and veal (Reg. 805/68, O.J. 1968(I), 187), certain products listed in
Annex II, coffee, tea, cider, cocoa, etc. (Reg. 827/68, O.J. 1968(I), 209),
tobacco (Reg. 727/70, O.J. 1970(I), 206), flax and hemp (Reg. 1308/70, O.J.
1970(II), 411), hops (Reg. 1696/71, O.J. 1971(II), 634), seeds (Reg. 2358/71,
O.J. 1971(III) 894), fruit and vegetables (Reg. 1035/72, O.J. 1972(II), 437),
sugar (Reg. 3330, O.J. 1974, L. 359/1), pigmeat (Reg. 2759/75, O.J. 1975, L.
282/1), eggs (Reg. 2771/75, O.J. 1975, L. 282/49), poultrymeat (Reg. 2777/75,
O.J. 1975, L. 282/77), rice (Reg. 1418/76, O.J. 1976, L. 166/1), fish
(Reg. 100/76, O.J. 1976, L. 20/1), products processed from fruit and vegetables
(Reg. 516/77, O.J. 1977, L. 73/1), dried fodder (Reg. 1117/78, O.J. 1978, L.
120/2), wine (Reg. 317/79, O.J. 1979, L. 54/1), sheep and goatmeat
(Reg. 1837/80, O.J. 1980, L. 183/1).
[38] Case 83/78 *Pigs Marketing Board*, (n. 10 above).
[39] Case 68/76 *Commission* v. *France* [1977] E.C.R. 515 at 531(24).

regulation setting up this organisation was adopted in 1962.[40] It provided for a transitional period during which the national market organisations remained in force and were progressively replaced by the European organisation. A definitive market organisation for cereals was established in 1967. Since the organisation is most typical of those for agricultural markets, it will be examined in some detail below.

However, not all market organisations are identical and they can be classified into three groups according, *inter alia* to the guarantees they offer the producers:

(a) for wheat, coarse grain, sugar and dairy products: a system of target and intervention prices, intervention purchases to be made under certain conditions, within the Community, and external protection in the form of variable levies;

(b) for beef and veal, pig and poultry meat and eggs: support is offered mainly through external protection;

(c) for fruit, vegetables and wine where the determinant factor is quality control,[41] only the standardised or graded products will be allowed on the market; in addition, measures to reduce production and customs duties are applicable.

While allowing European agriculture to develop at a tremendous pace and thereby ensuring a certain degree of self-sufficiency in foodstuffs which shielded the population from the traumatic experience of food shortage it had known during the war years, such market organisations were to grow out of hand. The main problem, which only appeared years later, being that the system was open-ended and the farmers produced with the

---

[40] Reg. 19, J.O. 1962, 933.
[41] See Case 29/82 *van Luipen* [1983] E.C.R. 151 concerning compulsory membership of a private control institution.

intervention price in mind rather than with regard for the market, *i.e.* without asking whether there was a demand for their products. The resulting surpluses caused the collapse of the Community's finances and brought about the reform of the CAP described above.

The common organisation of the market in cereals.[42] Broadly speaking, this organisation is based on a price system and a trading system. The former consists mainly of a target price and an intervention price, while the latter is based on a threshold price for imports from third countries and on export restitutions for exports, while both imports and exports require a licence; in other words, the market organisation provides guaranteed prices within the Community and protection against cheap imports from third countries. As can be seen, "prices" (*i.e.* fixed prices, not market prices) play an essential role in a market organisation[43]; this is because one of the basic ideas is that the income of the farmers should derive from their sales on the market and not from subsidies paid to them by public authorities (known as deficiency payments).

The "*target price*"[44] is the price at which it is expected cereal can be sold on the Community market during the next marketing year[45] which starts sometime during the next calendar year.[46] It is not a fixed price for the product in question since it does not bind anybody; it is *inter alia* destined to help the farmers plan their production by giving them an indication as to their possible income from the sales of that product on the Community market.

---

[42] Reg. 120/67 (O.J. 1967, 33); this regulation was superceded by Reg. 2727/75 (O.J. 1975, L. 281/1).

[43] See Case 223/78 *Grosoli* [1979] E.C.R. 2621.

[44] This target price is also, for all practical purposes, a maximum price, since, as will be seen, imported cereals can be brought into the Community at that price and are thus competitive at that price level.

[45] The marketing year begins after harvest-time; for cereals it runs from August 1 to July 31 of the following year (Reg. 2727/75, Art. 3).

[46] In other words, the target price is set ahead of the marketing period and before the "sowing" takes place.

The target price is established once a year,[47] before August 1, by the Council acting with a qualified majority, on a proposal from the Commission and after consulting Parliament.[48]

The *"intervention price"* or rather "basic intervention price" determines the price at which designated national authorities must buy the cereal offered to them[49]; it constitutes for the farmers a guarantee that their products, in case they cannot sell them on the market at a higher price, will at least be bought at the intervention price which is, of course, lower than the target price.[49] The basic and derived intervention prices are fixed annually, before August 1, simultaneously with the target price, by the Council acting by qualified majority, on a proposal from the Commission and after consulting Parliament.[50] They apply from August 1 until May 31 of the next year; from June 1 till July 31, the prices for the next season are applied.[51]

The *"threshold price"* is the price fixed for certain cereal products imported from third countries. This is necessary to protect the Community farmers against cheap, mostly subsidised, foreign products. The level at which the threshold price is established ensures that for the products imported through Rot-

---

[47] For the 1989/1990 period, the common wheat target price was set at 247.78 ECU/ton (O.J. 1989, L. 126). The target price applies for a standard quality determined by the Council for each cereal; it is fixed for Duisburg (Germany) at the wholesale stage, *i.e.* goods delivered to warehouse but not unloaded (Reg. 2727/75, Art. 2(3)). Duisburg was chosen because it is the area with the lowest production of cereals and therefore the highest prices. Since the intervention price fixed by the Council is a basic price, the intervention prices applicable in the other "commercialisation centres" of the Community are "derived" from the basic price and are thus necessarily lower (Reg. 2727/75, Art. 4(1)–(2)).

[48] This is the procedure provided for in EEC, Art. 43(2) to which Art. 2(4) of Reg. 2727/75 refers; in practice all price decisions are taken unanimously. Consultation of Parliament is not required in the case of the threshold price.

[49] For the 1989/1990 period, the basic common wheat intervention price was set at 179.44 ECU/ton (O.J. 1989, L. 126) as against a target price of 247.78. The level of the derived intervention prices is set in such a way that the differences between them correspond to the disparities in prices to be expected in a normal harvest, under natural conditions of price formation, thereby allowing for the free movement of cereals within the Community (Reg. 2727/75. Art. 4(1)).

[50] See n. 48 above.

[51] Reg. 2727/75, Art. 4(3).

terdam, the selling price on the Duisburg market is equivalent to the target price. Since those products have to be transported from Rotterdam to Duisburg, the threshold price is arrived at by deducting from the target price for the Duisburg area the transport costs of cereals from Rotterdam to Duisburg.

The threshold price for imported raw materials is fixed, for the same standard quality as the target price, by the Council acting by a qualified majority, on a proposal from the Commission, before March 15, for the following marketing year.[52] The threshold price for processed products is fixed by the Commission after consultation of a consultative committee.[53]

Since the prices of imported products are, generally speaking, lower than those of the Community products, a "*levy*" is imposed on them to arrive at the threshold price. This levy is equal to the difference between the threshold price and the most favourable c.i.f. price of imported products at Rotterdam. The levies are fixed daily by the Commission in the form of regulations.[54] Through this system imported products are made at least as expensive as Community products with the result that the consumer will continue to prefer home-grown products, although he pays higher prices than he would on the world market. This is a clear case of the short-term interest of the consumer running counter to the long-term necessity to maintain an efficient and competitive agriculture within the Community since some degree of self-sufficiency is one of the objectives of the CAP.

The target, intervention and threshold prices are subject to monthly increases to take into account additional storage and other financial costs accruing after the harvest.

"*Export restitutions*" are provided[55] to enable Community producers to export their surplus cereals on the world market where, as was said, prices are generally lower than within the Community. Restitutions are the same for the whole Community and may vary according to use and destination. They are equal to

[52] *Ibid.*, Art. 5(1)(5).
[53] *Ibid.*, Arts. 5(6) and 26.
[54] Reg. 2727/75, Art. 6.
[55] *Ibid.*, Art. 16.

the difference between quotations or prices on the world market and the Community prices; they therefore do not contain any element of subsidy: the exporter does not draw a financial benefit from the restitution.

Export restitutions are fixed at regular intervals by the Commission after consultation with a Management Committee.[56] Such a committee was set up within each market organisation to allow the Member States to follow at close hand the implementation of the CAP, without imposing the heavy procedure of formal Council decisions, but providing nonetheless the possibility of bringing matters before the Council in case of disagreement with a proposed Commission decision.

Finally, *"import and export licences"*[57] are required for all imports into and all exports from the Community. They are issued by the Member States to any applicant, irrespective of the place of his establishment within the Community. These licences are provided mainly for statistical purposes.

The implementation of a common market organisation requires an administrative machinery which the Commission does not possess; this task was therefore entrusted to the existing bodies of the Member States.[58] Not only are import and export licences issued by the national authorities, but they also collect the levies[59] and pay the refunds.[60] Similarly, the purchase of agricultural products at the intervention prices is the responsibility of the national intervention offices.[61] In case of conflict between farmers and those offices concerning the application of Community measures, the responsibility lies with the Member States, not with the Community institutions.[62] The responsibility of the

---

[56] See above Chap. 3, the Commission, (4) Exercise of powers conferred by the Council.

[57] Reg. 2727/75, Art. 12; see Case 109/82 *Interagra* v. *FORMA* [1983] E.C.R. 127.

[58] See Case 217/81 *Interagra* v. *Commission* [1982] E.C.R. 2233.

[59] See Joined Cases 178, 179 and 180/73 *Belgium and Luxembourg* v. *Mertens* [1974] E.C.R. 383.

[60] See Case 167/82 *Nordgetreide* v. *Hauptzollamt Hamburg-Jonas* [1983] E.C.R. 1149 and Case 217/81 *Interagra*, above n. 58.

[61] Reg. 2727/75, Art. 7.

[62] See Case 46/75 *IBC* v. *Commission* [1976] E.C.R. 65 and Case 250/78 *DEKA* v. *EEC* [1983] E.C.R. 421.

Community for all legislative acts in the agricultural field of course remains.[63]

Cereals are the most important agricultural production in the Community, which explains why they were the first common market organisation to be set up. Unfortunately, they were also, after a few years, the ones that caused the most trouble in respect of over-production and consequently of excessive budgetary costs resulting in the necessity to introduce drastic restrictions. The adjustments decided by the Council for the 1986/1987 marketing year consisted, in the case of cereals,[64] in applying a co-responsibility levy of 3 per cent of the intervention price to cereal producers; the proceeds of the levy are used to develop Community outlets and to give producers an indication of the nature of the market situation. It was a first, although still timid, step to introduce the market concept into the CAP. In 1987, the Commission proposed to introduce a maximum guaranteed quantity and this was done in 1988.[65] If the quantity is exceeded, the intervention price for the following marketing year falls by 3 per cent. In addition to this, from the start of the marketing year, an additional co-responsibility levy equal to 3 per cent of the intervention price for common wheat will be collected on a provisional basis, on top of the 3 per cent levy already being applied. If the maximum guaranteed quantity is exceeded by 3 per cent or more, the whole of the additional levy is credited to the Community budget.[66]

It is too early to say whether or not these additional measures will be sufficient to solve the problem of over-production within the Community, but the fact that they had to be applied shows that the original concept of the common market organisation did not allow for adaptation to rapidly changing circumstances.

---

[63] See Case 238/78 *Ireks-Arkady* v. *Council and Commission* [1979] E.C.R. 2955.
[64] Adjustments were introduced to some of the principal market organisations: Bull. 4–1986, 57.
[65] O.J. 1988, L. 110 and 132; Bull. 4–1988, 41 and 5–1988, 46.
[66] Twenty-second General Report (1988), 268.

2. Social-structural policy in agriculture

One of the objectives assigned to the CAP is to "increase agricultural productivity by promoting technical progress and by ensuring the rational development of agricultural production and the optimum utilisation of the factors of production, in particular labour."[67] The common organisation of agricultural markets aims at market equilibrium through a price system and a trade system; they do not, however, constitute a solution for the fundamental problems of agriculture within the Community.[68] At the most they are a palliative, providing a temporary breathing space needed to carry out the required structural reforms; or, as the Commission pointed out, the question of agricultural incomes cannot be dealt with exclusively by a price policy.[69]

Seeking a more durable solution, the Commission submitted to the Council in 1968 a "Memorandum on the Reform of Agriculture in the EEC" (Agriculture 1980).[70] Two and a half years later, the Council adopted a Resolution on new guidelines for the CAP,[71] closely following the measures proposed in the Memorandum. In the same Resolution, the Council stated that state aids in conflict with the common measures should be eliminated, and considered that success in the agricultural field depended on progress made in other domains such as economic and monetary union, regional policy and social policy. The Resolution was implemented by several directives establishing the basic

---

[67] EEC, Art. 39(1)(a).

[68] Those problems result mainly from: (1) a large and ageing agricultural population (increased since the accession of Greece, Portugal and Spain), (2) the limited size of the average farm which makes mechanisation and therefore rationalisation difficult and (3) outdated production and marketing methods. In respect to the latter see Reg. 355/77 (O.J. 1977, L. 51/1).

[69] Seventh General Report (1973), 247.

[70] An analysis of this document, also referred to as the "Mansholt Plan," is given in the Second General Report (1968), 135. It can be summarised as follows: starting from (1) the socio-economic situation in the Community's agriculture, the Memorandum sets out (2) the aims of an agricultural policy, (3) the concrete measures to be taken, and (4) an estimate of the costs.

[71] J.O. 1971, C. 52/1.

principles for joint action by the Community and the interested Member States in the socio-economic field.

The "first directive"[72] on the modernisation of farms provided for the introduction by Member States of a system of selective incentives to farmers who practise farming as their main occupation. To qualify for the incentives, the farmer must draw up a plan for the development of the farm business which shows that, on implementation of the plan, the modernised farm will be capable of providing for one or two persons the same revenue as that which is enjoyed by persons employed in non-agricultural work in the same region. In retrospect it seems rather preposterous to expect small farmers to be able to draw up such plans; the implementation of this directive was not a success.

The "second directive"[73] concerns measures to encourage the cessation of farming and the re-allocation of land for structural improvement. It provides for the grant of an annuity or a lump sum payment to those farmers aged between 55 and 65, who have practised farming as their main occupation and leave the land. At least 85 per cent of the land released in this manner must be made available either to farmers benefiting from the first directive or re-allocated for afforestation, recreational activities, public health or other purposes.

The "third directive"[74] provides for vocational retraining of persons engaged in agriculture who wish to take up an occupation outside agriculture.

Member States were given a year to implement these directives[75] and the drafts of the implementation measures were to be submitted to the Commission for its opinion.

Those three directives were superseded in 1985 by a Regulation on improving the efficiency of agricultural structures,[76]

---

[72] Dir. 72/159, O.J. 1972(II), 324. See Case 107/80 *Cattaneo Adorno* v. *Commission* [1981] E.C.R. 1469.

[73] Dir. 72/160, O.J. 1972(II), 332.

[74] Dir. 72/161, O.J. 1972(II), 339.

[75] See Case 113/82 *Commission* v. *Germany* [1983] E.C.R. 1173. In 1973, the Council adopted a directive for the regional differentiation of certain measures provided for in the three above mentioned directives: Dir. 73/440, O.J. 1973, L. 356/85.

[76] Reg. 797/85, O.J. 1985, L. 93; Bull. 3–1985, 44.

complemented by the Integrated Mediterranean Programmes.[77]
The main features of the regulation are:

(1) development plans (first reg.) are replaced by a more
flexible scheme: farm-improvement plans;

(2) greater importance is given to farm investment which is
designed to lower costs, achieve better working and
living conditions, improve the quality of products, switch
to products which are in demand, or safeguard the
environment;

(3) no investments which increase output of products of
which there are structural surpluses;

(4) aid schemes are introduced for the setting-up of young
farmers, farm relief and management services, etc.;

(5) vocational training in agriculture is adjusted and stepped
up and

(6) support for mountain and hill farming and farming in
certain less-favoured areas is increased.[78]

The regulation will apply for 10 years, *i.e.* until 1994. The
Community also has an agricultural research programme[79] and
various other possibilities to intervene in view of improving the
socio-structural situation of agriculture.[80]

In 1988 various new socio-structural measures were adopted by
the Council[81]: they provide for early retirement by farmers aged

[77] O.J. 1985, L. 197.
[78] See Nineteenth General Report (1985), 211.
[79] *Ibid.*, 157 and 213.
[80] For more details see the annual report of the Commission on the situation of
agriculture in the Community.
[81] O.J. 1988, L. 106.

over 55, amendment to the regulation on set-aside of farmland[82] and the extensification and conversion of production.[83] As the Commission pointed out "they are consistent with the new approach in structures policy, which aims to rationalise and control production in an attempt to modernise agricultural holdings and improve farmers' incomes."[84]

Future of rural society. Rural society has for a long time been undergoing far-reaching changes and is facing social and economic problems. In 1988, the Commission sent a Communication to the Council and Parliament defining guidelines and proposing measures to aid the rural community.[84]

3. Financing the CAP

As was pointed out above, all the CAP expenditures are borne by the Community; this applies both to the price system and to the socio-structural measures.[85] While expenditure on supporting agricultural markets grew yearly by some 23 per cent. until 1988, the 1989 budget saw for the first time a reduction in absolute figures.[86] This followed the decisions taken at the 1988 February meeting of the European Council[87] at which it was decided, and this is probably more important, that the overall expenditures on agriculture would grow annually by a lesser percentage than the budget itself, while the Structural Funds (including the guidance section of the EAGGF) would grow by a larger percentage.

If the budgetary problems created by the ever-increasing agricultural expenditure were one of the reasons for reforming the CAP, it should however be borne in mind that external

[82] O.J. 1985, L. 93.
[83] O.J. 1988, C. 51.
[84] Twenty-second General Report (1988), 267.
[85] Reg. 25, Art. 2(2), O.J. 1959–1962, 126.
[86] The budget for the EAGGF Guarantee Section was 27.5 billion ECU in 1988, 26.741 in 1989 and 26.452 in 1990.
[87] See above under "the common agricultural policy."

pressures also played a role: the multilateral trade negotiations within the GATT, the so-called Uruguay Round, forced the Community to prepare its negotiating position by making the adaptations described above. It is certain however that following a positive outcome of those negotiations, other restrictive measures will have to be introduced mainly in the price support sector and in respect of the external trade system, where both the levies and export restitutions will have to be adjusted.

Further Reading

F. Snyder, *The Law of the Common Agricultural Policy* (1985), London.

II. FISHERIES

Although fisheries are undoubtedly part of "Agriculture,"[88] they acquired a momentum of their own and now constitute an autonomous policy. Since the 1939–1945 world war, fisheries products have become an important food resource, and although this sector only provides a few hundred thousand jobs, compared with millions in agriculture, the industry is also of crucial economic importance to many otherwise disadvantaged coastal areas.[89]

However, it was not until 1970 that the first decisions concerning fisheries were taken:

    (1) the principle of common access to all fishing grounds in the Community was established[90];

---

[88] See Case 141/78 *France* v. *United Kingdom* [1979] E.C.R. 2923. The Treaty provisions concerning agriculture (Arts. 39–46) apply to the products listed in Annex II to the Treaty; this list includes "Fish, crustaceans and molluscs." Since fish is subject to the Treaty provisions on agriculture, a common policy is likewise required under Art. 38(4).

[89] See "The Common Fisheries Policy," European Files 11/83; this publication was used to write this section.

[90] See Reg. 2141/70 (O.J. 1970(III), 703), based upon EEC, Arts. 42 and 43, but also 7 and 235. This Reg. was superseded by Reg. 101/76, Art. 2(1) (O.J. 1976, L. 20/19).

(2) a common market organisation for fish was set up, based on the establishment of producer organisations and the operation of price support mechanisms and protection for the Community market[91];

(3) the structural policies of the Member States were to be co-ordinated with financial help of the Community with a view to modernising the Community fleets.[92]

In 1983 agreement was reached on the Commission proposals for a common fisheries policy, "Blue Europe,"[93] based on the following ground-rules for Community fishery activity:

(i) equality of access to resources in Community waters except for preferential arrangements for in-shore fishermen within the 12-mile limit;

(ii) compliance with a common policy for the conservation of resources;

(iii) the scope of agreements with non-Community countries to be reinforced and extended;

(iv) market support, and

(v) modernisation and development of the fisheries and aquaculture sector.

1. Conservation of resources—internal measures

The conservation of Atlantic, North-Sea, Antarctic, Baltic Sea, the Belts and the Sound fish stocks is controlled by the fixing of

[91] Reg. 2142/70 (O.J. 1970(III), 707), superseded by Reg. 100/76 (O.J. 1976, L. 20/1) and by Reg. 3796/81 (O.J. 1981, L. 379/1); a new version of the latter was adopted in 1988 (O.J. 1988, L. 305).
[92] Reg. 2141/70, see above n. 90.
[93] See Seventeenth General Report (1983), 193.

total allowable catches (TACs), fixed annually by the Council for all species threatened because of overfishing[94] and by technical conservation measures such as authorised mesh sizes, areas where fishing is prohibited, etc.[95]

The TACs are divided into national quotas according to an agreed-upon key based on traditional fishing activities, the specific needs of regions which are especially dependent on fishing and the loss of fisheries in the waters of non-Community countries.[96]

These measures do not absolve the Member States from their obligation to take certain national conservation measures. Besides implementing the Community regulations with respect to the Member States' vessels and waters, their responsibility extends to taking emergency conservation measures, measures to protect local stocks, measures to improve the management of quotas, measures to protect species and fishing grounds outside the field of application of the Community regulations and technical conservation measures.[97]

In 1982 the Council established certain control measures for fishing activities by vessels of the Member States,[98] which were implemented by measures issued by the Commission and which provide for:

(1) an inspection force composed of agents appointed by the Commission to assist in control operations carried out by the national authorities at sea and in the ports;

(2) decisions to curtail fishing which had been found to be exhausted;

---

[94] Reg. 172/83 (O.J. 1983, L. 24/30). For 1989 TACs and quotas see O.J. 1988, L. 369.

[95] Reg. 170/83 (O.J. 1983, L. 24/1) and Reg. 3094/86 (O.J. 1986, L. 288/1) amended by Reg. 3287/88 (O.J. 1988, L. 292/5), see Twenty-second General Report (1988), 292.

[96] See Arts. 3 and 4 of Reg. 170/83 (see n. 95 above) and Case 63/83 *Regina* v. *Kirk* [1984] E.C.R. 2689.

[97] See Seventeenth General Report (1983), 195 and Commission declaration concerning the duty of Member States in the absence of Council decisions (O.J. 1982, C. 199/2).

[98] Reg. 2057/82, O.J. 1982, L. 220/1.

(3) introduction of a logbook to be kept by the masters of vessels flying the flag of a Member State or registered in a Member State[99] and of a licensing system for fishing in a biologically sensitive area north of Scotland.[1]

2. Conservation of resources—external arrangements

Since 1976 the Community has been exclusively competent to handle international fishing negotiations. Fishing agreements were signed with a number of third countries[2] in order to safeguard traditional fishing rights of Community vessels or to seek new opportunities.

Multilateral agreements have also been concluded with a view to the Community's participation in the international agreements covering the North-West, North-East, East, Central and South-East Atlantic: the North-Atlantic Salmon Conservation Organisation (NASCO), the North-East Atlantic Fisheries Commission (NEAFC), the International Commission for the South East Atlantic Fisheries (ICSEAF), the Fishery Committee for the Eastern-Central Atlantic (CECAF), the International Whaling Commission, etc., etc.[3]

Through this vast network of international agreements the Community not only participated actively in the conservation efforts for endangered species, but managed to maintain for fishermen from the Member States access to the waters of non-Community countries by means of reciprocal fishing arrangements.

[99] O.J. 1983, L. 276.

[1] O.J. 1983, L. 206.

[2] See, *e.g.* the agreements with Guinea-Bissau, O.J. 1983, L. 84; Greenland (after withdrawal) O.J. 1985, L. 1; the U.S.A. O.J. 1984, L. 272; Equatorial Guinea, O.J. 1984, L. 188; Seychelles, O.J. 1984, L. 79; Sweden, O.J. 1984, L. 61; the Faeroes, O.J. 1984, L. 264; Senegal, O.J. 1985, L. 361; Morocco, O.J. 1988, L. 175; negotiations were also held with the Soviet Union, Bull. 9–1988, 41; for further information see the various General Reports.

[3] See Twenty-third General Report (1989), 270.

3. Community market organisation

In the section on agriculture, it was pointed out that the common market for agricultural products must be accompanied by the establishment of a common agricultural policy among the Member States[4] and that the CAP was to take the form of European market organisations.[5] Such a market organisation was set up for fish in 1970[6] and radically revised in 1981.[7] A new version was adopted in 1988[8] to bring the market organisation in line with the new conditions created by enlargement and the changes on the market for tuna and to involve producers' organisations in the operation of the Community intervention system.[9]

Basically, the market organisation provides marketing standards, participation of producers' organisations, a price system and intervention schemes for certain species and an external trade policy.[10]

4. Structural policy

The first rules laying down a common structural policy for the fishing industry were enacted in 1970.[11] Following enlargement, a new regulation was adopted in 1976.[12] Those provisions enabled the Community to support financially, through the agricultural fund, fish processing and marketing development projects, building of inshore fishing vessels, refitting of vessels and extension of fish farming schemes.

---

[4] EEC, Art. 38(4).
[5] EEC, Art. 40(2)(c).
[6] Reg. 2142/70 (O.J. 1970(III), 707).
[7] Reg. 3796/81 (O.J. 1981, L. 379).
[8] O.J. 1988, L. 305.
[9] Twenty-second General Report (1988), 296.
[10] See Eighteenth General Report (1984), 189.
[11] Reg. 2141/70 (O.J. 1970(III), 703).
[12] Reg. 101/76 (O.J. 1976, L. 20/19).

In 1977 common measures were adopted to improve the conditions under which agricultural and fishery products are processed and marketed,[13] and in 1983 the Council adopted common measures for restructuring, modernising and developing the fishing industry and for developing aquaculture[14] and measures to encourage exploratory fishing.[15] Once again new structural aspects of the fisheries policy were adopted, this time in 1986,[16] to finance the construction of fishing vessels, aquaculture and structural work in coastal waters, modernisation of fishing vessels and exploratory fishing voyages, while at the same time financing programmes to reduce the capacity of the Member States' fishing fleets to bring them into line with the available fish stocks.[17]

Further Reading

W. Howarth, "The Single European Market and the Problems of Fish Movements" (1990) 15 E.L.Rev., 34

III. TRANSPORT POLICY

Together with the basic freedoms and the agricultural policy, transport constitutes the "Foundations of the Community."[18] However, transport is basically a "service" and could therefore,

---

[13] O.J. 1977, L. 51.

[14] Reg. 2908/83 (O.J. 1983, L. 290 and Reg. 3166/83, (L. 316/1).

[15] Reg. 2909/83 (O.J. 1983, L. 290).

[16] O.J. 1986, L. 376.

[17] Twenty-second General Report (1988), 297 and Dir. 83/515 (O.J. 1983, L.290/15).

[18] As pointed out above, no particular meaning should, however, be attached to this classification: the competition and social policies for instance play at least as important a role in respect of the common market as does transport. Of all those policies it can be said that without them the freedoms would have no meaning: indeed, what use is it, *e.g.* to have the right to "move" goods freely across the Community if the transport or competition or social conditions make it practically impossible to do so? In other words, there exists such a close inter-relationship between all these areas that it is impossible to assign more importance to one rather than to another.

when carried out in another Member State,[19] come within the ambit of the provisions concerning the "freedom to provide services"; but because of its particular characteristics and its inter-relations with the policies of third countries, it was felt necessary to provide for some specific rules next to the general rules of the Treaty.[20]

What did the drafters of the Treaty mean when they referred to the "distinctive features of transport?"[21] Most kinds of transport require heavy investments which, due to widely varying demand, often remain idle and unproductive for long periods. There is an enormous discrepancy between the infrastructure needed for various means of transport: some, like railways and inland shipping, need heavy and specially designed infrastructure, used intermittently by a limited number, while others, like road transport, use the road network jointly with millions of other users. Another characteristic is that some means of transportation are in the hands of the State and are forced to offer services which are not always economically justifiable. Moreover, whether nationalised or not, all forms of transportation are subject to severe requirements with regard to public safety. Finally, air and sea transport extend far beyond the borders of the Community and are the subject of many international agreements and regulations.

1. Implementation of a transport policy

In accordance with the Treaty,[22] the provisions concerning transport only apply to "transport by rail, road and inland waterway." It is in this field that the Community institutions are required to

---

[19] It will be remembered that only "inter-state" activities are caught by the provisions of Community law.

[20] See EEC, Art. 61(1) and Case 167/73 *Commission* v. *France* [1974] E.C.R. 359(27–33).

[21] EEC, Art. 75(1).

[22] EEC, Art. 84(1).

develop a common transport policy comprising common rules for transport between the Member States, conditions allowing non-resident carriers to operate transport services in other Member States and all other appropriate measures.[23]

The Commission at first proposed to the Council the adoption of general principles covering all aspects of a common transport policy,[24] but it soon appeared that a global approach was politically impossible, not only because of differences in concept but also on account of variations in the level of development of, in particular, road transport. The Commission came to the conclusion that the only way to obtain at least some results would be to proceed gradually by presenting packages of concrete proposals which would allow the Council to reach compromises gained by limited mutual concessions. During the 60s and 70s, the approach to working out a common transport policy became increasingly pragmatic, but it was possible to work out at least some concrete solutions to problems affecting intra-Community transport.[25]

The Community managed to enact some rules concerning access to the market and concerning rates and conditions of carriage.[26] In regard to the latter, the Treaty specifically prohibits discrimination whereby carriers charge different rates for carrying the same goods over the same transport links[27]: wide powers were conferred upon the Commission whose agents may require information from any carrier and who may impose fines in case of refusal to provide information or when false information is provided or when discrimination is established.[28]

---

[23] EEC, Art. 75(1), (a), (b) and (c).

[24] Tenth General Report EEC (1967), 231.

[25] A first step was a procedure for prior examination by the Commission and consultation in respect of certain laws, regulations and administrative provisions of the Member States (O.J. 1959–1962, 96 and O.J. 1978, L. 54/16–18).

[26] See, *e.g.* Reg. on the establishment of common rules for certain types of carriage of goods by road between the Member States (O.J. 1983 L. 359/1) amended in 1988 (O.J. 1988, L. 176/5) and Dec. 82/529 on the fixing of rates for the international carriage of goods by rail (O.J. 1982 L. 234/5).

[27] EEC, Art. 79(1). See Reg. 3568/83 on the fixing of rates (O.J. 1983, L. 359/1).

[28] Reg. 11/60 (O.J. 1959–1962, 60), and Dir. 83/643 on physical inspections (O.J. 1983, L. 359/8); Case 272/85 *Antib* v. *Commission* [1987] E.C.R. 2218: discrimination in the inland waterway transport.

These were, however, only small steps and 25 years after the Treaty came into force there still was no Community transport policy! Parliament finally lost patience and on January 22, 1983 brought before the Court an action against the Council for failure to act in the field of transport.[29]

2. The judgment of the Court[30]

In its judgment of May 22, 1985, the Court declared that:

> "in breach of the Treaty the Council has failed to ensure freedom to provide services in the sphere of international transport and to lay down the conditions under which non-resident carriers may operate transport services in a Member State."[31]

Another element of importance in this field is the White Paper on the completion of the internal market[32] which includes the aim of a real common market in transport services among the objectives to be achieved if the Community's internal market is to be completed by 1992.[33]

The first concrete result was the adoption by the Council of a policy approach providing for the establishment of a free market without quantitative restrictions by 1992 at the latest and a transitional phase of gradual adjustment of bilateral quotas to make them non-discriminatory, together with increases in Community quotas.

With respect to access to the international road haulage market, the Council decided to eliminate all quantitative restric-

---

[29] This was the final stage in the procedure instituted by Parliament under EEC, Art. 175 by a Resolution (O.J. 1982, C. 267/62).

[30] Case 13/83 *Parliament* v. *Council* [1985] E.C.R. 1513.

[31] *Ibid.*, at 1603.

[32] Com(85) 310.

[33] Nineteenth General Report (1985), 235.

tions before January 1, 1993, and to establish a system of Community licences based solely on quantitative criteria.

3. Air transport

With regard to air transport, a judgment of the Court in the *Nouvelles Frontières* case[34] marked a turning point since it bolstered the Commission's objectives[35] set out in its second memorandum on civil aviation.[36] In the judgment just referred to, the Court concluded that "air transport remains, on the same basis as the other modes of transport, subject to the general rules of the Treaty, including the competition rules"[37] and therefore that Member States could not approve air tariffs and thus reinforce the effect thereof when those tariffs are the result of an agreement contrary to the Community competition rules.[38]

Considerable progress was made in this area in 1987[39] by the adoption of an air liberalisation package and in 1988 the Commission adopted three regulations granting block exemptions for certain types of restrictive agreements between airlines and between airlines and suppliers of related services.[40]

4. Sea transport

As a first step in the development of a common maritime transport policy, the Council reached agreement in 1986 on a

---

[34] Joined Cases 209 to 213/84 *Ministère Public* v. *Asjes and Others* [1986] E.C.R. 1457.

[35] Twentieth General Report (1986), 267.

[36] O.J. 1986, C. 182 and Nineteenth General Report (1985), 239.

[37] It should be noted however that transport in general was excluded from the application of Reg. 17 by Reg. 141 of 1962 (O.J. 1959–1962, 291); since then only transport by rail, by road and by inland waterway have been brought under the competition rules (Reg. 1017/68, O.J. 1968(I), 302), and therefore Arts. 88 and 89 continue to apply to air transport. In 1988 the Commission granted three so-called block-exemptions under Art. 85(3): Reg. 2671/88 on joint planning and capacity coordination, etc; Reg. 2672/88 concerning the system of informatised reservation and Reg. 2673/88 concerning assistance services (all in O.J. 1988, L. 239/9, 13, 17).

[38] *Ibid.*, at 1473.

[39] O.J. 1987, L. 374 and Bull. 12–1987.

[40] O.J. 1988, L. 239.

series of measures concerning the freedom to provide shipping services between Member States or between Member States and non-Community countries, unfair pricing practices and competition rules.[41]

5. Infrastructure

Although the Council failed to reach agreement on a proposal for a regulation on financial support for transport infrastructure projects of Community interest,[42] financial resources are provided on a yearly basis in the budget to support such projects.[43] No general action programme in the field of transport infrastructure exists as yet.

6. International co-operation

Because of the Community's geography, co-operation with Austria, Switzerland and Yugoslavia is extremely important for road and rail transport between Member States.

The Community has signed several agreements, such as the Agreement on the International Carriage of Passengers by Road by means of Occasional Coach and Bus service[44] and the Agreement on the International Road–Rail Combined Carriage of Goods (ATC).[45]

7. Conclusions

After years of procrastination some progress has finally been made in the direction of a common transport policy for the

[41] Twentieth General Report (1986), 271.

[42] Bull. 7/8, 1983.

[43] See the annual General Reports under the transport section and the Bulletins.

[44] O.J. 1986, L. 320.

[45] Bull 2–1987, 73.

Community; the first results were the consequence, not of the political will of the Member States to arrive at a common policy, but of decisions of the Court and indirectly of plans to complete the internal market by the end of 1992!

Further Reading

J. Balfour, "Freedom to provide Air Transport Services in the EEC" (1989) 14 E.L.Rev., 30.

IV. COMPETITION POLICY

Competition, according to the Commission, is the best stimulant of economic activity since it guarantees the widest possible freedom of action to all. An active competition policy, pursued in accordance with the provisions of the Treaties establishing the Communities, makes it easier for the supply and demand structures continually to adjust to technological development. Through the interplay of decentralised decision-making machinery, competition enables enterprises continuously to improve their efficiency, which is the *sine qua non* for a steady improvement of living standards and employment prospects within the countries of the Community. From this point of view, competition policy is an essential means for satisfying to a great extent the individual and collective needs of our society.[46]

Twenty years later, the Commission wrote[47] that:

"[a]n effective competition policy is the sole means of making the most of the potential offered by the completion of the large market and thus, by increasing competitive pressure, of producing a more competitive Community economy. More competition will also strengthen the posi-

---

[46] First Report on Competition Policy, 11.
[47] Eighteenth Report on Competition Policy, 13.

tion of European industry in both world and domestic markets. Without such a policy, there is the risk that Community consumers would be unable to enjoy the promised benefits of a large integrated market."

In other words, competition is not an end in itself, it constitutes another instrument in the hands of the Commission to ensure that the objectives of the Treaty are attained. One of those objectives, it will be remembered, is economic integration through the operation and development of the common market and convergence of the economic policies of the Member States.[48] The common market, in turn, is characterised by the basic freedoms, the most important of which is the free movement of goods. Free trade between Member States therefore is the overriding criterion for determining the compatibility of any market activity with Community obligations. This rule applies especially in the field of competition.[49] The Treaty does not define the concept of "competition,"[50] but refers to measures and actions which interfere with competition and are therefore prohibited, subject to exemptions granted by the institutions. Generally speaking, the Community rules of competition aim at preventing the Member States and legal or natural persons from maintaining or introducing obstacles to trade within the common market when, on the other hand, the traditional protective measures such as customs duties and quantitative restrictions were abolished.

The Treaty chapter on competition[51] contains, broadly speaking, two sets of rules: those applying to natural and legal persons and prohibiting trade restrictions through agreements or abuse of dominant positions and those applying to Member States, *i.e.*

---

[48] EEC, Arts. 2 and 3.
[49] Joined Cases 56 and 58/64 *Consten and Grundig* v. *Commission* [1966] E.C.R. 299 at 341.
[50] The preamble to the Treaty refers to "fair" competition, but this has no practical significance; for a definition of the kind of competition that must be protected from distortion (EEC, Art. 3(f)) see Case 26/76 *Metro* v. *Commission* [1977] E.C.R. 1875 at 1904(20).
[51] EEC, Arts. 85 to 94.

incompatibility with the common market of State aids which have effects comparable to those of quantitative restrictions. Other competition rules applying to Member States are to be found in the Treaty sections on State monopolies of a commercial character,[52] public enterprises[53] and fiscal discrimination.[54]

This does not mean, however, that Community competition policy is essentially negative. With regard to co-operation between undertakings, the Commission's declared intentions are to reinforce the competitive position of enterprises, and by adopting decisions exempting individual or categories of agreements from the prohibition of the Treaty, the Commission pursues its effort on behalf of certain forms of co-operation, *e.g.* by authorising the creation of joint ventures or exempting joint research and development agreements.[55] Similarly, it will be noticed that the Treaty does not prohibit all kinds of State aids and the Commission considers that, when judiciously applied, it is an indispensable instrument for regional development. All those aspects will be examined hereafter.

1. Competition rules applying to undertakings[56]

These rules are contained in two sets of provisions, one concerning "cartels" and the other regarding dominant positions. The first applies when several undertakings are involved, the second refers normally to the activities of a single one. Both sets of rules provide basically for a prohibition with, in the first case, the possibility of obtaining an exemption from the Commission, while in the second case it is up to the Commission to decide whether or not there is "abuse." Clearly, the Commission plays a major role in the implementation of those rules and is in a position to develop an active and positive policy in this field.

[52] EEC, Art. 37.
[53] EEC, Art. 90.
[54] EEC, Art. 95.
[55] Eighteenth Report on Competition Policy, 16.
[56] EEC, Arts. 85 to 89.

(1) *Agreements between undertakings—Article 85*[57]

Article 85 contains three elements:

(a) the prohibition

(b) the consequence of prohibition, *i.e.* nullity, and

(c) the possibility of obtaining an exemption from the prohibition.

(a) The Prohibition. In other words, cartels which may affect trade between Member States and which have as their object or effect distortion of competition are prohibited and automatically void, except where an exemption was granted by the Commission.

Parties to a cartel must therefore ensure that it does not impede the free movement of goods throughout the Community nor distort competition within the common market; if it were otherwise, it can safely be assumed that the cartel is void and any implementation thereof is at the parties' risk. This applies even when the Commission has been notified of the cartel as part of a procedure to obtain an exemption from the prohibition for the cartel in question.

Although those basic rules seem simple enough, they require explanations as regards the precise significance of the various terms used: "agreement," "undertaking," "decision of an association," "concerted practice," "may affect trade between Member States," "have as their object or effect" and "distortion of competition." Those terms will be successively examined hereafter.

Agreements and concerted practices. An agreement must be understood as a legally binding (and therefore enforceable)

---

[57] The Treaty refers to "agreements" between undertakings, "decisions" by associations of undertakings and "concerted practices"; unless otherwise indicated, they will be collectively referred to as "cartels."

contract. A practice, on the other hand, is a market behaviour which is only caught by the prohibition when it is the result of a concertation. Only binding agreements can be void as provided in the second paragraph of Article 85, while a concertation, not being binding, cannot be void. The difference between an agreement and a concertation is important with regard to the prohibition and the proof of the infringement.

In the case of a binding agreement, since it is sufficient that its "object" is to distort competition, independently of whether it actually did distort competition, the existence of a document or contract is proof enough of the infringement (it becomes more difficult with oral binding agreements). In other words, the question whether competition was actually distorted is irrelevant, as long as the clauses of the agreement clearly show the intention of the parties to distort competition.[58]

In the case of a concerted practice, concertation is not, in itself, prohibited; it is the behaviour which follows from a concertation which is, when it affects trade and distorts competition. As to the proof, the Commission must first show that the practice, *i.e.* the market behaviour, violates the Treaty and secondly that there was a "concertation" which led to this behaviour. The reality of such a concertation can be proven by the existence, *e.g.* of a "gentlemen's agreement" (which by definition is not binding).[59] Parallel price increases, for instance, are not in themselves prohibited; they could indeed be purely coincidental or the result of a particular market situation known

---

[58] See Case 56/65 *Société Technique Minière* v. *Maschinenbau Ulm* [1966] E.C.R. 235 at 249.

[59] Gentleman's agreements and other arrangements, binding in honour only, are not, in this writer's view, prohibited by the Treaty whatever their content; it is only the practice which can be prohibited. This view is not contradicted by the Commission's Dec. of July 16, 1969 (J.O. 1969, L. 192/5), *ACF Chemiefarma*, where the Commission considered a gentleman's agreement to be an agreement in the sense of Art. 85 because it was concluded together with a binding agreement which referred to the former. This view was accepted by the Court; Case 41/69 *ACF Chemiefarma* v. *Commission* [1970] E.C.R. 661 at 693(113–114). See also Opinion of the Advocate-General, *ibid.*, at 714. For an example of a concerted practice see Joined Cases 100–103/80 *Musique Diffusion Française* v. *Commission* [1983] E.C.R. 1825.

as oligopoly with price leadership.[60] But parallel price increases
are prohibited when they are the result of a concertation and the
proof of the existence of the latter will more often than not have
to be based on circumstantial evidence.[61]

Decisions of associations of undertakings. They must be understood to include the constitutive act of a trade association and its
internal rules,[62] decisions made in accordance with those rules
and which are therefore binding upon the members of the
association,[63] and also recommendations such as the fixing of
"target prices" by an association.[64] Whether an agreement must
be regarded as one between undertakings or one between associations of undertakings is irrelevant and so is the framework
within which decisions are taken and the classification given to
that framework by the national authorities.[65]

As for the term "association," it is not limited to any particular
form of association and it also includes associations of associations with or without legal personality and non-profit making
associations; a *de facto* association of associations was considered
by the Commission to be an association of undertakings.[66]

---

[60] See, *e.g. Pittsburg Corning* Dec. (J.O. 1972, L. 272/35). In Case 85/76
Hoffmann-La Roche v. *Commission* [1979] E.C.R. 461 at 520(39), the Court
refers to "parallel courses of conduct which are peculiar to oligopolies."
[61] See, *e.g.* Case 48/69 *I.C.I.* v. *Commission* [1972] E.C.R. 619 at 653 and Joined
Cases 40, etc./73 *Suiker Unie and Others* v. *Commission* [1975] E.C.R. 1663; in
both cases the Court admitted the existence of concerted practices; not
admitted in Joined Cases 29 and 30/83 *CRAM and Rheinzink* v. *Commission*
[1984] E.C.R. 1679 at 1702(19).
[62] *ASPA* Dec. (J.O. 1970, L. 148/11).
[63] *Bomee-Stichting* Dec. (O.J. 1975, L. 329/30).
[64] Case 8/72 *Cementhandelaren* v. *Commission* [1972] E.C.R. 977 at 991(19). See
also Joined Cases 209 etc./78 *van Landewyck* v. *Commission* [1980] E.C.R.
3125 at 3254(102).
[65] Case 123/83 *BNIC* v. *Clair* [1985] E.C.R. 391 at 423(17–20).
[66] *Cecimo* Dec. (J.O. 1969, L. 69/13) and Joined Cases 209 etc./78 *van Landewyck*, (n. 64 above).

Undertakings. They may or may not have legal personality.[67] In the latter case they must have some recognised legal status[68] otherwise they would not be able to carry out economic activities, *e.g.* conclude legally binding agreements, bring actions in the Court and be liable for the payment of fines. In other words, they must have "legal autonomy" which they can only have when they are a "legal entity." Whether or not they have the latter qualification must be determined in accordance with the applicable national law.

The term "undertaking" also covers natural persons, public enterprises and even Member States when they carry out commercial and economic activities.[69]

Besides being a "legal entity," an "undertaking" must also be an "economic entity," in other words have "economic independence."[70] The latter is, under certain conditions, not the case with undertakings belonging to the same group or concern and having the status of parent company and subsidiary. When the subsidiary is not free to determine its market behaviour independently of the parent company and the agreements concluded between them merely constitute an internal allocation of tasks, such undertakings form a single economic unit. Therefore, the agreement concluded between them is not an "agreement between under-

[67] This follows *inter alia* from the wording of EEC, Art. 52 which in regard to freedom of establishment refers to the right to set up and manage "undertakings, in particular companies and firms." The latter are, in turn, defined by Art. 58 as "constituted under civil or commercial law, including co-operative societies and other legal persons governed by public or private law, save for those which are non-profit making." It seems therefore that where the Treaty refers to entities having legal personality, the terms "company" and "firm" are used; while "undertaking," which is broader, covers also economic entities without legal personality.

[68] This is the case, *e.g.* with the Dutch "Vennootschap onder firma," the English "Partnership" and the German "offene Gesellschaft."

[69] The economic and commercial character of those activities is what distinguishes undertakings in the sense of Art. 85(1) from other bodies that are engaged, *e.g.* in artistic and scientific work. For individuals, see *Reuter/BASF* Dec. (O.J. 1976, L. 254/40) and for Member States, Case 83/78 *Pigs Marketing Board* v. *Redmond* [1978] E.C.R. 2347.

[70] See *Christiani and Nielsen* Dec. (O.J. 1969, L. 165/72) and Case 15/74 *Centrafarm* v. *Sterling Drug* [1974] E.C.R. 1147 at 1167(41) and Case 170/83 *Hydrotherm* v. *Compact* [1984] E.C.R. 2999 at 3016(11).

takings." The same applies when an agreement is concluded between two subsidiaries.[71]

If the relationship between a parent company and its subsidiary can thus result in the non-applicability of the prohibition of Article 85, it can, on the other hand, bring the parent company within the competence of Community competition rules for the market behaviour of the subsidiary. Indeed when this behaviour is determined by the parent company, it is the latter which will be considered as having violated the rules. Whether or not this parent company is situated within the Community becomes irrelevant because the violation has its effects inside the Community and is therefore caught by its rules.[72]

"Which may affect trade between Member States." This criterion serves, in the first place, to determine the field of application of the Community competition rules. Indeed, it is "to the extent that the agreement may affect trade between Member States that the interference with competition caused by that agreement is caught by the prohibition in Community law found in Article 85, while in the converse case it escapes those prohibitions."[73]

In several cases the Court held that "in order that an agreement between undertakings may affect trade between Member States it must be possible to foresee with a sufficient degree of probability on the basis of a set of objective factors of law or fact that it may have an influence, direct or indirect, actual or potential, on the pattern of trade between Member States such as

---

[71] See *Kodak* Dec. (J.O. 1970, L. 147/24).
[72] See, *e.g.* Case 48/69 *I.C.I.* v. *Commission* [1972] E.C.R. 619 at 662; Case 6/72 *Europemballage and Continental Can* v. *Commission* [1973] E.C.R. 215; Joined Cases 6–7/73 *Commercial Solvents* v. *Commission* [1974] E.C.R. 223; Case 27/76 *United Brands* v. *Commission* [1978] E.C.R. 207 and Case 85/76 *Hoffmann-La Roche* v. *Commission* [1979] E.C.R. 461. See also *Woodpulp* Dec. (O.J. 1985, L. 85/1).
[73] Case 56/65 *Société Technique Minière* (n. 58 above) at 249.

might prejudice the realisation of the aim of a single market in all the Member States."[74]

For instance, preventing undertakings from importing certain products into a Member State from another one, or prohibiting them from re-exporting those products to other Member States, indisputably affects trade between Member States; these measures constitute a limitation on the free movement of goods within the Community. With regard to agreements granting an exclusive right of sales, the Court stated that they do not necessarily, by their very nature, contain elements incompatible with the common market and that, in this respect, special attention should be given to whether or not the agreement is capable of partitioning the market in certain products between the Member States.[75] It is also clear from the wording of the Treaty and the terms used by the Court that the effect on trade does not have to be actual; it suffices that the agreement is "capable of constituting a threat"[76] to freedom of trade between Member States.

"Prevention, restriction or distortion of competition." Competition exists when the economic operators in the common market act independently and have freedom of choice.[77] "Economic operator" must be understood in the broadest sense possible to include all legal and natural persons performing an economic activity. Most typical is the free choice of the consumer: one can safely say that the moment this freedom is limited in one way or another, competition is distorted. As for the producers, competition arises whenever they have to take into account the market behaviour of other producers within the relevant market.[78]

---

[74] Case 42/84 *Remia* v. *Commission* [1985] E.C.R. 2545 at 2572(22); see also one of the first judgments: Joined Cases 56–58/64 *Consten and Grundig* (n. 49 above) 299 at 341. The Court added that the fact that an agreement encourages an increase, even a large one, in the volume of trade between States is not sufficient to exclude the possibility that an agreement "may affect" trade in the above mentioned manner. In Case 43/69 *Bilger* v. *Jehle* [1970] E.C.R. 127 at 135(5), the Court stated that trade may be affected even though the agreement does not concern imports or exports.

[75] Case 56/65 *Société Technique Minière* (n. 58 above) at 251.

[76] Joined Cases 56–58/64 *Consten and Grundig* (n. 49 above), 299 at 341.

[77] Joined Cases 40, etc./73 *Suiker Unie and Others* (n. 61 above) at 1942(173).

[78] For the concept "relevant market," see below "Abuse of a dominant position."

When the object of an agreement is to interfere with competition, distortion may result from all or some of the clauses; only those clauses which interfere with competition will be void, and not necessarily the whole agreement.[79] When the terms of the agreement do not disclose the intention to distort competition, the consequences of implementing the agreement must be considered and factors must be found which show that competition was, in fact, distorted.[80]

The Court has further developed and specified the meaning of "distortion of competition" by indicating that in order to be prohibited an agreement must distort competition "to an appreciable extent."[81] For instance, an "exclusive dealing agreement, even with absolute territorial protection, may, having regard to the weak position of the persons concerned in the market and the products in question, escape the prohibition of Article 85."[82] In other words the "*de minimis*" rule also applies in Community competition law.

Another point emphasised by the Court is that the anticipated effects on competition may not be purely theoretical, but that "the competition in question must be understood within the actual context in which it would occur in the absence of the agreement in dispute." It is therefore appropriate:

> "to take into account the nature and quantity, limited or otherwise, of the products covered by the agreement, the

---

[79] See Joined Cases 56–58/64 *Consten and Grundig* (n. 49 above) where the Court annulled the Commission's decision because it considered the whole agreement as void. See also Case 319/82 *Soc. de vente de Ciments et Bétons* v. *Kerpen & Kerpen* [1983] E.C.R. 4173 at 4184(12) where the Court reiterated that the consequences of the nullity of certain provisions, for other parts of the agreement, are not a matter for Community law, but must be determined by the national court on the basis of its own national law.

[80] See Case 56/65 *Société Technique Minière* (n. 58 above).

[81] *Ibid*. For more details as to the meaning of "appreciable" see the Commission's Notice concerning Agreements of Minor Importance (O.J. 1977, C. 313/3). See also the Commission's Decisions: *SOCEMAS* (J.O. 1968, L. 201/4) and *Intergroup Trading (Spar)* (O.J. 1975, L. 212/23) where the effects were considered to be minor. However in *Reuter/BASF* (O.J. 1976, L. 254/40) this was not the case.

[82] Case 5/69 *Völk* v. *Vervaecke* [1969] E.C.R. 295 at 303 and Case 30/78 *Distillers Company* v. *Commission* [1980] E.C.R. 2229 at 2265(28).

position and importance of the [parties] on the market for the products concerned, the isolated nature of the disputed agreement or, alternatively, its position in a series of agreements, the severity of the clauses intended to [limit trade] or alternatively, the opportunities allowed for other commercial competitors in the same products by way of parallel re-exportation or importation."[83]

Within the common market. According to the Treaty, distortion of competition must take place within the common market. It follows that an agreement between two undertakings situated within the Community but which limits competition in a third country is not prohibited by Community law.[84] It would be different, of course, if, as a result of this agreement, the behaviour of the parties were influenced in such a way as to cause distortion of competition and inter-state trade within the Community.[85] Another consequence is that an agreement concluded between undertakings situated outside the Community, but having effect on trade between Member States and competition within the Community, is prohibited by and prosecutable under Community law.[86] The same applies, of course, when one of the parties is situated within the Community.[87] Finally, it should be noted that the expression "within the Community" does not mean that agreements must concern all the Member States or even some of them. An agreement limiting competition in one Member State can have distorting consequences in other Member States and affect trade within the Community. This will practically always be the case when the agreement in question covers

---

[83] Case 56/65 *Société Technique Minière* (n. 58 above) at 250 and Case 99/79 *Lancôme* v. *Etos* [1980] E.C.R. 2511 at 2536(24).

[84] See, *e.g.* *Rieckermann* Dec. (J.O. 1968, L. 276/25).

[85] Same idea in Joined Cases 6–7/73 *Commercial Solvents* (n. 72 above) at 252(33).

[86] This is sometimes referred to as the extra-territorial application of Community competition law. It is doubtful whether this expression is correct in the above mentioned case since it is only as "operating within the Community," territorially speaking, that these undertakings are caught.

[87] See, *e.g.* *Franco-Japanese Ballbearings* Dec. (O.J. 1974, L. 343/19).

the whole territory of one Member State, since it creates a threshold effect with regard to imports.[88]

(b) The nullity. Cartels prohibited by the Treaty are automatically void[89]; no declaration to this effect is therefore needed.[90] This statement, however, is not as absolute as it sounds: indeed, a distinction needs to be made between "old" agreements and "new" ones. What distinguishes the two is whether they were concluded before or after March 13, 1962. This date refers to the moment when Regulation 17, the first regulation "to give effect to the principles set out in Articles 85 and 86,"[91] entered into force.[92] Nullity applies without reservation to all "new agreements" (those concluded after March 13, 1962[93]) prohibited by the Treaty, whether or not they were notified[94] to the Commission in a procedure to obtain an exemption from the prohibition[95] or whether they were exempted from notification.[96] In other words, as was pointed out before, those new agreements can only be implemented at the parties' own risk. It is up to them to determine whether their agreement is prohibited under the Treaty and consequently void. If the agreement is implemented anyway the possibility remains that even years later a national court may find that the agreement is void and always has been. The consequences of such a finding will also have implications for third parties.

---

[88] See, *e.g.* Case 8/72 *Cementhandelaren* (n. 64 above) at 991(29).
[89] EEC, Art. 85(2).
[90] Reg. 17, Art. 1: no prior decison is required to the effect that a cartel is prohibited; the same applies to the nullity.
[91] EEC, Art. 87(1), O.J. 1959–1962, 87.
[92] See EEC, Art. 191.
[93] Different dates applied, of course, for the new Member States: the date of accession was substituted for the original date the regulation came into force: January 1, 1973, for Denmark, Ireland and the U.K., January 1, 1981, for Greece, January 1, 1986, for Portugal and Spain; however, old agreements had to be notified within six months of the date of accession.
[94] Reg. 17, Art. 4; thus, notification has no suspensive effect with regard to nullity. As to what constitutes a proper notification, see Case 106/79 *Vereniging Boekhandels* v. *Eldi Records* [1980] E.C.R. 1137.
[95] See below "declaration of inapplicability of the prohibition of Art. 85(1)."
[96] Case 48/72 *Brasserie de Haecht* v. *Wilkin (No. 2)* [1973] E.C.R. 77 at 86(9–10).

The situation is different for "old agreements" (*i.e.* those that were in existence before March 13, 1962). The Court held[97] that in those cases the general principle of contractual certainty, particularly when the agreement had been notified in accordance with Regulation 17, requires that national courts may only declare the agreement to be automatically void after the Commission has taken a decision by virtue of that regulation. Since certain old agreements are exempted from notification, another distinction must be made between the latter (they are simply valid) and the old agreements which must be notified in order to be exempted from the prohibition; the latter are "provisionally valid," since they may still become void if the Commission refuses the exemption.[98] However this provisional protection ceases to exist from the date on which the Commission informs the parties that it has decided to close the file. From then on, the national courts before which the direct effect of the prohibition of Article 85(1) is invoked may decide whether or not the agreement violates the Treaty and is consequently void.[99]

(c) Exemption from the prohibition. A declaration that the provisions of Article 85(1) are inapplicable (or an exemption) may be granted, under certain limited conditions, either for individual agreements or for categories of agreements.[1]

Individual exemptions. Such exemptions may be granted by the Commission[2] and only by the Commission[3] which cannot act unless the agreement has been notified to it[4] and the following four conditions are all fulfilled:

---

[97] Case 59/77 *De Bloos* v. *Bouyer* [1977] E.C.R. 2359 at 2369(8).

[98] Case 13/61 *de Geus* v. *Bosch en Van Rijn* [1962] E.C.R. 45 at 52.

[99] Case 99/79 *Lancôme* (n. 83 above) at 2535. The same applies *a fortiori* to new agreements: Case 31/80 *L'Oréal* v. *De Nieuwe AMCK* [1980] E.C.R. 3775.

[1] EEC, Art. 85(3).

[2] Before Reg. 17 came into force, only the national authorities could grant such an exemption (see EEC, Art. 88); when Reg. 17 took effect, this exclusive right was transferred to the Commission (Reg. 17, Art. 9(1)).

[3] Case 31/80 *L'Oréal* (n. 99 above) at 3790(13).

[4] Reg. 17, Art. 4(1). For details concerning notification, see Reg. 27/62, First Regulation implementing Council Reg. 17 (O.J. 1959–1962, 132) amended by Reg. 2526/85 (O.J. 1985, L. 240/1) and Notice on Procedure Concerning Notification (O.J. 1983, C. 295/6). Once notified the agreement can no longer serve as a ground for imposing a fine.

(1) the agreement must contribute to improving the production or distribution of goods or to promoting technical and economic progress;

(2) consumers must get a fair share of the resulting benefit;

(3) the agreement may not impose restrictions which are not indispensable for the objectives under (1) and (2);

(4) the agreement may not allow the parties a chance to eliminate competition in respect of a substantial part of the products in question.

The exemption may not come into force on a date earlier than the date of notification[5]; it must be issued for a specific period and conditions and obligations may be attached to it. They may be renewed but also revoked even retroactively.[6]

Since it may take the Commission a very long time to make a decision granting an exemption, it introduced the so-called "comfort letter" simply stating that the Commission sees no reason to intervene. There are also cases where the Commission has written a more informal "comfort letter" stating that the Commission sees no reason to issue a formal decision.

Before granting an exemption or sending one of these letters, the Commission must invite comments from third parties by publishing a Notice.

Exemptions for categories of agreements. They comprise the so-called "Block exemptions" and the exemptions for certain categories (*e.g.* agriculture, transport). The block exemptions are granted by the Commission acting in pursuance of a Council decision: the Council decides by regulation on the principle of the exemption and delegates to the Commission the task of working out the details. This technique was used in two instances: the first

[5] Reg. 17, Art. 6(1).
[6] Reg. 17, Art. 8.

one for categories of agreements to which only two undertakings are party and which concern exclusive supply and purchase for resale or which include restrictions in relation to the acquisition or use of industrial property rights, the so-called "exclusive dealing agreements."[7] The second one for categories of agreements concerning the application of standards or types, research and development and specialisation.

On the basis of the first Council regulation (Reg. 19/65), the Commission adopted several regulations which will be briefly examined below. The first one was Regulation 67/67,[8] which after having been in force for over 15 years was replaced by Regulation 1983/83 applying Article 85(3) to categories of exclusive distribution agreements[9] and by Regulation 1984/83 applying Article 85(3) to certain categories of exclusive purchasing agreements.[10]

All the regulations granting block exemptions follow the same pattern: they stipulate, in detail, which restrictions may be imposed on each one of the parties, which restrictions do not infringe the prohibition and which ones are excluded from the exemption. It should be noted that an agreement which is not exempted under those regulations may be notified to the Commission in order to obtain an individual exemption.[11]

(1) *Bilateral exclusive distribution agreements (Reg. 1983/83)*

This regulation exempts from the Treaty prohibition agreements to which only two undertakings are party and whereby one party agrees with the other to supply certain goods for resale within the whole or a defined area of the common market only to that other party. This regulation does not apply to agreements for the resale of drinks in premises used for the resale and consumption of beer and to agreements for the resale of petroleum products.[12]

---

[7] Reg. 19/65 (J.O. 1965, 533; O.J. 1965–1966, 35).
[8] O.J. 1967, 10.
[9] O.J. 1983, L. 173/1 and corrigendum in O.J. 1983, L. 281/24.
[10] O.J. 1983, L. 173/5 and corrigendum in O.J. 1983, L. 281/24.
[11] See, *e.g. Carlsberg* Dec. O.J. 1984, L. 207/26.
[12] Reg. 1983/83, Art. 8.

(2) *Bilateral exclusive purchase agreements (Reg. 1984/83)*

This regulation exempts agreements to which only two undertakings are party and whereby one party, the reseller, agrees with the other, the supplier, to purchase certain goods specified in the agreement for resale only from the supplier or from a connected undertaking or from another undertaking which the supplier has entrusted with the sale of his goods.

This regulation also deals with beer supply agreements (brewery ties) and with petroleum products supply agreements. It should be noted that this regulation does not provide the reseller with an exclusive area as is provided in the former.

Both regulations described in (1) and (2) above are the object of a lengthy explanatory Notice from the Commission[13] whereby the latter gives a detailed interpretation of its own regulations; this rather unusual procedure has the advantage of providing interested parties with some necessary clarifications.

(3) *Patent licences (Reg. 2349/84)*[14]

Exemption is granted for certain patent licensing agreements and agreements combining the licensing of patents and the communication of know-how and to which only two undertakings are party.[15] Attention must be drawn to the special procedure by which agreements, not falling within the terms and conditions of the exemption, may nevertheless be notified to the Commission. They are automatically exempt if the Commission does not react within six months, the so-called "opposition procedure."

(4) *Motor vehicles distribution and servicing (Reg. 123/85)*

Exemption is granted for agreements between two undertakings only and in which one contracting party agrees to supply, within a

---

[13] O.J. 1984, C. 101/2.
[14] O.J. 1984, L. 219/15 and amended O.J. 1985, L. 113/34.
[15] Reg. 2349/84, Art. 4. For patents and licences see Case 24/67 *Parke, Davis* v. *Centrafarm* [1968] E.C.R. 55, Case 16/74 *Centrafarm* v. *Winthrop* [1974] E.C.R. 1183 and Case 258/78 *Nungesser* v. *Commission* [1982] E.C.R. 2015.

defined territory, only to the other party or only to the other party and to a specified number of other undertakings within the distribution system, for the purpose of resale certain motor vehicles.[16] This is a so-called "selective distribution" agreement about which more later.

(5) *Know-how licensing (Reg. 556/89)*[17]

This regulation concerns "a body of technical information that is secret, substantial and identified in any appropriate form." The regulation also covers mixed know-how and patent-licensing agreements not covered by Regulation 2349/84 and agreements containing ancillary provisions regarding trade marks and other intellectual property rights; agreements for territorial protection of the licensor and the licensee against any use of the licensed technology are exempt. It provides for a maximum degree of contractual freedom and for an opposition procedure.

(6) *Franchising (Reg. 4087/88)*[18]

Exempted are certain agreements concerning licences of industrial or intellectual property rights (trade marks or names or know-how) to be exploited for the purpose of selling goods or providing services to end-users in premises of uniform appearance and with the same business methods. The regulation applies to all economic sectors including those where specific block exemptions have been adopted. It is interesting to note that recommended prices and a post-term non-competition obligation not exceeding one year are admitted.

Two other regulations were made by the Commission in pursuance of the second Council regulation[19]:

---

[16] O.J. 1985, L. 15/16. See Eighteenth Report on Competition Policy, 43.
[17] O.J. 1989, L. 61/1. See *ibid.*, at 44.
[18] O.J. 1988 L. 359, 46.
[19] Reg. 2821/71 ((J.O. 1971 L. 285/46) O.J. 1971, 1032).

(a) *Specialisation agreements (Reg. 417/85)*[20]

Exemption is granted for agreements on specialisation whereby undertakings accept reciprocal obligations to leave the manufacture of certain products to other parties or to manufacture certain products or only have them manufactured jointly.

The exemption, however, only applies if the products which are the subject of the specialisation together with similar products of the participating undertakings do not represent more than 20 per cent of the market and the aggregate annual turnover of all the participants does not exceed 500 million ECU. If the latter is exceeded the agreement can be notified under the opposition procedure.

(b) *Research and Development agreements (Reg. 418/85)*[20a]

The prohibition does not apply to agreements entered into by undertakings for the purpose of:

(i) joint research and development of products or processes and exploitation of the results;

(ii) joint exploitation of results from a prior agreement between the same undertakings and

(iii) joint research and development excluding joint exploitation.

The exemption is valid for a limited number of years and where the undertakings are competitors, the combined market share of the products which are the object of the research may not exceed 20 per cent of the market.

All the above mentioned regulations expire after a period varying from 10 to 14 years, in the same way as individual exemptions must be limited in time, but they are renewable.

---

[20] O.J. 1985, L. 53/1. This regulation replaces Reg. 2779/72, itself replaced by Reg. 3604/82.

[20a] O.J. 1985, L. 53/5.

Application of competition rules to certain agreements. After this short analysis of the competition rules applying to undertakings, it might be useful to indicate briefly how they have been applied by the Commission and the Court to the main types of agreements.[21]

The following agreements are very likely to fall under the prohibition of Article 85(1):

(a) agreements relating to prices and conditions of sale[22];

(b) information agreements about prices, costs, investments, output, technology, etc.[23];

(c) agreements limiting production, except for genuine restructuring, specialisation or joint ventures;

(d) agreements on technical standards if they prevent the parties from selling differentiated products[24];

(e) agreements to limit or control markets, *e.g.* via market sharing[25];

(f) collective exclusive dealings: suppliers agree to deal exclusively through approved dealers[26];

(g) joint purchasing, *i.e.* fixing of purchase price or collective purchasing[27];

---

[21] This section is based on Bellamy and Child, *Common Market Law of Competition* (3rd ed. 1987) Sweet & Maxwell, with the kind permission of the authors.

[22] See, *e.g.* Joined Cases 240 etc/82 *Stichting Cigarettenindustrie* v. *Commission* [1985] E.C.R. 3831.

[23] See, *e.g. Vimpolter* Dec. (O.J. 1983, L. 200/44).

[24] See, *e.g. Transocean Marine Paint Association* Dec. (J.O. 1967, 163/10).

[25] See, *e.g.* Case 40/73 *Suiker Unie* v. *Commission* [1975] E.C.R. 1663.

[26] See, *e.g.* Case 243/83 *Binon* v. *AMP* [1985] E.C.R. 2015.

[27] See, *e.g. National Sulphuric Acid Association* Dec. (O.J. 1980, L. 260/24).

(h) joint selling[28];

(i) advertising and promotion if they restrict the undertakings' freedom to advertise or enable undertakings to engage in joint advertising and promotion; also the use of advertising to prevent imports[29] and

(j) trade exhibitions.[30]

Of particular interest are the "selective distribution agreements" whereby a producer limits the sale of his product to a few "selected" outlets. On the basis of the Court and Commission decisions[31] it can be admitted that the prohibition of the Treaty does not apply as long as certain conditions are met:

(1) selection takes place on the basis of non-discriminatory qualitative criteria concerning technical ability and suitability of premises;

(2) those criteria are reasonably necessary;

(3) all dealers who fulfil the conditions are admitted; and

(4) parallel imports and exports are possible.

Reference must also be made to "*intellectual property rights*" with respect to the Community competition rules. Normally those

---

[28] See, *e.g. Floral* Dec. (O.J. 1980, L. 39/51).

[29] *Ford Garantie Deutschland*, Thirteenth Report on Competition, 78.

[30] See, *e.g. SMM&T Exhibition Agreement* Notice (O.J. 1983, L. 376/1) and Case 83/85 *Ancides* v. *Commission* [1987] 3151.

[31] One of the first Commission decisions was *Omega* (J.O. 1970, L. 242/22) where the admissibility was based on the high technical quality of the product requiring well trained staff, etc., *id.* for *BMW* Dec. (O.J. 1975, L. 29/1). See also Case 107/82 *AEG* v. *Commission* [1983] E.C.R. 3151; Case 86/82 *Hasselblad* v. *Commission* [1984] E.C.R. 883 and Case 10/86 *VAG France* v. *Magne* [1986] E.C.R. 4084.

rights are used by their owner to prevent others from producing the product covered by the right, but also to reserve the use of this right to particular territories thereby dividing the Community again into so many separate markets of the Member States. Although the owner of the intellectual property rights acts in conformity with national law, by preventing imports and exports among the Community countries, he violates the basic principle of the free movement of goods. It is in relation to this principle that most cases concerning the use of those rights were brought before the Court.[32] But according to the latter such use is also contrary to the Community competition rules.[33] The position of the Court with regard to the use of intellectual property rights can best be summarised as follows: the Treaty provisions do not affect the existence[34] of the exclusive rights attached to patents, know-how, trademarks, copyrights, registered designs, plant breeder's rights and other similar rights; they do, however, limit their use in so far as they restrict trade between Member States.[35] On the other hand, the Court upholds the use of those rights when this is "justified for the purpose of safeguarding rights which constitute the specific subject matter of such property."[36]

A further restriction was introduced by the Court in the form of the principle of the exhaustion of rights: by putting a product on the market in a Member State the owner of the right "exhausts" his rights and can no longer set them against the free movement of the protected product within the Community.

(2) *Abuse of a dominant position: Article 86*

Competition and interstate trade can, as was seen, be adversely affected by several undertakings agreeing to do so, but they can

---

[32] See, *e.g.* Case 78/70 *Deutsche Grammophon* v. *Metro* [1971] E.C.R. 487 and Case 262/81 *Coditel* v. *Ciné Vog Films* [1982] E.C.R. 3381.

[33] Joined Cases 56–58/64 *Consten and Grundig* v. *Commission* [1966] E.C.R. 299 at 346, where the Court found that Community law does not allow the improper use of rights under national trade mark law in order to frustrate the Community's law on cartels.

[34] See EEC, Art. 222.

[35] Joined Cases 56–58/62 *Consten and Grundig* (n. 33 above).

[36] Case 78/70 *Deutsche Grammophon* (n. 32 above) at 500.

also be restricted by one or more undertakings who enjoy a quasi-monopoly situation called "dominant position." Both cases are, of course, prohibited by the Treaty.

The provisions concerning the agreements and those relating to the abuse are complementary[37] and, together, embody the Community competition rules applying to enterprises. It will be remembered that those provisions have as their object the "institution of a system ensuring that competition in the common market is not distorted."[38]

The Treaty provisions refer to "dominant position," "abuse" and "may affect trade between Member States." The latter was examined with respect to prohibited agreements in the previous section, and the other two will be briefly analysed here.

A "dominant position" exists, according to the Court, when an undertaking enjoys a position of economic strength "which enables it to hinder the maintenance of effective competition on the relevant market by allowing it to behave to an appreciable extent independently of its competitors and customers and ultimately of consumers."[38] It follows from the practice of the Commission[39] and the case law of the Court[40] that in order to

---

[37] As the Court pointed out in Case 6/72 *Europemballage and Continental Can* v. *Commission* [1973] E.C.R. 215 at 244(25) "The restraint of competition which is prohibited if it is the result of behaviour falling under Article 85, cannot become permissible by the fact that such behaviour succeeds under the influence of a dominant undertaking."

[38] Case 322/81 *Michelin* v. *Commission* [1983] E.C.R. 3461 at 3503(30).

[39] See, *e.g.* the following Commission Decisions: *GEMA* (J.O. 1971, L. 134/15), *Continental Can* (J.O. 1972, L. 7/25), *ZOJA* (J.O. 1972, L. 299/51), *General Motors* v. *Commission* [1975] E.C.R. 1367; Case 13/77 *GB–INNO–BM* v. *ATAB* [1977] E.C.R. 2115; Case 27/76 *United Brands* v. *Commission* [1978] E.C.R. 207; Case 77/77 *BP* v. *Commission* [1978] E.C.R. 1513; Case 85/76 *Hoffmann-La Roche* v. *Commission* [1979] E.C.R. 461; Case 22/78 *Hugin* v. *Commission* [1979] E.C.R. 1869; Case 7/82 *GVL* v. *Commission* [1983] E.C.R. 483 and Case 226/84 *British Leyland* v. *Commission* [1986] E.C.R. 3263.

[40] See, *e.g.* Case 6/72 *Europemballage and Continental Can* (n. 37 above); Joined Cases 6–7/73 *Commercial Solvents* v. *Commission* [1974] E.C.R. 223; Case 26/75 *General Motors* v. *Commission* [1975] E.C.R. 1367; Case 13/77 *GB–INNO–BM* v. *ATAB* [1977] E.C.R. 2115; Case 27/76 *United Brands* v. *Commission* [1978] E.C.R. 207; Case 77/77 *BP* v. *Commission* [1978] E.C.R. 1513; Case 85/76 *Hoffmann-La Roche* v. *Commission* [1979] E.C.R. 461; Case 22/78 *Hugin* v. *Commission* [1979] E.C.R. 1869; Case 7/82 *GVL* v. *Commission* [1983] E.C.R. 483 and Case 226/84 *British Leyland* v. *Commission* [1986] E.C.R. 3263.

determine whether a position is dominant, it must be viewed in relation to the "relevant product market" and the "relevant geographical market." The definition of the relevant product market is of essential significance because the possibilities of competition can only be judged in relation to those characteristics of the products in question by virtue of which those products are particularly apt to satisfy an inelastic need and are only to a limited extent interchangeable with other products.[41] In order to be regarded as constituting a distinct market, the products in question must be individualised not only by the mere fact that they are used for a given purpose, but by particular characteristics of production which make them specifically suitable for this purpose and within a given area.[42]

Whether or not an undertaking has a dominant position on a "relevant geographical market" depends on the structure of the product market, especially as far as production, supply and demand are concerned[43]; the limits of this market do not necessarily coincide with the territories of the Member States, although they normally do, mainly because statistics are only available per country; in any case the part of the common market on which the undertaking is supposed to have a dominant position must be "substantial."[44]

---

[41] For an example of non-interchangeable products see Case 85/76 *Hoffmann-La Roche* (n. 40 above) at 547(111).

[42] See Case 6/72 *Europemballage* (n. 40 above) at 217(14).

[43] See Case 247/86, *Alsatel* v. *Lorraine*, judgment of October 5, 1988 (not yet published), where the Court did not accept the existence neither of a relevant product market nor that of a national geographical market, but only a regional one. In the *Europemballage* case, the Court underlined "how necessary it is to define the market concerned in order that the relative strength of the undertakings in such a market might be considered (n. 42 above at 248(34)).
See also the definition of the "geographical reference market" in the regulation on the control of concentrations, Art. 9(7).

[44] See Case 40/73 *Suiker Unie and Others* v. *Commission* [1975] E.C.R. 1663 at 1977 and 1991.

As for "dominance," it is not merely a question of size,[45] but it can also derive from a combination of several factors which, taken separately, would not necessarily be determinative.

More difficult even is the definition of "abuse." It will be remembered that agreements between undertakings are prohibited when two conditions are fulfilled: trade between Member States must be affected and competition must be restricted. With regard to abuse of a dominant position the Treaty only mentions the first of these criteria and "abuse" must therefore be understood in relation to competition. Any behaviour of an undertaking (enjoying a dominant position) which interferes with one of the basic freedoms, or with the free choice of the purchaser or consumer, or with freedom of access to the market constitutes an abuse. The most obvious criterion is probably the freedom of choice left to the other participants in the market. According to the Court, the concept of abuse is an objective concept relating to the behaviour of an undertaking in a dominant position which is such as to influence the structure of the market and which, through recourse to methods different from those which condition normal competition has the effect of hindering the maintenance or growth of existing competition.[46]

The Treaty refers to abuse "of" a dominant position, but this does not mean that a link of causality must exist between the dominant position and the abuse. Indeed, the strengthening of the position of an undertaking may constitute an abuse and be prohibited regardless of the means and procedures by which it is achieved. In this respect it is important to note the adoption by the Council, at the end of 1989, of a Regulation on the control of

---

[45] A market share of 80 per cent clearly creates a dominant position. When the size of the market share is not decisive, additional criteria must be taken into consideration. See Case 85/76 *Hoffmann-La Roche* (n. 40 above at 524(48)) where the Court rejected as irrelevant a number of additional criteria mentioned by the Commission, but indicated those which it considered important, such as the relationship between the market share of the undertaking in question and the shares of the next largest, the technological lead, the existence of a highly developed sales network and the absence of potential competition. See also Case 22/78 *Hugin* (n. 40 above).

[46] See, *e.g.* Case 85/76 *Hoffmann-La Roche* (n. 40 above) at 541(91): use of economic power is not required.

concentration between undertakings[47] which will be examined below.

Control of concentrations. While recognising that the dismantling of the internal frontiers of the Community results in major corporate reorganisations in the form of concentrations and that this development must be welcomed as being in line with the requirements of dynamic competition, the Council considers that they may also seriously impede competition and must therefore be controlled. The Regulation on the control of concentrations presents the following features:

(1) Falling within the regulation are concentrations where the aggregate worldwide turnover of all the undertakings concerned is more than five billion ECU and the aggregate Community-wide turnover of at least two of them is more than 250 million ECU (those thresholds will be reviewed after four years); Article 1.

(2) A concentration is deemed to arise where two or more previously independent undertakings merge or where one or more persons already controlling one or more undertakings acquire direct or indirect control of the whole or parts of one or more other undertakings; Article 3.

(3) Those concentrations have to be notified to the Commission not more than one week after the conclusion of the agreement or the announcement of the public bid, or the acquisition of the controlling interest; Article 4.

(4) The Commission then appraises the concentration taking into account *inter alia* the structure of all the markets concerned and the actual and potential competition from

[47] Reg. 4064/89 (O.J. 1989, L. 395/1).

undertakings located within or outside the Community and the market position of the undertakings concerned and their economic and financial power, the opportunities available to suppliers and users, their access to supplies and markets, any legal or other barriers to entry, supply and demand trends for the relevant goods and services, the interests of the intermediate and ultimate consumers and the development of technical and economic progress; Article 2(1).

(5) A concentration which creates or strengthens a dominant position as a result of which effective competition would be significantly impeded in the common market or in a substantial part of it shall be declared incompatible with the common market; Article 2(2).

(6) The Commission may order suspension of a concentration until it reaches a final decision, but within given time-limits; Articles 7 and 10.

(7) Finally the Commission has powers to investigate and to impose fines or periodic penalty payments; Articles 13, 14 and 15.

With the adoption of this regulation the arsenal of Community instruments at the disposal of the institutions to ensure that competition is not distorted in the common market is now complete.

Regulation 17. Regulation 17[48] is the first regulation "to give effect to the principles set out in Articles 85 and 86."[49] Generally speaking it sets out the procedure to be followed when the Commission decides:

---

[48] J.O. 1962, 204; O.J. 1959–1962, 87.
[49] EEC, Art. 87.

(1) to give a "negative clearance"[50]: this is issued at the request[51] of undertakings which want to make certain that their agreement is not prohibited by Article 85 or 86. Before granting a negative clearance, or taking any other decisions which may affect third parties, the Commission must publish in the Official Journal the essence of the content of the application and invite interested parties to submit observations[52];

(2) to oblige undertakings to put an end to infringements, when it finds that they exist, either upon application of a Member State or a natural or legal person[53] or upon its own initiative.[54] In this connection attention should be drawn to the limitation period in proceedings under the competition rules[55];

(3) to issue a declaration granting an exemption from the prohibition of Article 85(1)[56];

---

[50] Reg. 17, Art. 2. Lists of decisions taken by the Commission can be found in the annual Reports on Competition Policy published in conjunction with the annual General Report. The first decision taken on the basis of Reg. 17 was a negative clearance: *Grosfillex-Fillistorf* (J.O. 915/64); a recent one concerned the *Channel Tunnel* (Bull. 10–1988, 29). The disuse of this procedure can be explained by the greater security which has existed since the Commission and the Court defined the various concepts of the competition provisions and the block exemptions and several Notices were issued.

[51] See Reg. 27 First Regulation Implementing Council Regulation 17, fixing form, content and other details concerning applications (J.O. 1962, 1118; O.J. 1959–1962, 132), last amended by Reg. 2526/85 (O.J. 1985, L. 240/1).

[52] Reg. 17, Art. 19(3).

[53] Reg. 17, Art. 3(2)(b). For the right to file a complaint with the Commission under that Art. see Case 125/78 *GEMA* v. *Commission* [1979] E.C.R. 3173 and for the rights of complainants see Joined Cases 142 and 156/84 *BAT and Reynolds* v. *Commission* [1987] E.C.R. 4566.

[54] Case 792/79R *Camera Care* v. *Commission* [1980] E.C.R. 119 at 131(18): the powers which the Commission holds under Art. 3 include the power to take interim measures which are indispensable for the effective exercise of its functions. See also Joined Cases 228–229/82R *Ford-Werke* v. *Commission* [1982] E.C.R. 3091 where interim measures were suspended.

[55] Enforcement procedures are subject to a limitation period of five years (Reg. 2988/74, Arts. 4–6, O.J. 1974, L. 319/1).

[56] Reg. 17, Art. 6. See above: "C. Exemption from the prohibition."

(4) to undertake investigations into undertakings; to this end officials authorised by the Commission are empowered, (a) to examine books and other business records, (b) to take copies of or extracts from the books and business records: the confidentiality of written communications between laywer and client is, however, protected when (i) such communications are made for the purpose and in the interests of the client's right of defence and (ii) they emanate from independent lawyers, *i.e.* lawyers who are not bound to the client by a relationship of employment (legal privilege[57]); (c) to ask for oral explanations on the spot and (d) to enter any premises, land and means of transport[58];

(5) to impose fines and penalties.[59]

In cases (1), (2) and (5), the Commission, before deciding, must make known to the undertakings concerned the points to which it objects and which it has taken into consideration, and give the undertakings an opportunity to express their views on them.[60] The Commission must also invite third parties to submit

[57] Case 155/79 *AM & S* v. *Commission* [1982] E.C.R. 1575 at 1611(22).

[58] This right to enter premises was contested recently, but to no avail, by several undertakings: Case 46/87R *Hoechst* v. *Commission* [1987] E.C.R. 1549 and Case 85/87R *Dow Chemical Nederland BV* v. *Commission* [1987] E.C.R. 4367. See also two Explanatory Notes to authorisation to investigate under Article 14(2) and (3) of Regulation 17/62, Thirteenth Report on Competition Policy, 270 and 271.

[59] Reg. 17, Arts. 15 and 16. See, *e.g.* two decisions of December 1988 imposing on 23 manufacturers of thermoplastics fines totalling 60.5 million ECU (Bull. 12–1988, 62) for taking part in a cartel. Fines have been imposed for submitting incomplete information (Bull. 11–1971,55) and periodic payments for each day an undertaking failed to fulfil an obligation imposed by the Commission: *MA-Statuut* (O.J. 1980, L. 318/1).

[60] See Reg. 99/63 on the Hearings provided for in Art. 19(1) and (2) of Reg. 17 (J.O. 1963, 2268; O.J. 1963–1964, 47); see Case 85/76 *Hoffmann-La Roche* (n. 40 above), where the Court indicated that the right to be heard is a basic principle of Community law in all procedures that may lead to the imposition of fines.
Note also the creation of the post of Hearing Officer and the Notice on procedures for applying the competition rules (O.J. 1982, C. 251/2). See Twelfth Report on Competition Policy, 38.

their observations and therefore must publish the essence of the decisions it intends to take. In those cases the Commission must also consult the Consultative Committee on Cartels and Monopolies composed of representatives of the Member States.

Commission Notices. To clarify its competition policy, the Commission has issued several notices; they somehow complete the block exemptions although, contrary to the latter, they have no binding effect, not even for the Commission. They simply provide guidance and information concerning the Commission's views on the implementation of the competition rules.

(a) *Exclusive Agency Contracts Made with Commercial Agents*: the Commission declared[61] that contracts concluded with commercial agents, in which those agents undertake for a specified part of the territory of the common market to negotiate transactions on behalf of an enterprise, or to conclude transactions in the name and on behalf of an enterprise, or to conclude transactions in their own name and on behalf of an enterprise, are not prohibited by the Treaty.

(b) *Co-operation Agreements*[62]: in this Notice the Commission first indicates that it encourages co-operation between small and medium-sized enterprises, where such co-operation enables them to work more rationally and increases their productivity and competitiveness on a larger market. It then lists eight categories of agreements which, in its view, do not restrict competition.

(c) *Import of Japanese products*[63]: the Commission reminds undertakings concluding agreements with Japanese firms and which are intended to restrict imports of Japanese products into the Community, that such agreements do not fall outside the Community competition rules because one or all of the parties are situated outside the Community. It urges the undertakings concerned to notify those agreements.

[61] J.O. 1962, 2921.
[62] O.J. 1968, C. 75/3.
[63] O.J. 1972, C. 111/13.

(d) *Subcontracting Agreements*[64]: this form of agreement is considered by the Commission as a form of work distribution which concerns in particular small and medium-sized firms and whereby technology is made available by one party to the other with restrictions as to its use. Under given conditions those agreements are not prohibited.

(e) *Agreements of Minor Importance*[65]: this Notice also follows from the desire of the Commission to promote co-operation between small and medium-sized enterprises. The Notice lists a number of criteria which allow undertakings to aquire the certainty that their agreement is not prohibited.

Relationship between Community and national competition rules. In one of its judgments[66] the Court had to answer the question whether or not Community and national competition law could be applied simultaneously to the same cartel. The Court ascertained that Community and national law consider cartels from different points of view. The former regards them in the light of the obstacles which may result for interstate trade, while the latter proceeds on the basis of considerations which are particular to it. This implies that, *e.g.* one and the same agreement may, in principle, be the object of two sets of parallel proceedings. However, if the ultimate general aim of the Treaty is to be respected, the parallel application of the national system can only be allowed in so far as it does not prejudice the uniform application throughout the common market of the Community rules on cartels and the full effect of the measures adopted in implementation of those rules.

The Court based its ruling on the fact that:

"the EEC Treaty has established its own system of law, integrated into the legal systems of the Member States, and which must be applied by their courts. It would be contrary

---

[64] O.J. 1979, C. 1/2.
[65] O.J. 1986, C. 231/2.
[66] Case 14/68 *Wilhelm* v. *Bundeskartellamt* [1969] E.C.R. 1.

to the nature of such a system to allow Member States to introduce or to retain measures capable of prejudicing the practical effectiveness of the Treaty. The binding force of the Treaty and of measures taken in application of it must not differ from one State to another as a result of internal measures, lest the functioning of the Community system should be impeded and the achievement of the aims of the Treaty placed in peril. Consequently, conflicts between the rules of the Community and national rules in the matter of the law on cartels must be resolved by applying the principle that Community law takes precedence."[67]

As long as this rule is applied, national authorities may take action against cartels in accordance with their national law, even when an examination of the same cartel, from the point of view of its compatibility with Community law, is pending before the Commission.[68]

However, in order to avoid conflict, the best solution is that as soon as the Commission starts proceedings, the national authorities, and this includes tribunals, should suspend their procedure. But it is for the national judge to decide whether or not there is cause to suspend proceedings in order to allow the parties to

---

[67] *Ibid.*, at 14(6).

[68] This means that when, *e.g.* an agreement is void under Community law, national authorities may not declare it to be valid on the basis of national law. The question whether national authorities may declare void an agreement for which the Commission has granted an exemption under Art. 85(3) remains unresolved; in this writer's opinion, to admit this possibility would amount to a differentiated application of Community competition law according to the Member State. The agreement in question would be void in one country and valid in all the others. This seems contrary to Community law in general. However, when applying national law, national authorities are under no obligation to take into account possible infringements of Community law, as long as the Commission has not opened proceedings. Furthermore, nothing prevents those authorities from either prohibiting under national law agreements which are void under Community law, or from imposing fines upon the undertakings concerned, even if fines were already imposed by the Commission. Conversely, the Commission is not prevented from imposing fines after an undertaking has been fined under national law. See Case 7/72 *Boehringer* v. *Commission* [1972] E.C.R. 1281 at 1289: only when two cases are identical, fines should be offset against one another.

obtain the Commission's standpoint, unless of course it is established that the agreement does not have any perceptible effect on
competition or trade between Member States or that there is no
doubt that the agreement is incompatible with Article 85.[69]

2. Competition rules applying to Member States

As was mentioned at the beginning of this section on competition, obstacles to the free movement of goods can result from
illegal behaviour of undertakings as well as from interference by
national authorities. Both are prohibited by the Treaty. Having
abolished customs duties and taxes with equivalent effect, on the
one hand, and quantitative restrictions and measures having
equivalent effect, on the other, Member States can still affect
trade and competition. This can be done by establishing or
maintaining state monopolies, by using public enterprises to
bypass the Treaty rules, by granting unlawful subsidies to enterprises or by discriminating between national and other undertakings through fiscal measures. Those various measures and the
corresponding Treaty rules will be examined below.

(1) *State monopolies of a commercial character*[70]

Members States are required by the Treaty to "adjust" their
monopolies of a commercial character,[71] so as to ensure that, by

---

[69] In Case 48/72 *Brasserie de Haecht* v. *Wilkin-Janssen* [1973] E.C.R. 77 at 87(11),
the Court considered that "whilst the principle of legal certainty requires that in
applying the prohibition of Article 85, the sometimes considerable delays by the
Commission in exercising its powers should be taken into account, this cannot
however absolve the (national) court from the obligation of deciding on the
claims of interested parties who invoke the automatic nullity."

[70] EEC, Art. 37. A state monopoly is a body through which a State, in law or in
fact, directly or indirectly supervises, determines or appreciably influences the
marketing of products in its territory and their imports or exports between
Member States.

[71] The term "commercial" indicates that production monopolies are not affected
by the Treaty. Indeed, in an open common market those monopolies do not
constitute an obstacle to free trade. Neither are the common agricultural
organisations affected by Art. 37 (see above under "CAP"), since, under
Art. 38(2) they have precedence over other Treaty provisions. See Case 83/78
Pigs Marketing Board v. *Redmond* [1978] E.C.R. 2347. The same applies to
service monopolies: Case 161/82 *Commission* v. *France* [1983] E.C.R. 2079.

the end of the transitional period,[72] no discrimination regarding the conditions under which goods are procured and marketed exists between nationals of the Member States.

At the time the Treaty came into force about a dozen such monopolies existed in the original six Member States.[73] The time-table provided for in the Treaty was not respected and although most monopolies were either simply abolished or adapted, it was only in 1983 that the Commission could report that it considered the measures taken by the French Government such as to bring the tobacco monopoly in line with the Treaty provisions were adequate, although the Commission still receives complaints about other monopolies.[74] The accession of Greece, Portugal and Spain added new state monopolies to the list of those still to be adapted.[75] As can be seen, adaptation did not come easily and the Commission had to start several procedures[76] to force the Member States to abide by the Treaty rules in this domain.

(2) *Public undertakings*[77]

A public undertaking is any undertaking, whatever its public or private status, on whose economic behaviour the State can exert influence, *e.g.* by virtue of its direct or indirect financial participation or by legal provisions governing its establishment. In other words, the essential criteria for determining whether an undertaking is a "public" one, in the sense of the Treaty, is the "control" a national authority can and does exercise over it.[78] The

---

[72] December 31, 1969 for the original six Member States; other dates were of course provided in the different accession treaties, *e.g.* January 1, 1993 for Portugal (Act of Acc., Art. 208(1)).

[73] See First Report on Competition Policy, 160.

[74] Twelfth Report on Competition Policy, 149. See however Bull. 3–1983: opening of procedure against France concerning the alcohol monopoly. *Ibid.* for the oil and potash monopolies in France, see Sixteenth Report, 203.

[75] For details see the Reports on Competition Policy. Spain has until the end of 1991 and Portugal until the end of 1992 (Acts of Accession, Arts. 48(1) and 208(1)).

[76] See, *e.g.* Case 78/82 *Commission* v. *Italy* [1983] E.C.R. 1955.

[77] EEC, Art. 90.

[78] See Dir. 80/723, Art. 2 (O.J. 1980, L. 195/35) and Case 118/85 *Commission* v. *Italy* [1987] E.C.R. 2599 at 2621(8).

logical consequence of the subordinate position of the undertaking in question is that the public authority which controls it, is responsible for its market behaviour.[79] Furthermore, when this undertaking acts illegally with regard to the Treaty, it is irrelevant whether it did so on instructions from the controlling national authority[80] or not. In the latter case the authority is responsible for not having taken the necessary measures to prevent the undertaking from violating the Treaty.[81] But in both cases it is the Member State, to be understood here as any public authority, which is considered responsible for the violation.

This explains why Article 90 imposes obligations exclusively upon the Member States, not on the undertakings. It also explains why the last paragraph of that Article provides that the Commission, in order to "ensure the application of the provisions of this Article shall where necessary, address appropriate directives or decisions to the Member States." The first directive issued by the Commission in pursuance of that provision was challenged by the addressees in Court, but to no avail,[82] and the Commission has, since then, affirmed its authority in this field.[83]

---

[79] A parallel can be drawn between this relationship and that existing between a parent company and its subsidiary; see above under "Agreements between Undertakings."

[80] Member States might indeed be tempted to implement, through an undertaking they control, measures which would have been illegal under the Treaty had they carried them out themselves. Art. 30 constitutes a good example: it prohibits *inter alia* restrictions on import; if in a notice for public procurement the Member State were to indicate that it will only accept bids proposing national products, it would violate Art. 30. If an undertaking were to do the same, no action could be taken, so the Member State could instruct the "public" undertaking to do it in its stead.

[81] See EEC, Art. 90(1): "maintain in force any measure contrary to the rules contained in this Treaty": the authority could be accused of having maintained rules which do not prevent Treaty violations.

[82] See Dir. 80/723 on the transparency of financial relations between Member States and public authorities (O.J. 1980, L. 195/35), see Tenth Report on Competition Policy, 163 and Joined Cases 188–190/80 *France, Italy and U.K.* v. *Commission* [1982] E.C.R. 2545 and Case 118/85 *Commission* v. *Italy* [1987] E.C.R. 2599.

[83] See Case 226/87, *Commission* v. *Greece*, judgment of June 30, 1988 (not yet published) and Dec. 87/359 addressed to Spain concerning reduced air fares (O.J. 1987, L. 194/28); for more details see the Report on Competition Policy.

In 1989 the Commission issued another Directive[84] requiring Member States to establish a system of free competition in the Community market for telecommunications terminal equipment, and in particular, for telephone sets, modems and telex terminals.[85]

An interesting provision of Article 90 is that concerning undertakings "entrusted with the operation of services of general economic interest."[86] Such undertakings shall be subject to the Treaty rules, in particular those on competition, only "in so far as the application of such rules does not obstruct the performance in law or in fact, of the particular task assigned to it."[87]

Owing to the very important role played by the public undertakings within the common market *inter alia* as producers of goods and services, it is to be expected that the provisions of Article 90 will continue to be applied with increased vigour.

(3) *Aids granted by States*[88]

As the Commission pointed out,[89] the Community's efforts to complete a single unified internal market by 1992 lends added weight and importance to the enforcement of the competition rules, and in particular the rules on State aid. Indeed, this common market implies that all those who operate within it do so only with their own resources and at their own risk. Those resources can be artificially increased and those risks reduced by agreements between undertakings as well as by State intervention.

The Treaty states that aid granted by a Member State or through State resources which distorts or threatens to distort

---

[84] O.J. 1988, L. 131/73.
[85] See Eighteenth Report on Competition Policy, 215.
[86] See Case 10/71 *Ministère Public Luxembourgeois* v. *Muller* [1971] E.C.R. 723. Art. 90 is relevant only for those enterprises which are in competition with undertakings not controlled by the State. See also Cases 155/73 *Sacchi* [1974] E.C.R. 409 and 127/73 *BRT* v. *Sabam and NV FONIOR* [1974] E.C.R. 313.
[87] See Case 30/87 *Bodson* v. *Pompes Funèbres*, judgment of May 4, 1988.
[88] EEC, Arts. 92–94.
[89] Sixteenth Report on Competition Policy, 136.

competition is incompatible with the common market in so far as it affects trade between Member States. It seems difficult to imagine State aid favouring certain[90] undertakings which does not distort competition nor affects trade between Member States,[91] but the incompatibility of aid with the common market is "neither absolute nor unconditional."[92]

However, State aid can also constitute an instrument of structural development policy when certain legitimate objectives of economic growth cannot be attained solely by the interplay of market forces, or not within an acceptable time-limit, or not without unacceptable social frictions. The Treaty, therefore, having stated the principle of incompatibility of State aid with the common market, provides for certain categories of aid which either are, or may be considered[93] by the Commission as being compatible with the common market.[94]

In order to allow the Commission to supervise the implementation of Article 92 and declare certain aid measures compatible with the common market, Member States are under obligation to

---

[90] The reference to "certain" undertakings establishes a distinction between what is commonly considered an "aid," *i.e.* measures favouring a limited number of undertakings, and "general economic measures" which favour all the undertakings operating within a given territory; the latter measures are not caught by Art. 92. Distortions resulting on the common market from those measures must be eliminated through approximation of legislation (see below).

[91] See Case 730/79 *Philip Morris* v. *Commission* [1980] E.C.R. 2671: the Court rejected by implication the applicant's argument that in order to show that an aid falls within the terms of Art. 92(1), the Commission must apply the tests which determine the existence of restrictions on competition under Arts. 85 and 86 (relevant market, market structure, etc.). The Court held that simpler grounds (a more favourable treatment of some firms affects inter-State trade) are adequate. See however Case 323/82 *Intermills* v. *Commission* [1984] E.C.R. 3809: the granting of aid cannot be regarded as automatically contrary to the Treaty. With regard to the application of Art. 92(3), the Court confirmed that the Commission enjoys a measure of discretionary power.

[92] Case 74/76 *Iannelli* v. *Meroni* [1977] E.C.R. 557 at 574(11).

[93] This category of aid can be extended by the Council in pursuance of Art. 92(3)(d): see Sixth Dir. 87/167 on aid to shipbuilding (O.J. 1987, L. 69/55).

[94] Any aid therefore which does not fall within one of those categories is automatically incompatible (it will be noticed that, contrary to Art. 85, the Treaty does not use the term "prohibited"); see, *e.g.* Belgian aid to undertakings in difficulty which the Commission ordered to be abolished (J.O. 1972, L. 10/22).

notify the Commission of any plans to grant or alter aid.[95] Until the Commission has decided on the compatibility of the plans, the Member States concerned may not put its proposed measures into effect. If it does so anyway or does not notify the aid measure, the latter is considered incompatible and the Member State may be required to withdraw the aid and recover the amounts already paid.[96]

Furthermore, Member States must notify the Commission "in sufficient time to enable it to submit its comments" and the latter has, according to the Court, two months to make a decison.[97]

If, in the meantime, the Commission comes to the conclusion that the aid cannot be considered compatible with the common market, it opens a procedure which allows all interested parties to express their opinion. To achieve this, the Commission publishes a Notice in the Official Journal and must then take a position on the observations submitted by "concerned" third parties.[98]

Once the Commission has opened the procedure, it must close it with a formal decision. This decision is notified to the Member State and also to third parties who have intervened in the procedure.[99]

A Member State may apply to the Council to have an aid declared compatible with the common market; when the application to the Council is made after the Commission has opened the procedure, the latter is suspended for three months.[1]

---

[95] EEC, Art. 93(3). The obligation to notify applies also to aid which the Member State considers not to be incompatible; see Commission Notice of 1983 to that effect: O.J. 1983, C. 318.

[96] See Fifteenth Report on Competition Policy, 140 and Cases 70/72 *Commission* v. *Germany* [1973] E.C.R. 813 at 828(10) and 94/87 same parties, judgment of July 2, 1989 (not yet published).

[97] Case 122/73 *Nordsee* v. *Germany* [1973] E.C.R. 1511 at 1522(4) and Case 171/83R *Commission* v. *France* [1983] E.C.R. 2621.

[98] See Case 169/84 *Cofaz* v. *Commission* [1986] E.C.R. 408; as for the publication of the Notice see Fifteenth Report on Competition Policy, 140. See also Case 84/82 *Germany* v. *Commission* [1984] E.C.R. 1451.

[99] The Commission instituted a system in 1985 whereby third parties who intervened will receive a copy of the decision; Fifteenth Report on Competition Policy, 140.

[1] EEC, Art. 93(2).

The decisions of the Commission are, of course, subject to the control of legality by the Court,[2] but on the other hand, in case a Member State refuses to abide by the Commission's decision, the latter can refer the matter directly to the Court without applying the preliminary procedure provided for by Articles 169 and 170.[3]

As was pointed out before, the Commission can declare incompatible any aid measure implemented by a Member State in violation of the above mentioned procedure. The Commission can also ask the Court to adopt interim measures requiring the Member State to cease the infringement.[4] Furthermore, any interested party can also ask the national judge to declare the aid illegal since the last sentence of Article 93 has direct effect.[5]

Apart from a category of aid measures which are compatible under the Treaty, all others must, before being implemented, be declared compatible by the Commission. The Treaty provides, in this respect, for several kinds of aids which will be briefly examined below.

(1) *Regional development aids.* The Treaty distinguishes between aid "to promote the economic development of areas where the standard of living is abnormally low or where there is serious underemployment"[6] and aid "to facilitate the development of certain economic areas"; for the latter the Treaty requires that this aid "does not affect adversely trading conditions to an extent contrary to the common interest."[7] The latter is a typical expression whereby large discretionary powers are granted to the Commission but which, to become operational, have to be

---

[2] See, *e.g.* Case 730/79 *Philip Morris* v. *Commission* [1980] E.C.R. 2671; it was the first time a potential beneficiary of an aid contested the Commission's refusal to recognise the aid compatible.

[3] *i.e.* without first giving the Member State the opportunity to submit observations and without sending a reasoned opinion.

[4] Case 31/77R and 53/77R *Commission* v. *U.K.* and *U.K.* v. *Commission* [1977] E.C.R. 921.

[5] Case 120/73 *Lorenz* v. *Germany* [1973] E.C.R. 1471 at 1483(8).

[6] EEC, Art. 92(3)(a).

[7] EEC, Art. 92(3)(c).

specified. This was done by the Commission in 1988 with its Communication on the application of Article 93(3)(a) and (c).[8]

The first group of regions was defined as those where the per capita gross domestic product (GDP) does not exceed 75 per cent of the Community average in purchasing power parity (PPP). Those regions lie mainly on the Southern and Western periphery of the Community. Given the severe problems existing there, the Commission has decided that it may allow operating aid in certain circumstances.[9]

The second group comprises regions which often suffer from the decline of traditional industries and are frequently located in the more central prosperous parts of the Community; the Commission uses two indicators: income and structural unemployment, both assessed in a national context. The better the position of a Member State relative to the Community situation, the wider must be the disparity of a region in order to justify aid.[10]

The criteria set out in the Communication serve as indicators for the Member States to evaluate the chance of having their schemes declared compatible by the Commission, while the latter uses them in the evaluation it makes of those schemes.

(2) *Aid to certain industries.* The application of Community rules to industrial aid, as opposed to regional aid, is, generally speaking, easier since their scope is much more limited and the measures more clearly defined.[11] In this field also the Commission undertook to clarify its policy by a Communication to the Council describing the general principles for industry aid and outlining the specific criteria used in the scrutiny of national schemes.[12]

---

[8] O.J. 1988, C. 212. The method set out in this Communication replaces the Principles of co-ordination of national regional aid schemes of 1971 (O.J. 1974(2nd)IX, 57).

[9] Eighteenth Report on Competition Policy, 147.

[10] *Ibid.*, at 148.

[11] EEC, Art. 92(3)(c) development of certain economic activities.

[12] Eighth Report on Competition Policy, 132 and Bull. 5–1978, 28.

The main problem areas are shipbuilding,[13] textiles,[14] steel,[15] coal[16] and motor vehicles (for which the Commission produced guidelines[17]).

(3) *Cumulation of aids with different policy objectives.*[18] This system has been applied since 1985 and comprises alternative notification thresholds. It enables the Commission to have a better view on the effects of cumulations on trade between Member States.

(4) *General Aid Schemes.* These are general measures granting assistance to undertakings, but which are not justified by the need to develop the region where they invest or to restructure the industrial sector to which they belong. Those schemes do not fall within one of the categories provided for in the Treaty as being suitable for a consideration of their compatibility with the common market. Consequently, the Commission is unable to take a definitive position on such aid schemes. It therefore requires the Member States, when applying those schemes, to notify in advance the regional or sectoral programmes envisaged to implement them or, failing this, the significant cases of aid to be granted.

On the occasion of the publication of the first survey on State aids, the Commission ascertained that these aids or "schemes having horizontal objectives" were found to be at least as important in terms of financial resources as the combined total of schemes that were regionally or sectorally specific.[19]

In 1988 the Commission completed this first survey on State aids. It gave for the first time an overview of the total expendi-

---

[13] Sixth Council Dir. 87/167 (O.J. 1987, L. 69).
[14] See Case 84/82 *Germany* v. *Commission* (n. 98 above) and Competition Reports.
[15] Dec. 3484/85 (O.J. 1985, L. 340) prolonged by Dec. 89/28 (O.J. 1989, L. 14); this sector is particularly difficult due to the large State shareholdings (Thirteenth Report on Competition Policy, 136).
[16] Dec. 2064/86, Sixteenth Report on Competition Policy, 143 and O.J. 1986, L. 177.
[17] *Ibid.*, 145.
[18] Fifteenth Report on Competition Policy, 125.
[19] Eighteenth Report on Competition Policy, 144.

ture on State aids by each Member State. It will allow the Commission a review of overall policy in this field, as required by the Treaty.[20]

Mention was made at the beginning of this section on the competiton rules applying to Member States of the possibility of discrimination via fiscal measures; they will be examined below under Fiscal Policy. Mention must also be made of aids to Transport, Agriculture and to Fisheries; they were examined in the sections concerning those areas of activity.

Conclusions with regard to competition policy. Community competition policy must be seen as an instrument in the hands of the institutions to ensure that the objectives set out in the Treaty are attained, and not as an end in itself. As pointed out before, the prohibitions concerning undertakings are of great importance, especially when placed in the perspective of the completion of the internal market by 1992. Logical interpretation and systematic application are essential for the necessary legal certainty. Furthermore, without the knowledge that the rules are strictly and objectively implemented, it will be difficult to convince the undertakings that fulfilling Treaty obligations is in their own interest and in that of their purchasers and consumers.

The same considerations apply, of course, to the incompatibility with the common market of State aid, the adjustment of the State monopolies and the behaviour of public enterprises. The Member States have a right to know how the Commission intends to interpret and apply the relevant provisions. They must also have the assurance that the Commission will prosecute any failure by a Member State to fulfil its Treaty obligations in this particular sensitive field. Now that with the completion of the internal market all technical barriers to trade are slowly but surely disappearing the temptation to use, *e.g.* State aids as a protective measure increases.

More important than those prohibitions are the discretionary powers of the Commission both with regard to undertakings and

[20] EEC, Art. 93(1).

Member States. By granting exemptions, the Commission is in a position to develop a constructive competition policy which serves the interests of the Community as a whole. Agreements, mergers, dominant positions, etc., tend to reinforce the competitive position of the Community undertakings both in the internal and in the world market. Economic strength and technological progress require co-operation between undertakings and between the latter and the public authorities. Similarly, by considering State aid compatible with the common market under given conditions, the Commission is able to develop, in close co-operation with the Member States, a Community structural policy which will contribute to the development of economic activities throughout the whole Community.

The policy thus developed through the implementation of the Community competition policy is further strengthened by the financial contributions from the various instruments which the Commission administers. Mention must be made in this respect of the orientation section of the agricultural fund, the regional fund, the social fund, the ECSC funds, the Euratom funds and the Community borrowing and loan facilities. The European Investment Bank also contributes to this effort.

The ultimate goal of all those policies and instruments is the same, *i.e.* to strengthen the structure of the regions and the Community industry. It is essential to keep this in mind in order to see the competition rules in their true relation with the Community objectives.

Further Reading

Annual Commission Reports on Competition Policy.
C. Bellamy and G. Child, "*Common Market Law of Competition*" (3rd ed. 1987), Sweet & Maxwell.
C. S. Kerse, "*EEC Antitrust Procedure*" (2nd ed. 1988), European Law Centre Ltd.
R. P. Whish, "*Competition Law*" (2nd ed. 1989), Butterworths, London.
C. Quigley, "The Notion of State Aids in the EEC" (1988), 13 E.L.Rev., 242

S. Hornsby, "Competition Policy in the 80s: More Policy Less Competition" (1987) 12 E.L.Rev., 79

P. J. Slot, "The Application of Articles 3(f), 5 and 85 to 94 EEC" (1987) 12 E.L.Rev., 179

J. Joshua, "Proof in Contested EEC Competition Cases: A Comparison with the Rules of Evidence in Common Law" (1987) 12 E.L.Rev., 315

Jones, Van der Woude, Lewis, *EEC Competition Law Handbook 1989/90*, (1990) Sweet and Maxwell, London.

Common Market Law Reports, Antitrust Supplement

R. Merkin, *Encyclopedia of Competition Law*, Sweet and Maxwell.

J. F. Beseler and A. Williams, *Anti-Dumping and Anti-Subsidy Law: The European Communities*, (1986), Sweet and Maxwell, London

S. Hounsby, "National and Community Control of Concentrations in a Single Market" (1988) 13 E.L.Rev., 295

V. REGIONAL POLICY

In operation since 1975, regional policy as such was introduced into the Treaty by the SEA[21]; there always were, however, a certain number of provisions[22] referring to the development of regions with particular problems.[23] The European Investment

---

[21] SEA, Art. 23 which added a new Title V "Economic and Social Cohesion" to the Treaty.

[22] See, *e.g.* the fifth paragraph of the Recitals: to ensure "harmonious development by reducing the differences existing between the various regions and the backwardness of the less favoured regions." Art. 2 refers to economic development "throughout the Community." Art. 39 instructs the institutions to take into account, when setting up the CAP, the "structural and natural disparities between the various agricultural regions"; Art. 80: rates and conditions of transport shall take account of "the requirement of an appropriate regional economic policy, the need of under-developed areas and the problems of areas seriously affected by political circumstances"; and finally Art. 92(3): may be considered compatible with the common market State aid "to promote the economic development of areas where the standard of living is abnormally low or where there is serious underemployment."

[23] At the time the Treaty was signed, there were mainly two areas with development problems: the Mezzogiorno in Southern Italy and the Zonenrandgebiet, a stretch of land along the dividing line between the two Germanies.

Bank, for instance, was set up to provide the necessary resources *inter alia* for "developing less developed regions."[24] Moreover, the drafters of the Treaty were convinced that the functioning of the common market, with the resulting development of economic activities, continuous and balanced expansion and accelerated raising of the standards of living would more or less automatically reduce, if not eliminate, regional disparities. Unfortunately, as was pointed out in Chapter V on the common market, the latter never became a full reality because Member States simply did not abide by the rules of the Treaty concerning, *e.g.* the free movement of goods which, more than 30 years after the signing of the Treaty, is not yet effective.

The partial establishment, functioning and development of the common market did, however, achieve spectacular results in most of those areas as evidenced by a doubling, even trebling of their per capita income. Nevertheless, this was not enough for achieving some kind of equality among the regions, in a Community where similar developments were taking place in the well developed areas. The result was that, although the gap between richer and poorer regions may not have widened, it remained relatively stable.[25] It goes without saying that such discrepancies are no longer socially and politically acceptable and create a major problem for the Community as a whole. Even worse, it becomes very difficult, if not impossible, to achieve the necessary economic convergence[26] between the Member States. Indeed, as long as some of them, and their number has increased with each enlargement, have to devote a large fraction of their resources to the development of their less favoured regions, they will be subject to inflation, balance of payment problems and exchange rate fluctuations.

It is also clear that regional imbalances may have a disruptive effect on the completion of the internal market. Indeed, Member

---

[24] EEC, Art. 130(a).

[25] Depending on the method of calibration: Gross National Product per inhabitant or Purchasing Power Parity.

[26] It will be remembered that economic convergence is one of the two means provided for in Art. 2 of the Treaty, to achieve the objectives of the Community.

States have shown dangerous tendencies to have recourse to protective measures where, *e.g.* low productivity and inflation have resulted in increased prices and diminished competitiveness for their industries.

It was at the October 1972 Paris conference of Heads of State or Government that it was agreed that a high priority should be given to the aim of correcting the structural and regional imbalances which might affect the realisation of economic and monetary union.[27] They undertook to co-ordinate their regional policies and invited the Community institutions to create a European Regional Development Fund (ERDF).[28]

It was not until March 1975, however, that the Council adopted the regulation setting up the ERDF[29] and a decision creating a Regional Policy Committee.[30] It is interesting to note that no provisions were made to develop a Community Regional Policy. This had to wait till February 1979 when amendments to the regulation[31] were adopted together with a Resolution concerning guidelines for such a policy.[32] A new Regulation was adopted in 1984 covering both the instruments for a Community regional policy and the fund.[33]

The modifications of the Treaty by the SEA in 1986 introduced the concept of co-ordination of the activities of the structural funds and provided for "such amendments to the structure and the operational rules of the European Agricultural Guidance and Guarantee Fund, Guidance Section (EAGGF Guidance Section), the European Social Fund (ESF) and the ERDF as are necessary to clarify and rationalise their tasks in order to contribute to the achievement of the objectives set out in Article 130a and in

[27] Bull. 10–1972, 9. This was the first "summit" at which Denmark, Ireland and the U.K. participated.
[28] See the Commission's "Report on Regional Problems in the Enlarged Community" Bull. suppl. 8/73.
[29] Reg. 724/75 (O.J. 1975, L. 73/1); it is based upon Art. 235. Initially the ERDF was endowed with the equivalent of 375 million ECU; in 1989 it was 4.5 billion ECU.
[30] O.J. 1975, L. 73/47.
[31] O.J. 1979, L. 35/1.
[32] O.J. 1979, C. 36/10.
[33] O.J. 1984, L. 169/1.

Article 130c of the Treaty, to increase their efficiency and to co-ordinate their activities between themselves and with the operations of the existing financial instruments,"[34] *i.e.* the loan granted through the EIB, the NIC, the ECSC and Euratom. To this end the Commission was required to submit a comprehensive proposal and it was on that basis that the Council adopted a series of Regulations in 1988.

The basic regulation defines the tasks of the Structural Funds[35] and sets out the principles for co-ordinating their activities as between themselves and in relation to the EIB and other financial instruments. It is complemented by four regulations which provide for the actual co-ordination and implementation of the basic regulation itself with regard to each of the three structural funds.[36] The Commission also published a Notice to the Member States on monitoring compliance with public procurement rules in the case of projects and programmes financed by the structural funds and financial instruments.[37]

If the reform of the structural funds results from the modifications introduced in the Treaty by the SEA, it also coincides with the enlargement of the Community to include Portugal and Spain. The latter brought a substantial widening of the already considerable regional disparities in the Community of Ten.[38] This led to a doubling of the population in the least-favoured regions (those with a per capita GDP of less than 50 per cent of the Community average). For the Community it meant the need to use its resources taking into account, *inter alia* the levels of development and unemployment, the importance of declining industries, the relative share of the agricultural sector, the peripheral situation, and the single market.

The reform of the structural funds, which came into force on January 1, 1989, is based on five principles:

---

[34] EEC, Art. 130d.
[35] Reg. 2052/88 (O.J. 1988, L. 185/9).
[36] Regs. 4253–56/88 (O.J. 1988, L. 374/1–25).
[37] See "Guide to the reform of the Community's structural funds" published by the Commission, catalogue no. CB–56–89–223–EN–C, on which this section is based and from which passages are taken.
[38] O.J. 1989, C. 22/3.

(1) *Assistance concentrated on five priority objectives:*

- objective 1: promoting the development and adjustment of the regions whose development is lagging behind (less than 75 per cent of Community average);

- objective 2: converting regions severely affected by industrial decline (criteria: unemployment rate, industrial employment rate and its decline);

- objective 3: combatting long-term unemployment (above 25 years, unemployed for more than 12 months);

- objective 4: facilitating the occupational integration of job-seekers below 25;

- objective 5: consequence of the reform of the CAP:
  5(a) dapting production, processing and marketing structures in agriculture;
  5(b) promoting the development of rural areas (criteria: high proportion of agricultural employment, low level of agricultural income, low level of per capita GDP).

For each one of those objectives an integrated approach of the financial instruments is provided for.

(2) *Partnership*

This is the key principle underlying the reform. It is defined as "close consultation between the Commission, the Member States concerned and the competent authorities designated by the latter at the national, regional, local or other level, with each party acting as a partner in pursuit of a common goal." This partnership covers "the preparation, financing, monitoring and assessment of operations."

Since Community action must "complement" actions in the field, continual dialogue with all the economic operators is required. The nature of partnership will depend on the institutional structure and traditions of each Member State. It will therefore necessarily take many forms.

(3) *Consistency, particularly with the Member States' economic policies*

Investment decisions are frequently influenced by the general economic situation of the region and country where they are to take place. The "plans" and "Community support frameworks" must provide information for assessing the extent to which structural measures are linked to and consistent with, the economic and social policies of the Member States.

(4) *Improved administration of the funds*

At the Brussels European Council meeting in February 1988 it was agreed to double the commitment appropriations of the three structural funds between 1987 and 1993, in real terms. In ECU terms this means a rise from ECU 7 to 14 billion. This doubling is to be accompanied by a more rigorous approach to the administration of the funds. The reform sets out to achieve a better combination of Community loans and grants; this would bring in other financial institutions which, besides additional resources, would provide their expertise in financial engineering. Other measures proposed as part of the reform will also result in better use of financial resources.

(5) *Simplification, monitoring and flexibility*

This will be achieved through uniformity of procedures for the three funds and a machinery for monitoring and assessing Community structural action is set up.

1. Operational arrangements

The new approach provides for four stages:

 (i) requirements are spelled out by the competent national authorities in multi-annual "plans";

 (ii) priorities are determined by the Commission in "Community support frameworks" (CSFs);

 (iii) the operational stage is carried out in partnership with the national authorities and consists in implementing the CSFs through the use of assistance;

 (iv) the CSFs and the assistance granted are monitored and assessed.

2. The Regional Development Fund.

The first fund regulation was adopted by the Council in 1975,[39] and after an important revision in 1979,[40] remained in force until 1984. A new regulation entered into force on January 1, 1985 and provided for some interesting novelties at that time such as the programme financing, economic evaluation of programmes and projects, technical assistance, a higher rate of Community financial participation and the abolition of the "quota-free" section introduced in 1979. A new fund regulation entered into force on January 1, 1989.[41]

Some of the main features of the ERDF are the following:

 – to be eligible for fund assistance, measures must be consistent with and must relate to the priorities laid down in the

---

[39] Reg. 724/75 (O.J. 1975, L. 73/1).
[40] Reg. 214/79 (O.J. 1979, L. 35/1).
[41] Reg. 4254/88 (n. 36 above).

Community support frameworks (CSFs) in response to the
regional plans proposed by the Member States.

– the fund is implemented through:
   operational programmes
   individual large-scale projects
   global grants
   part-financing of national aid schemes

– the eligible measures include:
   public infrastructure
   industry and services
   SMEs structures and services
   technical assistance and preparatory studies
   pilot projects

– the maximum rate of assistance is
   for Objective 1 regions: 75 per cent,
   for others 50 per cent.

– with certain exceptions, Community assistance is conditional upon financing by national authorities.

In implementing the rules concerning the Fund, the Commission is assisted by an Advisory Committee on the Development
and Conversion of Regions. It is made up of Member States'
representatives and chaired by the Commission.[42]

3. Consultative Council of Local and Regional Authorities.

This council was set up by the Commission in 1988. It has 42
members holding elective office at regional or local level and
appointed by the Commission on a proposal from the main
European organisations concerned.[43]

---

[42] Reg. 4253, Art. 27 (*ibid.*).
[43] The Assembly of Regions in Europe, The Council of European Municipalities
and Regions and the International Union of Local Authorities.

Mention must also be made of the Regional Development Programmes which provide a frame of reference for fund assistance and are a key instrument for co-ordinating Member States' regional policies and the Regional impact assessment of Community policies,[44] various specific programmes,[45] Community programmes, indigenous development potential and studies which were created under the former regulation. Also the Integrated Mediterranean Programmes (PIMs) and the European Business and Innovation centres.[46]

4. Conclusion.

As the main Community structural instrument, Community regional policy is fast becoming the essential element of the strategy provided by the Community for implementing the internal market by 1992.

Further Reading

P. Romus, *L'Europe Regionale*, (1990), Brussels.

VI. INDUSTRY POLICY

The manufacturing and service industries are the object of several explicit Treaty provisions. The right of establishment, the freedom to provide services, the free movement of capital, etc., are all of direct concern to them. So are the provisions regarding the Community competition policy, *i.e.* agreements, dominant positions, concentrations, State aid and the so-called "public" undertakings. And since the entry into force of the SEA, the Treaty provides for strengthening "the scientific and technologi-

---

[44] See Twenty-second General Report (1988), 228.
[45] *e.g.* Resider and Renaval, see *ibid*.
[46] For all these aspects of regional policy implementation see the annual General Reports.

cal basis of European industry and to encourage it to become more competitive at international level"; this will be examined hereafter. There is however no reference to industry as a whole and its role within the Community.

The coal and steel industries which fall within the ambit of the ECSC and atomic energy, the development of which is promoted by the Euratom Treaty, are no exception to this rule; they are the result of the first approach to European integration which was purely sectoral. Those two sectors are now administered by the Commission on the basis of their respective Treaties.

This absence of an industrial policy corresponds of course to the more or less liberal conceptions prevailing with regard to economic policies in the fifties. They find their expression in the fundamental freedoms which constitute the characteristics of the common market, reinforced by the competition rules. Maybe this was feasible as long as the economies of the Member States continued to develop, but as soon as the recession of the seventies set in, several industries, supported by their governments, requested Community intervention. But no comprehensive industry policy was decided upon.

Instead, various specific measures were adopted, applicable either to industry as a whole, *e.g.* public contracts,[47] or to particular sectors. The latter approach seemed to be the only possible one. Over the years various measures were adopted either by the Community or, as was seen in the section on State aid, by the Member States with the authorisation or support of the Community. It concerned mainly the reconversion of the steel and coal industry, of shipbuilding, textile, automobile, chemicals, aerospace, etc., etc.[48] Five main areas of Community activity in the industrial sector will be examined hereafter: Enterprises, Intellectual and Industrial Property Rights, Procurement, Research and Technology and, finally, Telecommunications, Information Technology and Innovation.

---

[47] For "works" contracts: Dir. 71/305 (O.J. 1971 (II) 682), Dir. 72/277 (J.O. 1972, L. 176/2), Dir. 78/669 (O.J. 1978, L. 225/41) and for "supply" contracts, Dir. 77/62 (O.J. 1977, L. 13/1), Dir. 80/767 (O.J. 1980, L. 215/1) and Dir. 88/295 (O.J. 1988, L. 127/1).

[48] See the annual General Reports.

1. Enterprises

Particular emphasis is put by the Community on improving the business environment and promoting the development of small and medium-sized enterprises. To that effect a Resolution[49] was adopted by the Council in June 1988 *inter alia* urging the Commission to make speedier progress with the small-business action programme.[50]

Various actions were undertaken by the Commission within the framework of this programme. In 1987 it set up the Centres for European Business Information,[51] *i.e.* information offices with the purpose of promoting communications between businesses and the Commission by enabling businessmen to obtain ready answers to their questions on Community policies. Also, the Commission set up the European Business and Information Centres Network[52] designed to provide practical assistance for the expansion of the small business sector which will create new jobs and provide means of exploiting the potential for growth internally generated in regions where industry is stagnating or in decline.[53]

Within this framework must also be mentioned the Business Co-operation Network.[54] It provides a link between business advisers to enable them to respond very quickly to offers of and requests for co-operation. Finally, the Commission launched "Europartnership 1988" designed to promote the development of small firms in Ireland by encouraging co-operation agreements between them and firms from other Community regions.[55]

[49] O.J. 1988, C. 197/6. For details see Bull. 6–1988, 31.
[50] See Council Resolution of October 1986 (O.J. 1986, C. 287) and Bull. 5–1987, 18 and 2–1988, 30.
[51] See Bull. 4–1987, 17.
[52] O.J. 1987, C. 33 and Bull. 1–1987, 21.
[53] *Ibid.*
[54] Twentieth General Report (1986), 152.
[55] Twenty-first General Report (1987), 137.

2. Industrial and Intellectual Property Rights

The Treaty refers to industrial and commercial property in connection with legitimate prohibitions or restrictions on imports or exports of goods.[56] The expression "industrial and commercial property" can be held to cover all the rights mentioned in the Paris Convention on the Protection of Industrial Property, the Munich Convention on the European Patent and the Luxembourg Convention on the Community Patent.

The owners of such rights enjoy a legal and absolute monopoly (but not necessarily a dominant position), since they can, as any property owner, claim exclusive use. But by doing so they can prevent trade between Member States since the protection is generally afforded by each Member State separately.[57] As the Court put it, in the absence of unification of national rules relating to such protection, industrial property rights and the differences between national rules are capable of creating obstacles to the free movement of products covered by such rights.[58]

The exercise of a property right granted and guaranteed by national law thus constitutes an obstacle to the full application of certain fundamental Community rules. The question therefore arose of how to reconcile the use of those individual rights with the principle of free trade. The answer given by the Court is that the "existence" of the right is not affected by the Treaty, but that the "exercise" of such rights can, under certain conditions, be prohibited by Community law.[59] Consequently, such exercise

---

[56] EEC, Art. 36; such restrictions are provided for as long as they do not "constitute a means of arbitrary discrimination or a disguised restriction on trade between Member States." See under Community Competition Policy where the position of the Court with regard to the use of such rights was discussed.

[57] Except of course when a patent is issued under the Convention on the Community Patent which has the same effects, as regards the rights conferred by it, in all the Member States (O.J. 1976, L. 17/1).

[58] Case 24/67 *Parke, Davis* v. *Centrafarm* [1968] E.C.R. 55 at 71. See also Case 53/87 *Cicra* v. *Renault*, judgment of October 5, 1988 (not yet published): the Court accepted opposition to the import of decorative parts on the basis of national law.

[59] See the cases reported above under Community Competition Policy; also Case 40/70 *Sirena* v. *Eda* [1971] E.C.R. 69.

must be strictly limited to what is necessary to safeguard what constitutes the "specific subject-matter" of those rights.[60]

The question arose however of what is left of this specific subject-matter once the owner has used his rights in one of the Member States. The Court refers to "exhaustion of rights."[61] It was considered to be illegal for a manufacturer of a protected article to prevent the sale of that product in a given Member State when this product had been placed on the market by him or with his consent in another Member State.[62] In other words, once the owner of a right has exercised it in such a way that its use by others in a given Member State is legal, he can no longer claim territorial exclusivity within the common market. The situation can, however, be different in regard to products coming from third countries.[62]

The various rules with regard to property rights and free movement of goods were restated by the Court as follows:

(1) the Treaty does not affect the existence of property rights recognised by the law of the Member States;

(2) the exercise of those rights may, nevertheless, depending on the circumstances, be restricted by the prohibitions of the Treaty;

(3) in as much as an exception to the fundamental principles of the Treaty is provided, it applies only to the extent

---

[60] See Cases 15/74 *Centrafarm* v. *Sterling Drug* and 16/74 *Centrafarm* v. *Winthrop* both [1974] E.C.R. 1147 and 1183, where the Court defined what is the subject-matter of a patent (Case 15/74 at 1162) and of a trade mark (Case 16/74 at 1194); from Case 24/67 *Parke, Davis* (n. 58 above) it follows that one can legally oppose the import and distribution of an unpatented product, otherwise one's own patent becomes useless. The same principle applies where the holder of a specific right prevents the import of a product from another Member State where there is no longer a protection: Case 341/87 *EMI*, judgment of January 24, 1989 (not yet published). See also Case 119/75 *Terrapin* v. *Terranova* [1976] E.C.R. 1039: the protection of a trade mark implies also the right to prevent confusion between two products bearing similar names. It is for the national courts to determine whether a risk for confusion does in fact exist.

[61] Case 15/74 *Centrafarm* (n. 60 above).

[62] See *EMI* Cases 51/75, 86/75 and 96/75, all [1976] E.C.R. 811, 871 and 913.

necessary to safeguard rights which constitute the specific subject-matter of that property;

(4) the owner of the right cannot rely on national law to prevent the importation of a product which has been marketed in another Member State by the owner or with his consent;

(5) it is the same when the right relied on is the result of a sub-division, either voluntary or publicly imposed, of a trademark which originally belonged to a single owner;

(6) even when the rights belong to different proprietors, national law may not be relied on when the exercise of those rights is the purpose, means or result of a prohibited agreement;

(7) it is compatible with the Treaty provisions concerning free trade for the owner of a trademark to prevent the importation of products from another Member State and legally bearing a name giving rise to confusion with the trademark. However, this does not apply when there is an agreement or link between the owner and the producer in the other Member State; their respective rights must also have arisen independently.[63]

As was mentioned in the section on Competition Policy, the Commission issued regulations providing block exemptions for patent licensing[64] and for know-how licensing agreements.[65]

Attention must also be drawn to the Directive to approximate the laws of the Member States relating to trademarks,[66] a

---

[63] Case 119/75 *Terrapin* (n. 60 above).
[64] Reg. 2349/84 (O.J. 1984, L. 219/15, amended O.J. 1985, L. 113/34). See Case 65/86 *Bayer*, judgment of September 27, 1988 (not yet published): the no-challenge clause is admissible under certain conditions.
[65] Reg. 556/89 (O.J. 1989, L. 61/1).
[66] Twenty-second General Report, 134.

Directive on the legal protection of the topographies of semicon-
ductor products[67] and another on the legal protection of bio-
technological inventions.[68]

3. Procurement

Within the framework of the completion of the internal market,
the Commission aims at improving the transparency of public
works[69] and public supply contracts[70] in order to open up public
procurement to intra-Community competition and permit the
introduction of more effective surveillance of the application of
Community rules.

The Commission was rather successful both in the legislative
and in the jurisdictional field. As far as legislation is concerned,
its action programme based on the White Paper concerning the
completion of the internal market provides for several Directives
to be adopted by the Council. In 1988 the Council adopted a
regulation modifying an earlier one on the co-ordination of
procedures for the award of public supply contracts[71] and in 1989
a similar one for public works contracts.[72] The Council also
reached agreement on a directive concerning appeal procedures
in the field of public procurement.

As far as the case-law is concerned, the Court found that
Ireland had failed to fulfil its Treaty obligations concerning the
free movement of goods by asking for tenders which practically
only an Irish undertaking could answer. This case was all the
more interesting since it concerned one of the sectors (water,
energy, transport and telecommunication utilities) which are still
excluded from the existing directives on public procurement. This

---

[67] O.J. 1987, L. 24/36.
[68] O.J. 1989, C. 10.
[69] For a list of existing Directives, see n. 47 above.
[70] *Ibid*.
[71] Dir. 88/295 (O.J. 1988, L. 127/1).
[72] Dir. 89/440 (O.J. 1989, L. 210/1).

means that even in the absence of those directives the Member States have the obligation not to exclude undertakings from the other Community countries.[73]

In May 1987, the Commission set up an Advisory Committee on the Opening-up of Public Procurement[74] and in November it published a "Users Guide to the Community Rules on open Government Procurement.[75]

In 1988 the Community signed the Protocol[76] amending the GATT Agreement on Government Procurement.[77]

Public procurement contracts represent a very important percentage of the transactions taking place in the field of supply and works. Unless this sector is opened to intra-Community competition, the single market will not achieve its objectives. Much remains to be done and it can only be hoped that the Council will be able to adopt the necessary directives in this field before the end of 1992.

4. Research and Technology

In September 1987 the Council adopted[78] the Framework Programme of Community activities in the field of research and technological development (1987–91). It comprises eight activities[79] and serves as a basis for the main Community activities

[73] See also Case 103/88 *Costanzo* v. *Comune di Milano*, judgment of June 22, 1989 (not yet published): *inter alia* direct effect of Dir. 71/305. Another interesting case was the one concerning Denmark and the construction of a bridge on the *Storebaelt*; at the last minute the Commission withdrew its request for an interim Court decision after the Danish Government recognised publicly its mistake.

[74] Twenty-first General Report (1987) 87.

[75] *Ibid.*, at 88.

[76] Dir. 88/295 (O.J. 1988, L. 127/1).

[77] O.J. 1987, L. 345.

[78] O.J. 1987. L. 302/1. See Twenty-first General Report (1987), 143.

[79] Those eight activities are: quality of life, information and communication, modernisation of industrial sectors, exploitation and optimum use of biological resources, energy, science and technology for development, exploitation of the sea bed and of marine resources and improvement of European S/T co-operation.

in this field. Most of those are carried out in the form of multi-annual programmes, both within the Community and in co-operation with third countries.[80]

In November 1988 the Commission adopted a first report on the state of science and technology in Europe.[81] It is worthwhile quoting here the summary published by the Commission[82]:

"A good deal has already been done to improve Europe's situation by increased spending on research and development and by improving industrial performance through innovation. Nevertheless, the overall effort remains unbalanced and piecemeal. Three Member States (Germany, France and the United Kingdom) account for three-quarters of total research and development spending in the Community and there are very pronounced regional variations. Transnational co-operation (Community programmes, Eureka, COST, ESA, CERN, etc.) accounts for only a small proportion of the total research effort.

Europe's efforts in this area are well below those of its two main competitors (the United States and Japan), both of which are spending more and also taking action to remedy their own weaknesses. Europe's position is also threatened by the new efforts of emerging science and technology powers (especially the newly industrialized countries)."

The report highlights five areas of major relevance for the European economy:

— information technology and telecommunications,
— new materials and technology for industry,
— aerospace,

[80] The European co-operation on scientific and technical research (COST) is one of those programmes being carried out with a large number of third countries; see the General Reports.
[81] Bull. 11–1988, 24.
[82] Twenty-second General Report (1988), 162.

— biology and biotechnology, and
— energy.

Some research is carried out by the Community itself in the Joint Research Centre which was set up in pursuance of the Euratom Treaty.[83] The latest five year programme (1988–91) adopted by the Council[84] provides for research in the nuclear and non-nuclear fields. The areas of Community activity are those indicated in the Framework Programme and carried out, as was indicated, mainly through multi-annual programmes.

The Commission, of course, promotes the utilisation of the results of Community-sponsored research and development; in June 1989, the Council adopted a specific programme for the dissemination and utilisation of research results (Value).[85]

5. Telecommunications, Information Technology and Innovation

In 1984 the Community adopted a three-year plan for the transnational development of the support structure for innovation and a five-year programme for the development of the specialised information market,[86] which provided a general framework to develop activities in those fields.

The same year the Council adopted the European Strategic Programme for Research and Development in Information Technology (ESPRIT) which became operational the same year.[87]

Other areas on which the efforts of the Community have focused are: the future shape of the Community's telecommunications industry (RACE),[88] the organisation of a large

---

[83] Euratom, Art. 8(1).
[84] Twenty-second General Report (1988), 164.
[85] Twenty-third General Report (1989), 164.
[86] Eighteenth General Report (1984), 229.
[87] *Ibid.*, at 104; it covers five main areas of activity: micro-electronics, software technology, advanced information processing, office automation and computer-integrated manufacturing.
[88] Research and development in Advanced Communication for Europe; see General Reports.

European market for information equipment and services and implementation of a programme on the development of telecommunications infrastructure and services in the less-favoured areas of the Community (STAR).[89]

The Community's efforts in those fields aim at developing a powerful common market for telecommunciations and information technology equipment and services.

Further Reading

Encyclopedia of U.K. and European Patents, London.

Melville, *Forms and Agreements on Intellectual Property and International Licensing*, (1990), London.

N. Hunnings, "Industrial Property Law in the Common Market," London, (1973–1988). E.L.C. at Sweet and Maxwell, London

M. Milmo, "European Commercial Cases" E.L.C. at Sweet and Maxwell, London

J. Dine, "The Community Company Law Harmonisation Programme" (1989) 14 E.L.Rev., 322.

F. Weiss, "Public Procurement in the EEC – Public Supply Contracts" (1988) 13 E.L.Rev., 318.

J. Scherer, "European Telecommunication Law: The Framework of the Treaty" (1987) 12 E.L.Rev., 354.

VII. SOCIAL POLICY

The free movement of workers and related social security advantages were examined earlier in this book in the Chapter on the Common Market.[90] Under the Title "Social Policy,"[91] which in the Treaty is divided into a chapter on Social Provisions and one on the Social Fund, Member States agreed to promote "improved working conditions" and an "improved standard of living."[92]

---

[89] Special Telecommunication Action for Regional Development.
[90] EEC, Arts. 48–51.
[91] EEC, Arts. 117–128, including Arts. 118a and 118b added by the SEA.
[92] EEC, Art. 117(1). See also Treaty Preamble and Art. 3(i).

The task of the Commission in this field is to promote close co-operation between the Member States particularly in matters relating to employment, labour law and working conditions, basic and advanced vocational training, social security, prevention of occupational accidents and diseases, occupational hygiene and the right of association, and collective bargaining between employers and workers.[93]

Curiously enough the initial provision of this Title is drafted as a recital of the Preamble: the Member States

> "believe that such a development will ensue not only from the functioning of the common market, which will favour the harmonization of social systems, but also from the procedures provided in this Treaty and from the approximation of provisions laid down by law, regulation and administrative action."[94]

More recently with the plans for completing the internal market by 1992, its social dimensions were emphasised both in the Treaty[95] and by the European Council.[96] Consequently, the Commission adopted a Working Paper on the Social Dimension of the Internal Market[97] which constitutes the framework for its activities in the coming years with regard to social policy.

1. Employment

As the Commission pointed out:

> "any social policy, whether Community or national, must have as its first priority an endeavour to help solve the grave

[93] EEC, Art. 118.
[94] EEC, Art. 117(2).
[95] EEC, Arts. 118a and 118b and Art. 130a.
[96] European Council in Hanover in June 1988 (Bull. 6–1988, 8).
[97] Bull. 9–1988, 8.

problem of unemployment and reduce the unevenness of its impact. Over the last few years, the Community's unemployment rate has remained almost unchanged at 11 per cent of the labour force, which means that more than 16 million Europeans wishing to work are unable to find employment."[98]

Furthermore, many of the unemployed are under 25 and more than half live in 42 regions (out of 161) where the rate is over 12 per cent.

In December 1986 the Council adopted a Resolution relating to an action programme on employment growth,[1] called co-operative growth strategy for more employment. According to the Commission it is necessary to adapt this strategy to the current economic situation which is showing a return to expansion with favourable effects on employment.

2. Social Policy and the Internal Market

Not only must all the obstacles to free movement of persons[2] and freedom of establishment be eliminated, but mutual recognition of professional qualifications has to be implemented. Since the creation of a large number of new jobs, as a consequence of the completion of the internal market, will go hand in hand with the loss of others, and since the new jobs will require different qualifications, supporting Community measures are needed.[3] One of those measures is the reinforcement of vocational training.

3. Vocational Training

Various programmes were adopted by the Community in this field, *e.g.* COMETT, programme for co-operation between universities

---

[98] *Ibid.*
[99] See Reg. providing exceptional financial support for Greece in the social field, amended in 1988 (O.J. 1988, L. 362/1).
[1] O.J. 1986, C. 340.
[2] The Commission decided to promote access to employment in public service, focussing on bodies responsible for running commercial services, public health care services, teaching in State educational establishments and research for non-military purposes in public establishments (O.J. 1988, C. 72).
[3] n. 97 at 9.

and industry in training for technology,[4] ERASMUS, European Community Action Scheme for the Mobility of University Students.[5]

The European Centre for the Development of Vocational Training issues guidelines for activities programmes which cover, *e.g.* correspondence of vocational training qualifications, establishment of a European directory of careers, study activities and research and publications.

4. Other Measures and Community Activities

— Social security with various programmes (fight against poverty, economic and social integration of the least-favoured groups, social protection);

— social security for migrant workers (amendment of existing regulations, Administrative Commission on Social Security for Migrant Workers);

— social integration of the disabled (action programme Helios[6]);

— labour law and living conditions (migration policy in relation to third countries,[7] ECSC subsidised housing scheme[8]), with the help of the European Foundation for the Improvement of Living and Working Conditions;

— Social dialogue and industrial relations[9];

— Health and Safety (public health *inter alia* "Europe against Cancer" programme,[10] safety at work,[11] ECSC health and safety[12] and Euratom health and safety measures).

---

[4] O.J. 1989, L. 13.
[5] O.J. 1987, L. 166. Second programme for the academic year 1990–1991 was accepted in 1989 (O.J. 1989, L. 395/23).
[6] O.J. 1988, L. 104/38.
[7] O.J. 1988, L. 183.
[8] Twenty-second General Report (1988), 221.
[9] EEC, Art. 118b.
[10] O.J. 1987, C. 50.
[11] O.J. 1988, L. 183.
[12] O.J. 1986, L. 137.

5. Social Fund (SF)

The Treaty provides for the establishment of a "European Social Fund" in order to improve employment opportunities for workers in the common market and to contribute thereby to the raising of the standard of living.[13]

The SF is administered by the Commission, assisted by a Social Fund Committee composed of representatives of governments, trade unions and employers organisations.[14] The fund resources are provided by the Community budget from the Community's own resources. The main function is to reimburse Member States, or bodies governed by public law, 50 per cent of the expenditure incurred for (a) ensuring re-employment by means of vocational retraining[15] and resettlement allowances and (b) granting aid for the benefit of workers whose employment is reduced or temporarily suspended as a result of the conversion of an undertaking to other production.[16]

In pursuance of the provisions introduced into the Treaty by the SEA,[17] the SF was, together with the other structural funds, amended to increase its effectiveness and to co-ordinate its activities with the other funds.[18]

Accordingly the operations eligible under the SF now are: vocational training operations, accompanied where necessary by vocational guidance, and subsidies towards recruitment into newly created stable jobs and towards the creation of self-employed activities.[19] The "priority objectives" are the same for the three structural funds although their participation in the

---

[13] EEC, Art. 123.
[14] EEC, Art. 124.
[15] With regard to vocational training and the Council's power of decision see Case 242/87 *Commission* v. *Council*, judgment of May 30, 1989 (not yet published).
[16] EEC, Art. 125.
[17] EEC, Art. 130d.
[18] Reg. 2052/88 on the task of the structural funds and on co-ordination of their activities (O.J. 1988, L. 185/9) and the implementing Regs. 4253/88 and 4255/88 (O.J. 1988, L. 374/1 and 21).
[19] Reg. 4255/88, Art. 1(1).

realisation of them differs greatly. The SF is the only one to contribute to the attainment of all five objectives.[20]

The SF may partly reimburse Member States for expenditure to cover:

(a) the income of persons receiving vocational training;

(b) the costs for vocational training operations and for subsistence and travel of those covered;

(c) the granting of subsidies towards recruitment into newly created stable jobs and towards the creation of self-employed activities;

(d) other activities provided for in the Regulation.

Applications for assistance must be presented in the form of operational programmes, global grant schemes or actions.[21]

Resources available for commitments under the 1989 budget amounted to 3.387 million ECU.

6. Equal Opportunity for Men and Women

The Treaty provides that each Member State must ensure and maintain the application of the principle that men and women should receive equal pay for equal work.[22] According to the Treaty "pay" means the ordinary basic wage or salary and any other consideration, whether in cash or in kind, which the worker receives.

Several directives were adopted by the Council to implement the principle of equality between men and women[23] and many

---

[20] See Reg. 2052/88, Arts. 1 and 2.

[21] Reg. 4255/88, Art. 6.

[22] EEC, Art. 119.

[23] Dir. 75/117 (O.J. 1975, L. 45/19), see Case 237/85 *Rummler* v. *Dato-Druck* [1986] E.C.R. 2101; Dir. 76/207 (O.J. 1976, L. 39/40), see Case 318/86 *Commission* v. *France*, judgment of June 30, 1988 (not yet published); Dir. 79/7 (O.J. 1979, L. 6/24).

judgments of the Court have clarified the concept.[24] In a recent case[25] the Court decided that when there are important differences between the pay of men and that of women, and they cannot be explained, it is up to the employer to prove that there is no discrimination.

The Commission submitted to the Council, which approved them by Resolution, medium-term programmes: 1982–1985[26] and 1986–1990.[27] The latter, in the words of the Commission, provides for an overall and diversified strategy, aimed at improving the application of existing provisions, in education and training, employment, the new technologies, social security and protection, the sharing of family and job responsibilities and changing attitudes.[28]

To borrow once again the words of the Commission, "although progress has been made, much remains to be done and a comprehensive and wide-ranging policy will be needed to achieve results in the field of equal opportunities."[29]

Further Reading

N. Hunnings, "EEC Employment Cases" (1988) E.L.C. at Sweet and Maxwell, London.
A. Riley, "The European Social Charter and Community Law" (1989) 14 E.L.Rev., 80.
M. Gould, "The European Social Charter and Community Law – A Comment" (1989) 14 E.L.Rev., 223.

VIII. ECONOMIC AND MONETARY POLICY

In this field also the SEA introduced new provisions into the Treaty. A new Chapter was inserted in Part Three, Title II, reading

---

[24] The most famous cases are without doubt the *Defrenne* cases: Case 80/70 *Defrenne* v. *Belgium* [1971] E.C.R. 445 and Case 43/75 *Defrenne* v. *Sabena* [1976] E.C.R. 455. See also Case 61/81 *Commission* v. *U.K.* [1982] E.C.R. 2601 and Case 165/82 *Commission* v. *U.K.* [1983] E.C.R. 3431.
[25] Case 109/88, *Handels Forbund* v. *Danfoss*, Judgment of October 17, 1989 (not yet published).
[26] O.J. 1982, C. 186/2.
[27] O.J. 1986, C. 203/2.
[28] Nineteenth General Report (1985), 181.
[29] Bull. 1985, 53.

as follows: "Co-operation in Economic and Monetary Policy (Economic and Monetary Union)." The Treaty now refers explicitly to "convergence" of economic and monetary policies.[30] It will be remembered that in order to achieve the objectives of the Community, two means were provided by the Treaty: the creation and development of the common market and the convergence of the economic policies of the Member States. More concretely, the Treaty calls for "the application of procedures by which the economic policies of Member States can be co-ordinated and disequilibria in their balances of payments remedied."[31] It also provides for measures to be taken by the institutions and the Member States with regard to conjunctural policy[32] and balance of payments.[33] In order to promote co-ordination of the policies of the Member States in the monetary field, a Monetary Committee[34] and a Committee of the Governors of the Central Banks[35] were set up.

Finally, a Committee for Budgetary Policy started functioning in 1965, in order to try to co-ordinate various questions concerning the presentation, the duration, the composition, etc., of the national budgets.

The Treaty provides for Community action, *i.e.* granting of mutual assistance, where a Member State is in difficulty as regards its balance of payments.[36] In pursuance of those provisions, the Community several times borrowed in order to provide

---

[30] See EEC, Art. 2, although the expression used there is "progressively approximating"; "converging" sounds definitely more modern!

[31] EEC, Art. 3(g).

[32] EEC, Art. 103. Several Reg., Dirs. and Decs. were issued in pursuance of this provision; see, *e.g.* Dec. 74/120 (O.J. 1974, L. 63/16), modified in 1979 (O.J. 1979, L. 35/8). A Committee for Conjunctural Policy was also set up.

[33] EEC, Arts. 104–109. The most used of these provisions is Art. 105 (co-operation between appropriate administrative departments and between Central Banks); see, *e.g.* Dec. 64/300 concerning co-operation between the Central Banks (O.J. 1963–1964, 141) and the programmes for medium-term economic policy (O.J. 1982, L. 236/1).

[34] EEC, Art. 105(2). Its mandate was enlarged in 1964 to include international monetary aspects.

[35] Eighth EEC General Report (1964–65), para. 134.

[36] EEC, Art. 108.

financial assistance to Member States, or authorised them to take or maintain certain safeguard measures.[37]

In 1974 the Council adopted a Decision on the Attainment of a High Degree of Convergence of the Economic Policies of the Member States[38] in pursuance of which the Commission publishes an Annual Report on the Economic Situation of the Community. This Report is adopted yearly by the Council together with the orientations of economic policy for the following year.[39]

1. Economic and Monetary Union

Those various measures do not, of course, constitute an overall Community policy in the economic and monetary fields. This was tried, some years back, in the form of an Economic and Monetary Union. On the basis of a report drawn up by a committee under the chairmanship of Mr. Pierre Werner, the then Prime Minister of Luxembourg, the Council and the Representatives of the Member States expressed their political will to establish this Union. It would be set up in phases starting on January 1, 1971.[40] The final objective was the establishment of an area within which persons, goods, services and capital would move freely.[41] It would form an individualised entity within the

---

[37] Safeguard measures in Ireland and the U.K. (O.J. 1978, L. 45/29–30); Greece (O.J. 1988, L. 218/19). With regard to loans see Reg. concerning the Community loan mechanism designed to support Member States' payments balances (O.J. 1985, L. 118) and Community loans to France (O.J. 1983, L. 153/44) and to Greece (O.J. 1985, L. 341/17). See also special financial assistance to Portugal for an industrial development programme (O.J. 1988, L. 185/21).

[38] O.J. 1974, L. 63/16.

[39] O.J. 1988, L. 377/1; *inter alia* adoption of guidelines for 1990.

[40] Council Dec. (J.O. 1970, L. 59/44; O.J. (2nd), 11) and Resolution (J.O. 1971, C. 28/1; O.J. (2nd) IX, 40). Measures were to be taken during the first stage ending on December 31, 1973; these included: co-ordination of short-term economic policies, measures in the regional and structural field, co-ordination of monetary and credit policies, narrowing of fluctuations of exchange rates, etc.

[41] The reader will have noticed that those are practically the same words as the ones defining "internal market" in Art. 8a, introduced in the Treaty by the SEA (but nearly 20 years later).

international system. It would also, in the economic and monetary fields, have powers and responsibilities allowing its institutions to administer the Union. Community instruments would be created whenever necessary.

The first stage was rather successfully implemented, but the oil and ensuing economic crises of the 70s made the transition to the second stage impossible.[42]

As was pointed out at the beginning of this section, the words "Economic and Monetary Union" are back (although within brackets) but this time in the Treaty itself. This proves not only that the idea never was abandoned, but that economic integration without monetary integration is not viable. The Treaty now clearly states that convergence of economic and monetary policies is "necessary for the further development of the Community." The Treaty even refers to the necessary institutional changes.

At its meeting in Hanover in June 1988, the European Council gave new impetus to the realisation of the economic and monetary union. It set up a Committee composed of the governors of the Central Banks and monetary experts, under the chairmanship of the President of the Commission. It was instructed to study and propose concrete steps that would lead towards economic and monetary union.[43]

The report was produced in April 1989.[44] It first points out that economic and monetary union implies far more than a single market. It requires major steps in all areas of economic policy-making, and presupposes a high degree of integration, a common monetary policy and consistent economic policies. The realisation of the Union would require amendments of the Treaty and changes in the national legislations. Among the reasons mentioned was that within the Union there can be only one monetary policy, the conduct of which would require the creation of a

---

[42] See however Bull. 10–1977, 15: "The Prospect of Economic and Monetary Union" and Bull. 2–1978, 16 for an action programme presented by the Commission.

[43] Twenty-second General Report (1988), 88.

[44] For a summary, see Bull. 4–1989, 8.

European System of Central Banks (ESCB). The latter would consist of a new Community institution and the existing national central banks, co-existing within this federal structure. It would be independent of the national and Community authorities. Its primary objective would be to ensure price stability and to support the Community's general economic policies.

According to the Report, a single currency is not strictly necessary to monetary union.

The relationship between the existing institutions and the ESCB must be clearly defined and some decision-making authority will have to be transferred from the national to the Community level, respecting the principle of subsidiarity.

Further action would be needed:

   (i) strengthening of competition policy and other measures to improve market mechanisms;

  (ii) common policies for structural adjustment and regional development, and

 (iii) tighter macroeconomic policy co-ordination, including binding budgetary rules.

Although no timetable is given, the union would be completed in three stages.

The first stage would consist in strengthening economic and monetary policy co-ordination within the existing institutional framework and preparation and ratification of the Treaty amendments.

Stage two would involve the setting up of the new monetary institution and strengthening of the provisions concerning economic policy co-ordination.

Stage three would start with the irreversible locking of the exchange rates and the transfer of economic and monetary authority to the Community institutions including the ESCB.[45]

---

[45] Bull. 4–1989, 8.

At the European Council meeting in Strasburg in June 1989, it was decided that the first stage would start on July 1, 1990 and the Commission, the Committee of Central Bank Governors and the Monetary Committee were asked to carry out the preparatory work for the organisation of an Intergovernmental Conference to lay down the subsequent stages.[46] In other words, whether one likes it or not, Economic and Monetary Union is on its way.

2. The European Monetary System (EMS)

The EMS was set up by the European Council at its Bremen meeting in July 1978. Its objective is to create a zone of monetary stability in Europe by eliminating erratic parity changes between the Member States' currencies. The system has four main characteristics: a European monetary unit, an exchange rate and intervention mechanism, a credit mechanism and a transfer mechanism. It came into operation on March 13, 1979.[47] The peseta was included in June 1989.

The European Monetary or Currency Unit (ECU) is at the centre of the system. It serves as a *numéraire*: each currency has a central rate expressed in this unit. It serves as the basis for the "divergence indicator" (see next mechanism) and as denominator for claims and liabilities arising under the intervention and the credit mechanisms. Finally, it serves also as a means of settlement between the monetary authorities of the Community.

The Exchange Rate and Intervention Mechanism. The central rates of the national currencies, expressed in ECUs, are used to establish a grid of bilateral exchange rates. The system provides for fluctuation margins of 2.25 per cent around those established rates (it was 6 per cent for Italy and still is for Ireland). The intervention mechanism is supported by unlimited very short-term credit facilities. Settlements are made through the European Monetary Co-operation Fund (EMCF).

---

[46] Bull. 6–1989, 11.
[47] Regs. 3180/78 and 3181/78 (O.J. 1978, L. 379/1–2).

The existing *Credit Mechanisms*: short-term monetary support and short-term and medium-term credit are maintained and strengthened.

Under the *Transfer Mechanism*, the NCI (new borrowing and lending instrument) and the EIB made about 1 million ECU per year available to Italy and Ireland, on special conditions, for the financing of selected infrastructure projects and programmes.

As the Commission pointed out[48] the exchange-rate stability provided by the EMS constitutes a vital factor in the development of the ECU, which is being used increasingly by the private sector on financial markets and in international transactions in Europe, and is now maturing into a currency in its own right.

The system has evolved over the past 10 years, its rules have been adapted and its procedures have been implemented flexibly. The Basel/Nyborg agreement[49] of September 1987 provided a more balanced implementation of the exchange-rate commitment in order to spread the burden of protecting monetary stability against external shocks more evenly among the Member States. A system of macroeconomic indicators geared to the needs of the EMS was created. By ensuring closer co-ordination of monetary policies within the Community, the Basle/Nyborg agreement marked a new phase for the EMS and considerably improved the way in which it functions. There has been no EMS realignment since January 1987. By the end of that year all 12 Member States were participating in the system of swaps used to create official ECUs, as well as taking part in the EMS surveillance and monitoring procedures. The Bank of International Settlements (BIS) and the Swiss National Bank have been accorded the status of Other Holder of official ECUs.

The EMS has led to a reduction in the variability of nominal and real exchange rates among the currencies participating in the exchange-rate mechanism, to lower levels of inflation and to smaller interest-rate differentials. It has also played a vital role in bringing monetary policies and performances closer together.

[48] Bull. 3–1989, 8.
[49] Bull. 9–1987, 12.

Nevertheless, divergences between EMS countries remain with regard to budget policies and current account imbalances. On the other hand, the success of the internal market requires closer economic and monetary co-operation. The EMS will have an important role to play in ensuring that the internal market functions smoothly.

3. The Development of the ECU

The ECU is composed of the participating national currencies weighted to represent the percentage shares of trade as between Member States, the so-called "basket." The proportions within this basket were changed at the occasion of the inclusion of the peseta and the escudo.[50]

While the financial use of the ECU by the private sector has expanded rapidly, it has also become a major financial instrument at the international level, overtaking most of its component currencies in its international financial use. However, the temporary nature of the official ECU and its treatment more as a reserve asset are factors holding back its development. Until these drawbacks are rectified, the official ECU will not be much more than an accounting unit.

The exact value of the ECU in various currencies is published daily by the Commission in the Official Journal.

The Community financial activities were increased by the creation of the *New Community Borrowing and Lending Instrument* (NCI) in 1978.[51] The aim is to borrow funds on the capital markets on behalf of the Community and to lend the proceeds for the purpose of promoting investment and creating jobs. Priority should be given to investments carried out by small and medium-sized undertakings, particularly those designed either to diversify

---

[50] Reg. 1771/89 (O.J. 1989, L. 189/1). See Twenty-third General Report (1989), 87.
[51] O.J. 1978, L. 298/9; 1982, L. 78/19; 1983, L. 112/26 and 1987, L. 71/34.

rural economies or to safeguard the rural environment or to develop new technologies.[52] Since those borrowing and lending activities have to be closely co-ordinated with those of the EIB and other financial instruments of the Community (ECSC and Euratom), all of them are administered by the Bank.

Finally, mention must be made here of the *European Financial Area* which should constitute an area within which all financial transaction can be accomplished without any other procedure than the one applying in the Member State of origin.

In December 1985, the Council adopted Directives co-ordinating laws, regulations and administrative provisions relating to undertakings for collective investment in transferable securities (Ucits) and abolishing exchange restrictions on the free movement of units issued by Ucits.[53]

IX. TAX PROVISIONS AND VAT

1. Indirect Taxes

The objective of the Treaty[54] is to ensure free movement of goods by prohibiting the direct or indirect[55] imposition by Member States of internal taxation of any kind, on products from other Member States, in excess of that imposed directly or indirectly on similar[56] domestic products. Also prohibited are internal taxes

---

[52] Twenty-second General Report (1988), 96.
[53] O.J. 1985, L. 372/39 and 375/3. They entered into force on October 1, 1989, but only the U.K., France, Luxembourg and Ireland had transposed the Dirs. into national law!
[54] EEC, Art. 95.
[55] These terms must be widely interpreted: Case 28/67 *Molkerei-Zentrale West-falen* v. *Hauptzollamt Paderborn* [1968] E.C.R. 143.
[56] Similarity exists when the products in question are normally to be considered as coming within the same fiscal, customs or statistical classification: Case 27/67 *Finck-Frucht* (n. 57 below) or when the products have the same characteristics and meet the same needs from the point of view of the consumer: see Cases

imposed on products from other Member States of such a nature as to afford protection to other products.[57]

This prohibition is akin to the one examined in Chapter Three: elimination of measures with effects equivalent to quantitative restrictions.[58] The prohibition of discrimination through taxation[59] was also mentioned in the section on Competition Policy; it could indeed be considered as a measure of public authorities affecting competition and interstate trade.[60] The Treaty provisions prohibiting tax discrimination can be invoked before the national courts and tribunals, *i.e.* they have direct effect.[61]

The tax provisions do not, however, restrict the freedom of the Member States to establish the system of taxation which they consider the most suitable.[62] This includes tax systems which differentiate between products on the basis of objective criteria such as the nature of the raw materials used,[63] although the Treaty prohibits, for instance, a system of taxation affecting differently whisky and other spirits.[64] Since the Treaty refers to products "from other Member States," products from third countries are not included.[65]

168/78 and 170/78 *Commission* v. *France* and the *U.K.* (see n. 57 below).

[57] EEC, Art. 95(2); this provision also has direct effect: Case 27/67 *Fink-Frucht* v. *Haüptzollamt Munchen* [1968] E.C.R. 223. The function of Art. 95(2) is to cover all forms of indirect tax protection in the case of products which, without being similar, are nevertheless in competition, even partial, indirect or potential, with certain products of the importing country: Case 168/78 *Commission* v. *France* [1980] E.C.R. 347 and Case 170/78 *Commission* v. *U.K.* [1983] E.C.R. 2265, where the Court considered discriminatory the imposition of higher taxes on wine than on beer.

[58] EEC, Art. 30.

[59] Case 168/78 *Commission* v. *France* [1980] E.C.R. 347.

[60] The Court found that Art. 95 constitutes, in the field of taxation, the indispensable foundation of the common market.

[61] Case 57/65 *Lütticke* v. *Hauptzollamt Saarlouis* [1966] E.C.R. 205.

[62] Case 127/75 *Bobie* v. *Hauptzollamt Aachen-Nord* [1976] E.C.R. 1079.

[63] Case 140/79 *Chemial Farmaceutici* v. *DAF* [1981] E.C.R. 1.

[64] Case 216/81 *Cogis* v. *Amministrazione delle Finanze dello Stato* [1982] E.C.R. 2701. See Sixteenth General Report (1982), 315.

[65] Case 148/77 *Hansen* v. *Hauptzollamt Flensburg* [1978] E.C.R. 1787; not to be confused with Case 153/80 *Rumhaus Hansen* v. *Hauptzollamt Flensburg* [1981] E.C.R. 1165, where the Court held that Art. 95 also applies to tax advantages granted under the legislation of a Member State; those must be extended to

Where exports are concerned, the Treaty prohibits repayment of internal taxation beyond the actually imposed charges.[66]

2. Harmonisation of Indirect Taxes

In its White Paper on the completion of the internal market,[67] the Commission pointed out that taxation will be one of the areas most affected. The remission of tax on exports and the taxing of imports in intra-Community trade, and the attendant checks, constitute what have come to be known as "tax frontiers." The removal of those frontiers, which is essential if a single market is to be achieved, calls for a substantial harmonisation of VAT and excise duties so as to avoid distortion of competition and diversion of trade.

The Commission made several proposals to the Council for the harmonisation of VAT rates, but owing to the wide existing differences, it has not been possible until now to arrive at an agreement at the Council level. The latest proposals were sent in May 1989. In December, the Council reached agreement on the gradual alignment of VAT rates. Where the standard rate is concerned, Member States undertook not to depart, before January 1, 1993 from the 14 to 20 per cent rate band proposed by the Commission. In addition, before that date, the Council will decide on the rate band or minimum rate applicable from the same date within the 14 to 20 per cent range. Furthermore, before that the

products originating in other Member States. When such an advantage is made conditional upon the possibility of inspecting production on national territory it is discriminatory by nature and prohibited by Art. 95: Joined Cases 142–143/80 *Amministrazione delle Finanze dello Stato* v. *Essevi and Salengo* [1981] E.C.R. 1413. See also Case 38/82 *Hauptzollamt Flensburg* v. *Hansen* [1983] E.C.R. 1271.
[66] Case 45/64 *Commission* v. *Italy* [1965] E.C.R. 857 and [1969] E.C.R. 433. Where a cumulative multi-stage tax system applies (*e.g.* VAT), Member States may establish average rates: Art. 97. See Dir. 68/221 (O.J. 1968(I) 114).
[67] Nineteenth General Report (1985), 90.

Council will decide on the level and scope of the reduced rate[68] and zero rates which can continue to be applied without distorting competition.

As regards excise-duty rates, the Council has not gone beyond the stage of examining Commission proposals.[69]

3. Turnover Tax (VAT)

The principle of VAT was defined in the First VAT Directive.[70] It consists in the application to goods and services, up to and including the retail stage, of a general tax on consumption. This tax is exactly proportional to the "production" price of the goods and services, regardless of the number of transactions which take place during the production and distribution process, before the stage at which tax is charged. This implies that on each transaction VAT will be calculated on the price of the goods and services chargeable at that stage. At each stage the VAT already paid for the various cost components will be deducted from the VAT to be paid at that stage.[71]

The Second VAT Directive specifies the method of implementing those principles. It is now uniformly applied in all the Member States. Unfortunately the latter were allowed to determine their own rates, with the consequences just described.

The system was introduced on July 1, 1972 by the Third VAT Directive.[72] A small part of the VAT revenue accrues to the Community as own resources.[73]

---

[68] There are indeed two "rate bands": the "normal" one, *i.e.* 14 to 20 per cent (the width of this band will have to be reduced) and the "reduced" one (something in the area of 5 to 9 per cent). Furthermore, there are three Member States (U.K., Ireland and Portugal) which apply a zero rate on products like food and childrens clothes; the question is whether those can be allowed to remain.

[69] Twenty-third General Report (1989), 125.

[70] O.J. 1967, 14.

[71] Case 15/81 *Schul* v. *Inspecteur der invoerrechten en accijnzen* [1982] E.C.R. 1409 at 1426(10).

[72] O.J. 1969 (II) 55. The Fourth and Fifth concern introduction of VAT in Italy (J.O. 1971, L. 203/41 and 1972, L. 162/18).

[73] See above "Financing Community activities."

Of the many other VAT Directives adopted by the Council,[74] mention must be made of the Sixth establishing a uniform base of assessment.[75] Many other Directives were nothing more than temporary derogations from that Directive.[76]

Finally, mention should be made of various other Directives: on the excise duties for tobacco products,[77] duty free allowances in international travel,[78] exemption for fuel held in commercial motor vehicle tanks,[79] common rates of capital duty[80] and mutual assistance of Tax Authorities.[81]

4. Direct Taxes

The Treaty does not provide for harmonisation of direct taxes, but the general harmonisation provisions[82] provide the necessary powers.[83] Several proposals for Directives were made to the Council by the Commission; very few were adopted.[84] However, the Council and the Representatives of the Member States

---

[74] Eighth: concerns refunds to non-Community persons (O.J. 1979, L. 331/11); Ninth: postponing the Sixth (O.J. 1978, L. 194/16); Eleventh: excluding the French overseas territories (O.J. 1980, L. 590/41). Concerning the Sixth and Ninth see Case 70/83 *Kloppenburg* v. *Finanzamt Leer* [1984] E.C.R. 1075.

[75] O.J. 1977, L. 145/1.

[76] See, *e.g.* Eighteenth VAT Dir. concerning various temporary derogations which are to be ended (Bull. 7/8–1989, 2.1.33).

[77] Dir. 72/464 (J.O. 1972, L. 303/1, last modified in 1986 (O.J. 1986, L. 164/26). For duties on alcoholic beverages see Case 170/78 *Commission* v. *U.K.* [1980] E.C.R. 417.

[78] Dir. 69/169 (J.O. 1969, L. 133/6; O.J. 1969 (I), 232). See Case 158/80 *Rewe* v. *Kiel* [1981] E.C.R. 1805. See also three Dirs. on tax-free allowances on imports (O.J. 1983, L. 105/38); Dir. 83/183 was modified by Dir. 89/604 (O.J. 1989, L. 348).

[79] Dir. 68/297 (J.O. 1968, L. 175/15; O.J. 1968 (II), 313, modified O.J. 1985, L. 183/22).

[80] Dir. 73/80 (O.J. 1973, L. 103/15).

[81] Dir. 77/799 (O.J. 1977, L. 336/15).

[82] EEC, Arts. 100–102, included Arts. 100a and 100b added by the SEA.

[83] See Programme for the Harmonisation of Direct Taxes, Bull. Suppl. 8/1967.

[84] See General Reports. A general reference to direct taxes no longer appears in those Reports since 1985.

recognised that harmonisation was necessary to achieve the effective liberalisation of the free movement of goods, persons, services and capital and to accelerate economic integration.[85]

Further Reading

N. Hunnings, "EEC VAT Cases", (1987) E.L.C. at Sweet and Maxwell, London.

X. ENERGY POLICY

A Community energy policy as such is not provided for under any of the European Treaties, although coal, previously a main source of energy, has been the object of Community measures since 1952. That year the ECSC Treaty entered into force. Furthermore the development of nuclear energy has been the objective of the Euratom Treaty since 1958.

Back in 1968, the Commission forwarded to the Council a document entitled "First Guidelines for a Community Energy Policy."[86] It put the emphasis on the need to adapt the structure of the Community industry so as to enable it to meet expanding demand under the required conditions as regards costs and security of supply.[87] The basic principles of the Memorandum were approved by the Council[88] which only issued two Regulations concerning notification of imports and investment projects in the energy field.[89]

After nine years of procrastination, the Member States and the Community were caught totally unprepared for the first oil shock of 1973. Yet even this major event, which was to change

---

[85] Council Resolution of March 22, 1971 (J.O. 1971, C. 28/1; O.J. Ser. IX, 40).
[86] Second General Report (1968), 251.
[87] Third General Report (1969), 251.
[88] Fourth General Report (1970), 207.
[89] J.O. 1972, L. 120/3–7; O.J. 1970 (II), 462–466. See also Reg. 1025 (J.O. 1970, L. 124/6; O.J. 1970 (II), 309 and O.J. 1974, L. 32/1) and two Regs. introducing registration of imports (O.J. 1979, L. 220/1 and L. 197/1); registration was suspended in 1981 (O.J. 1981, L. 52/1).

fundamentally the world's economic conditions, could not incite the Governments of the Nine to formulate, let alone implement, a common energy policy. The only action that could be obtained was a Directive on measures to mitigate the effects of difficulties in the supply of crude oil and petroleum products.[90] It was, however, left to the individual Member States to take the necessary measures.

In order to increase the independence of the Community in matters of energy, the Council adopted a framework Regulation on the granting of financial support for projects to exploit alternative energy sources.[91] Those projects may relate, *e.g.* to geothermal sites,[92] liquefaction and gasification of solid fuels, solar energy, wave energy or tidal energy. Another Regulation was adopted on the granting of support for demonstration projects which offer substantial improvement in the efficiency with which energy is used.[93] Those programmes were renewed, complemented and extended over the years and the more rational utilisation of energy became the subject of a series of Resolutions,[94] Directives[95] and Recommendations.[96]

In 1980 the Council adopted a Resolution on Community Energy Objectives for 1990 and convergence of the Member States' policies. New energy objectives for 1995 were adopted by the Council in September 1986.[97] The primary objectives are to limit reliance on oil to around 40 per cent of energy consumption and to keep net oil imports at less than one third of the Community's total energy consumption, to improve energy efficiency[98] by at least 20 per cent, to reduce the proportion of electricity generated from oil to less

---

[90] O.J. 1973, L. 228/1.
[91] O.J. 1978, L. 158/3; see Bull. 6–1982, 57.
[92] See Bull. 7/8–1982, 51.
[93] O.J. 1978, L. 158/3.
[94] *e.g.* Resolution of January 15, 1985 concerning the improvement of Member States' programmes on the economy of energy (O.J. 1985, C. 20/1).
[95] *e.g.* Commission Directive of July 29, 1987 (O.J. 1987, L. 238/40).
[96] *e.g.* Commission Recommendation concerning third party financing (O.J. 1988, L. 122/75) and Twenty-second General Report (1988) 310.
[97] O.J. 1986, C. 241.
[98] Dec. 89/364 concerning an action programme for improving the efficiency of electricty use (O.J. 1989, L. 157).

than 15 per cent, to increase the share of solid fuels and to maintain the share of natural gas in the energy balance and substantially to increase the contribution made by new and renewable energy sources instead of conventional fuels.[99]

1. Solid Fuels

In March 1989, the Commission adopted a report on the solid fuels market in the Community in 1988 and the outlook for 1989.[1] The ECSC Consultative Committee, consulted on this report, deplored the decline in the share of solid fuels in the Community's energy balance.[2]

In order to increase the competitiveness of solid fuel production capacity, the Commission authorised the granting of aid[3] to the coal industry in Belgium, France, Spain, the United Kingdom and Germany.[4]

2. Nuclear Energy

With a share of 35 per cent. of electricity production and 14 per cent of total energy requirements, nuclear energy is steadily increasing its contribution to the attainment of the Community's major energy policy objectives for 1995 in terms of supply security and diversification and the limitation of the role of oil and gas in electricity production. There are now 115 nuclear power reactors operating in the Community.[5]

The Community (Euratom) has concluded several agreements with third countries concerning transfer of nuclear materials, etc.

---

[99] Twentieth General Report (1986), 274.
[1] Bull. 3–1989, 49.
[2] Twenty-third General Report (1989), 292.
[3] See Dec. 2064/86 establishing Community rules for State aid to the coal industry (O.J. 1986, L. 177).
[4] Twenty-third General Report (1989), 292.
[5] Twenty-first General Report (1987), 268.

Co-operation agreements were concluded with the United States,[6] Japan, Canada, Brazil, etc.

The Community guarantees, by appropriate measures of control, that nuclear materials are not diverted for purposes other than those for which they are intended. In other words, Euratom does not guarantee peaceful uses unless materials have been intended for such purpose by their supplier or consumer.[7] On April 5, 1973, an agreement was signed between the International Atomic Energy Agency (IAEA), Euratom and seven Member States which do not have nuclear weapons.[8] The agreement was concluded pursuant to the Treaty on the Non-Proliferation of Nuclear Weapons. Euratom consequently adapted its safeguard system. Similar agreements were signed between the IAEA on the one hand, and Euratom, France and the United Kingdom, on the other.[9] Joint teams of Euratom and IAEA inspectors operate regularly in all the major plants in the Community.

The Community also develops nuclear research carried out either through contracts or in the Joint Nuclear Research Centre. The latter has branch establishments in Ispra, Italy, Petten in the Netherlands, the Central Nuclear Measurement Bureau in Geel, Belgium and Karlsruhe, Germany. The technical and scientific information obtained through the implementation of the Community's research programme is disseminated on a non-discriminatory basis.[10]

3. The Supply Agency

The property of all special fissionable materials within the territory of the Member States is vested in the Community,[11] in so

---

[6] O.J. 1974, L. 139.

[7] See Regs. 2, 8 and 9 (J.O. 298/59, J.O. 651/59 and J.O. 482/60, respectively O.J. 1959–1962, 23, 27 and 43); see also Commission Reg. O.J. 1976, L. 363/1.

[8] O.J. 1978, L. 51/1 and Bull. 2–1977, 61.

[9] Bull. 7/8, 69.

[10] See Commission Announcement J.O. 1963, 2569.

[11] Euratom, Art. 86.

far as this material is subject to Euratom's safeguard control. The latter does not extend to materials "intended to meet defence requirements."[12]

The Treaty provides for the creation of a Supply Agency having a right of option on all ores, source materials and special fissile materials produced in the territories of the Member States. It also has the exclusive right to conclude contracts relating to the supply of ores, source material and special fissile materials coming from inside or outside the Community.[13] The Statutes of the Agency were laid down by the Council[14] and various regulations have specified the conditions under which nuclear materials can be required, sold or transferred.[15]

Currently, the supply of natural uranium, special fissile material and enrichment services to Community users and the provision of services for the whole fuel cycle do not present any problems.[16]

The Community depends on imports for some 70 per centof its supplies of natural uranium.[17]

However short, this survey clearly shows that the Community is still far from having a comprehensive energy policy.

Further Reading

K. Lenaerts, "Nuclear Border Installations: A Case Study" (1988) 13 E.L.Rev., 159.

XI. ENVIRONMENT

The SEA added a Chapter VII on Environment to the Treaty which previously did not contain any provision concerning this

---

[12] *Ibid.*, Art. 85.
[13] *Ibid.*, Art. 52(2)(b). In 1989, *e.g.* the Agency concluded 185 contracts, 95 for uranium procurement and 90 for the supply of enrichment services and special fissile materials. See Case 7/71 *Commission* v. *France* [1971] E.C.R. 1003.
[14] J.O. 534/58, O.J. 1952–1958, 78.
[15] See J.O. 777/60, O.J. 1959–1962, 46 (manner in which demand is to be balanced against supply); J.O. 116/62 and J.O. 4057/66, O.J. 1965–1966, 297 (implementation of supply provisions) and J.O. 1460/60 and 240/64 (communications of the Agency).
[16] Twenty-third General Report (1989), 295.
[17] *Ibid.*

important matter. The Community therefore acted often through agreements, action programmes,[18] resolutions, etc., but also through decisions, regulations and about 100 Directives, based on Article 235.

The Treaty now assigns the following objectives to the Community:

> (i) to preserve, protect and improve the quality of the environment;
>
> (ii) to contribute towards protecting human health;
>
> (iii) to ensure a prudent and rational utilisation of natural resources.

Of great interest also are the basic principles provided for in the Treaty:

> — preventive action should be taken,
> — environmental damage should as a priority be rectified at source,
> — the polluter should pay,
> — environmental protection requirements shall be a component of the Community's other policies,[19]
> — Community action shall be taken to the extent to which the objectives can be better attained at Community level than at the level of the individual Member States (the principle of subsidiarity).[20]

---

[18] First programme: 1973; second 1977; third 1983; those programmes aimed mainly at controlling the discharge of dangerous substances into water, control of chemicals and the protection of nature (birds, etc.). The objective of the fourth programme (1989–1992) is to integrate the preventive approach into all sectors of activity.

[19] A clause concerning the protection of the environment was inserted into the Community Support Frameworks (CSFs) adopted during the reform of the structural funds; see above under "Regional Policy."

[20] EEC, Art. 130r(4).

The Treaty also provides that the Community and the Member States, each within their respective sphere of competence,[21] shall co-operate with third countries and with the relevant international organisations.[22] The activity of the Community in the field of environment in fact started with the Summit Conference in Paris in 1972, where the Heads of State or Government emphasised the importance of a Community environment policy.[23] Since then, the Commission not only has concluded a large number of international agreements,[24] but also participates in the work of many international organisations and in all the major conferences regarding the protection of the environment.[25]

Protection of the environment covers an enormously vast domain and the Community has for many years been active in many areas: acquatic environment,[26] air pollution, noise abatement, control of chemicals, industrial hazards and biotechnology, conservation of the natural heritage, waste management, urban environment, public awareness, information and training. In each one of those areas, the Community has enacted a great number of Directives.[27] Those now constitute a growing "corpus" of Community laws and the task to supervise their implementation by all the Member States is one of the most demanding imposed upon the Commission.[28]

[21] From the principle of subsidiarity and this provision it is clear that there has not been a transfer of exclusive competence to the Community in the field of environment.

[22] EEC, Art. 130r(5).

[23] Sixth General Report (1972), 12; Bull. 10–1972, 20.

[24] See, *e.g.* the signing in March 1989 of the Basle Convention on Transboundary Movements of Hazardous Wastes (Bull. 3–1989, 39); the Bonn Agreement on the Prevention of Pollution of the North Sea (Seventeenth General Report (1983), 160) and the Convention on International Trade in Endangered Species of Wild Flora and Fauna (O.J. 1982, L. 384/1, modified O.J. 1989, L. 66/24).

[25] Conference on Security and Co-operation October 1989 (Twenty-third General Report (1989), 229).

[26] Case 14/86 *Pretore di Salò* v. *Persons Unknown* [1987] E.C.R. 2565.

[27] Details concerning those Dirs. and other Community acts are to be found in the annual General Reports.

[28] In 1989, *e.g.* the Commission received 350 complaints about breaches of environmental legislation.

Further Reading

J. Temple Lang, "Implications of the European Community's Environment Policy for Turkey" (1988) E.L.Rev., 403.
D. Vandermeersch, "The Single European Act and the Environment Policy of the European Economic Community" (1987) 12 E.L.Rev., 407.

XII. CONSUMERS

The history of Consumer Protection in the Community starts with the Council Resolution of April 14, 1975 concerning a preliminary programme for a protection and information policy of the consumer.[29] Among other things it provides for the consumer's health and safety, protection of the economic interests of the consumer (misleading advertising, unfair commercial practices, etc.,) advice, help and redress, consumer information and consumer consultation and representation.

In the following years an impressive array of Decisions, Directives, Regulations, Resolutions and Recommendations were issued by the institutions on the above mentioned subjects.[30] Also a Consultative Committee of the Consumers was set up.[31]

In what is sometimes referred to as the "White Paper Bis," *i.e.* the Communication on the completion of the internal market of foodstuffs, the Commission points out four areas in which it will continue to legislate. One of them is the information needs of the consumers and their protection other than health protection. It concerns mainly labelling[32] and nutritional labelling.[33]

In November 1989, the Council adopted a resolution setting out future priorities for relaunching the policy for the protection

[29] O.J. 1975, C. 92/1.
[30] The full list of all the Community acts can be found in the Repertory of applicable Community legislation, published twice a year by the Commission.
[31] O.J. 1973, L. 283/18.
[32] O.J. 1989, L. 186/17, amending Dir. 79/112 (O.J. 1979, L. 33/1).
[33] O.J. 1988, C. 282.

and promotion of consumer interests.[34] It identified as particular sensitive areas the integration of consumer policy in other Community policies, improvement of consumer representation at Community level, promotion of the general safety of goods[35] and services and better information on their quality, and improved access to legal redress.

It might be noted that in February 1989, the Commission set up a new, autonomous department, the "Consumer Policy Service." This shows its determination to develop consumer protection as part of the completion of the internal market.

Further Reading

S. Weatherill, "Consumer Safety Legislation in the United Kingdom and Article 300 EEC," (1988) 13 E.L.Rev., 87.

L. Krämer, *EEC Consumer Law*, (1986) Brussels.

T. Bourgoignie, D. Tauber, *Consumer Law, Common Markets and Federalism*, (1987) Berlin.

---

[34] Bull. 11–1989, 40.

[35] See proposals for a Directive on general product safety. The basic cprinciple is the obligation of suppliers to put on the market only products which are safe, and of the Member States to ensure that this obligation is complied with: by monitoring the market and, if necessary, restricting sales or withdrawing dangerous products (Twenty-third General Report (1989), 239).

CHAPTER 7

EXTERNAL RELATIONS

I. COMMUNITY'S JURISDICTION

Under this heading will be examined the Community's commercial policy, development policy, its relations with international organisations and the bilateral and regional relations. However, before going into details, some general remarks seem necessary. Indeed, the ECSC Treaty explicitly provides that, in international relations, the Coal and Steel Community enjoys the "legal capacity it requires to perform its functions and attain its objectives."[1] The Euratom Treaty confers upon the Atomic Energy Community the authority to enter, within the limits of its powers and jurisdiction, "into obligations by concluding agreements or contracts with third States, an international organisation or a national of a third State."[2] But the EEC Treaty only refers to the "establishment of a commercial policy towards third countries"[3] and the "association of the overseas countries and territories"[4] and contains a few other specific provisions.[5]

However, the absence of a provision conferring upon the Community a general competence to conclude international agreements has not prevented it from developing a particularly

---

[1] ECSC, Art. 6. This international capacity is thus strictly limited.
[2] Euratom, Art. 101.
[3] EEC, Art. 113.
[4] EEC, Arts. 131–135.
[5] EEC, Art. 111 (tariff negotiations with third countries) and Art. 228.

active external policy. This was made possible, as will be seen, with the help of the Court.

The Community is a body created by an international treaty concluded between sovereign States with the task *inter alia* of exercising activities in the international field. As far as those States are concerned this body enjoys international legal personality and participates in activities which come within the ambit of international law. However, it is therefore only to the extent that other subjects of international law recognise the Community as a member of the international community, that it can take initiatives and play an active role in the international sphere. This recognition is no longer a problem. It was rather among the Member States that, until recently, some disagreement existed on the extent of the Community's jurisdiction in international affairs.

The question was raised mainly with regard to the Community's treaty-making power; in other words: how much of the Member States' treaty-making power was transferred to the Community? That some powers were transferred is not questioned, but it was not clear whether those powers are to be exercised exclusively by the Community or in conjunction with the Member States.

As far as the first question is concerned, the views of the Court were clearly formulated in 1971[6] and repeated in later judgments.[7] They were based on Article 210 of the Treaty which provides that "the Community shall have legal personality." According to the Court, this provision placed at the head of Part Six of the Treaty devoted to "General and Final Provisions,"

---

[6] Case 22/70 *Commission* v. *Council* (better known as the *ERTA* case: *Accord Européen de Transport (European Transport Agreement)*) [1971] E.C.R. 263 at 274(14). See also the Opinions of the Court given under EEC, Art. 228: Opinion 1/75 [1975] E.C.R. 1355: compatibility with the EEC Treaty of a draft "Understanding on a Local Cost Standard" drawn up under the auspices of the OECD; Opinion 1/76 [1977] E.C.R. 741: compatibility of a draft agreement establishing a European lying-up fund for inland waterway vessels; Opinion 1/78 [1979] E.C.R. 2871: compatibility of the draft International Agreement on Natural Rubber negotiated in the UNCTAD.

[7] See, *e.g.* Joined Cases 3, 4 and 6/76 *Cornelis Kramer and Others* [1976] E.C.R. 1279.

means that in its external relations the Community enjoys the capacity to enter into international commitments over the whole field of objectives defined in Part One of the Treaty, which Part Six supplements. The following statement is also important:

> "to establish in a particular case whether the Community has authority to enter into international commitments, regard must be had to the whole scheme of Community law no less than to its substantive provisions. Such authority arises not only from express conferment by the Treaty but may equally flow implicitly from other provisions of the Treaty, from the Act of accession and from measures adopted within the framework of those provisions, by the Community institutions."[8]

In other words, whenever Community law has created for the institutions powers within the internal system for the purpose of attaining a specific objective, the Community has authority to enter into the international commitments necessary for the attainment of that objective, even in the absence of an express provision in that connection.[9] This is particularly so in all cases where internal power has already been used in order to adopt measures which come within the attainment of common policies.[10]

With regard to the second question (exclusive or shared jurisdiction) the Court admits a "mixed procedure," *i.e.* both the Community and the Member States are the contracting parties when an agreement covers matters for which the Community is competent and others coming within the ambit of the Member States.[11] But, "each time the Community with a view to implementing a common policy envisaged by the Treaty, adopts provisions laying down common rules, whatever form these may take, the Member States no longer have the right, acting individually or even collectively, to undertake obligations with third countries which affect those rules."[12]

---

[8] *Ibid.* at 1308(17–18).
[9] Opinion 1/76 Lying-up fund (n. 6 above) at 755.
[10] *Ibid.*
[11] *Ibid.* at 756(7).
[12] Case 22/70 *ERTA* (n. 6 above) at 274(17).

As long as the Community has not exercised its right to conclude agreements, the Member States retain the power to do so.[13] But this authority is only of a transitional nature and Member States are bound by Community obligations in their negotiations with third countries: they may not enter into or renew any commitment which could hinder the Community in the carrying out of the tasks entrusted to it by the Treaty.[14]

The emergence of a Community competence should not, however, be seen as a sudden break; Community law being evolutive, the transfer of power from the Member States to the Community is necessarily gradual.[15]

Then there is also the question of the consequences for the Community and Community law of existing collective international commitments undertaken by the Member States. Here also the Court has, through various judgments, formulated the basic principles. For instance with regard to tariffs and trade policy the Member States have progressively transferred to the Community their jurisdiction. By doing so they have also conferred upon the Community the international rights and obligations connected with the exercise of this jurisdiction, particularly with regard to the General Agreement on Tariffs and Trade (GATT). It follows that the Community itself is bound by that agreement.[16] This constitutes a clear case of substitution of the Community for the Member States in the implementation of multilateral treaties bearing on the subject-matter of the Treaty.

---

[13] See answer to Parliamentary question no. 173/77 (O.J. 1978, C. 72/1).

[14] Joined Cases 3, 4 and 6/76 *Kramer* (n. 7 above), at 1310(40). See also EEC, Art. 111(4) obliging Member States to bring about adjustments to existing tariff agreements with third countries and EEC, Art. 234: existing agreements concluded between one or more Member States and one or more third countries are not affected by the entry into force of the Treaty.

[15] Case 22/70 *ERTA* (n. 6) above) at 281(81–92).

[16] Joined Cases 21–24/72 *International Fruit Company* v. *Produktschap voor Groenten en Fruit* [1972] E.C.R. 1219 at 1227(18). The Community has assumed those powers in pursuance of EEC, Arts. 111 and 113. See also Case 38/75 *Nederlandse Spoorwegen* v. *Inspecteur der invoerrechten en accijnzen* [1975] E.C.R. 1439 at 1450(21); Joined Cases 267–269/81 *Amministrazione delle Finanze dello Stato* v. *SPI and SAMI* [1983] E.C.R. 801 and Joined Cases 290–291/81 *Singer and Geigy* v. *Amministrazione delle Finanze dello Stato* [1983] E.C.R. 847.

As for the rights which derive for the Community from those agreements, their exercise depends on recognition of the Community by the other contracting parties.

The internal problems of the Community in this field may not of course obliterate the interests of third countries. In the various Court statements referred to above, this principle was underlined several times.[17] However, third States may not intervene in internal matters of the Community and, more particularly, in the determination of the very complex and delicate relationship between the Community and its own Member States.[18]

A last question to be examined here concerns the effects of international commitments undertaken by the Community. In the first place, it should be noted that such commitments constitute "acts of the institutions of the Community" and as such can be challenged in the Court as to their compatibility with the Treaty.[19] In the second place, provisions of international agreements concluded by the Community in conformity with the procedures provided for in the Treaty, "shall be binding on the institutions of the Community and on Member States."[20] Such provisions are directly applicable in the Community. They can also have direct effect and override conflicting provisions of Member States' domestic law.[21]

II. COMMERCIAL POLICY

The Treaty provides for the "establishment of a common customs tariff and a common commercial policy towards third coun-

---

[17] See, *e.g.* Opinion 1/75 Local Cost Standards (n. 6 above) and Opinion 1/76 Laying-up fund (*ibid.*).

[18] Ruling 1/78 [1978] E.C.R. 2151 compatibility with the Euratom Treaty of a draft Convention of the IAEA on the Physical Protection of Nuclear Materials, Facilities and Transport.

[19] EEC, Arts. 173 and 177.

[20] EEC, Art. 228(2). See also Opinion 1/76 Laying-up fund (n. 6 above), at 6 and 7.

[21] Case 87/75 *Bresciani* v. *Amministrazione Italiana delle Finanze* [1976] E.C.R. 129 at 141(23). See also Case 65/77 *Razanatsimba* [1977] E.C.R. 2229.

tries."[22] It was pointed out earlier that the two are complementary, the customs tariffs being one of the main instruments of any commercial policy. It was also shown that the elimination of all trade barriers between the Member States required a "common" customs tariff towards third countries. It follows that the commercial policy itself had to be "common" and therefore transferred from the national ambit to the Community's jurisdiction.[23] Measures of commercial policy of a national character are no longer possible in principle and may only be taken by virtue of specific authorisation by the Community.[24]

Consequently, customs tariffs, for instance, can only be modified by the Community. The Treaty provides for two procedures to do so; the autonomous modifications[25] and those which take place pursuant to agreements with third countries. For such agreements, the Commission makes recommendations to the Council which authorises it to negotiate them. They are concluded by the Council after consultation of Parliament.[26]

In case the implementation of the common commercial policy were to lead to economic difficulties in a Member State, the Commission may authorise that State to take the necessary protective measures[27] which can deviate from the provisions regarding free movement of goods.[28] Those provisions must however be interpreted restrictively since they derogate from provisions which are fundamental to the operation of the com-

[22] EEC, Arts. 3(b) and 9(1).
[23] Opinion 1/75 Local Cost Standards (n. 6 above), at 1364.
[24] Case 41/76 *Donckerwolcke* v. *Procureur de la République* [1976] E.C.R. 1921 at 1937(32). See Council Dec. 89/525 authorising the prorogation or tacit renewal of certain commercial agreements concluded by Member States with third countries (O.J. 1989, L. 273/1).
[25] EEC, Art. 28. "Autonomous" means that it takes place without an agreement with third countries. See also Art. 25.
[26] EEC, Art. 113(3); these negotiations are conducted in close consultation with a special Committee (the "113 Committee") composed of national officials appointed by the Council.
[27] EEC, Art. 115.
[28] Case 62/70 *Bock* v. *Commission* [1971] E.C.R. 897 at 909(14).

mon market and they maintain an obstacle to the full implementation of the common commercial policy.[29]

With regard to *imports* into the Community, the European Council of June 1982 stated that in the matter of trade protection, the Community should aim to act "with as much speed and efficiency as its trading partners" and "defend vigorously the legitimate interests of the Community in the appropriate bodies."

In 1979 the Council had established common rules for imports and rules for imports from State-trading countries.[30] Those were replaced by new rules[31] providing for:

   (i) a Community investigation procedure,

   (ii) criteria relating to the "injury" concept,

   (iii) harmonisation of the protective arrangements and

   (iv) a list of residual restrictions.[32]

The second "line of defence" of the Community is against dumped or subsidised imports. The basic instruments were clarified and consolidated in 1984.[33] It is not uncommon that anti-dumping duties are imposed on products from third countries, while in some cases the Commission accepts exporter's undertakings to increase their prices.[34]

Every year the Commission presents to the Council and to Parliament a report on the application of the Community's anti-dumping and anti-subsidy measures and the relevant GATT

---

[29] *Ibid.* See particularly Case 29/75 *Kaufhof* v. *Commission* [1976] E.C.R. 431 at 443(6) where the Court annulled a Commission decision granting an authorisation under Art. 115 because the Commission failed to examine the justification put forward by the Member State and whether the measures were necessary.

[30] Regs. 925 and 926/79 (O.J. 1979, L. 131).

[31] Reg. 288/82 (O.J. 1982, L. 35/1; they were modified in 1988 O.J. 1988, L. 209 and 230).

[32] Sixteenth General Report (1982), 234.

[33] Reg. 2176 (O.J. 1984, L. 201/1, modified 1988, L. 388/1).

[34] Twenty-third General Report (1989), 311.

codes. The Commission noted that industry is making increasing use of those provisions and codes to defend itself against unfair trading practices.[35]

As far as *exports* are concerned, the principle of freedom of export for almost all the headings of the common customs tariff was established by the Council back in 1969; the list of products excluded from this liberalisation was shortened over the years.[36] Specific measures were taken from time to time concerning particular products.[37] In this context mention must be made of auto-limitation decisions with regard to export of steel products to the United States.[38]

Another important item of commercial policy in this field is the *export credit* system with or without insurance or guarantee, applied by various Member States. In 1977 the Council adopted a decision concerning the application by the Member States of certain guidelines for the granting of export credits to non-member countries.[39]

III. MULTILATERAL RELATIONS

In the field of multilateral trade negotiations within the framework of the General Agreement on Tariffs and Trade (GATT), the Community's role has grown considerably over the years. It certainly played an important role in the so-called Kennedy Round in 1967.[40] Similarly, the Community participated actively in the "Tokyo Round" negotiations which started in 1973. After

---

[35] Nineteenth General Report (1985), 272.

[36] Reg. 2603/69 establishing common rules for export (J.O. 1969, L. 324/25; O.J. 1969, 590, amended O.J. 1982, L. 382/1.)

[37] Reg. 428/89 concerning the export of certain chemical products (O.J. 1989, L. 50/1); see also Decision 89/303 (O.J. 1989, L. 122/29.)

[38] See, *e.g.* Reg. 61/85 (O.J. 1985, L. 386/96).

[39] For the OECD Understanding on Export Credits for Ships and the Arrangement on Guidelines for Officially Supported Export Credits ("Consensus"), see Sixteenth General Report (1982), 238. O.J. 1977, L. 270. See also Dir. 84/568 (O.J. 1984, L. 314).

[40] See Tenth EEC General Report (1966), 310 and First General Report (1967), 381).

the results were approved by the Council, the Commission signed them on behalf of the Community.[41] The implementation of such agreements comes within the sphere of the common commercial policy. But the Community presently plays what turns out to be the leading role in the Uruguay Round negotiations which started in 1986.[42] This is due mainly to the fact that for the first time agriculture was included in the negotiations; but the negotiations also broke new ground by covering trade in services, intellectual property and trade-related investments. The Uruguay Round negotiations should be concluded by the end of 1990.

Special arrangements exist with regard to various products: steel (mention was made of the special agreement with the United States),[43] shipbuilding, textiles (26 bilateral agreements were renegotiated in 1986 under the Multifibre Arrangement (MFA),[44] non-ferrous metals and high-technology products.

IV. RELATIONS WITH INDUSTRIALISED COUNTRIES

1. United States

The relations between the United States and the Community are rather ambiguous. On the one hand, both sides claim to attach great importance to closer co-operation and to a strengthening of their relations, and on the other hand they are involved in what seem petty disputes,[45] threats, retaliation measures, counter-retaliations, GATT panels, etc.

These two economic powers are however bound to co-operate very closely in the economic and political fields. This they successfully do, for example, within the Western Economic Summits held every year.

---

[41] O.J. 1980, L. 71/1.
[42] See Twentieth General Report (1986), 300.
[43] See Twenty-third General Report (1989), 316.
[44] *Ibid.* at 317.
[45] *Ibid.* at 320.

2. Canada

Less tense than with the United States, the economic relations with Canada are nonetheless clouded by numerous disagreements. Nevertheless the Commission could report that trade between the Community and Canada continued to grow.[46]

3. Japan

Although imports into Japan increased to the benefit of Community exporters, this was not sufficient to stabilise the trading deficit. While the Japanese market for manufactured products has become more open through the removal of specific barriers to entry, it remains less open than comparable markets in other industrialised countries. The reason why the trading surplus persists seems to lie mainly in the existence of structural impediments to imports which have attracted the attention of Japan's main trading partners.[47]

4. Australia and New Zealand

The relations of the Community with Australia and New Zealand are affected principally by the opposition of those two countries to what they consider to be a subsidised common agricultural policy. While those same countries apply very restrictive measures to the imports of manufactured products, they seem unable to understand that the Community cannot allow itself to rely on imports for most of the agricultural products it needs. A certain degree of self-sufficiency is politically and economically imperative and the Community must therefore maintain its two-tier price system which includes levies on imports and restitutions for the exports of agricultural and processed products.

[46] *Ibid.* at 323.
[47] *Ibid.* at 325.

5. EFTA

The countries of the European Free Trade Association are the main trade partners of the Community and the relations between the two groups are of the utmost importance for both of them. Responding to an invitation from the Community, the EFTA countries are now "ready to explore together with the EEC ways and means to achieve a more structured partnership." The Community now hopes to open negotiations with EFTA with a view to reaching a comprehensive agreement that would strengthen their co-operation in a European Economic Area of 18 countries. This would enable EFTA to participate in certain Community activities, and in the disciplines and benefits of the internal market. Independent decision-making processes of each organisation would be respected and a strict balance between rights and obligations maintained.[48]

The Community has concluded separate agreements with Austria, Switzerland, Sweden, Norway, Iceland and Finland.[49]

On July 17, 1989, Austria applied for accession to the Communities and the Council decided to set in motion the procedures provided for in the Treaties.

6. State-trading countries

Several agreements have been concluded by the Community with State-trading countries even before the recent evolution towards more democracy in Eastern Europe. A trade and co-operation agreement with Hungary was signed in September 1988.[50] One on trade and commercial and economic co-operation with Poland

---

[48] *Ibid.* at 328.
[49] For a list of the most recent ones see Repertory of applicable Community legislation and other acts of the Community institutions.
[50] O.J. 1988, L. 327/1. See also n. 13 below.

was signed in February 1989[51]; it concerns elimination of quantitative restrictions and mutual concessions on agricultural products.
In December 1989 the Council approved guidelines for the
negotiation of an economic co-operation and trade agreement
with the German Democratic Republic.[52] Also an agreement with
Czechoslovakia on trade in industrial products came into force on
April 1, 1989[53] and an agreement with the Soviet Union was
signed in Brussels on December 18, 1989.[54] Negotiations were
also started with Bulgaria for a trade and commercial economic
co-operation agreement.[55] By the end of July 1990 bilateral
agreements had been signed with all the East European countries. Following the dramatic turn of events in these countries,
the so-called Group of 24 (industrialised countries) set up a fund
to help the economic reconstruction of Poland & Hungary
(PHARE). The Commission was entrusted with the task of
coordinating this aid. The operation will be extended to the other
East European countries insofar as the conditions for democrat-
isation are met. Mention must also be made of the Bank for East
Europe Reconstruction and Development (BERD), created in
May 1990 and in which the Community participates.

The Community also intends to establish official relations with
the COMECOM (Council for Mutal Economic Assistance).[56]

V. RELATIONS WITH MEDITERRANEAN, GULF AND ARABIAN PENINSULA, ASIAN AND LATIN AMERICAN COUNTRIES

1. Mediterranean countries

As far as the Mediterranean countries are concerned, a Commission Communication entitled "Redirecting the Community's

---

[51] Bull. 9–1989, 48.
[52] Bull. 12–1989, 87.
[53] O.J. 1989, L. 88/1.
[54] Bull. 12–1989, 87.
[55] Bull. 4–1989, 67.
[56] Twenty-third General Report (1989), 336.

Mediterranean policy" was approved by the European Council in Strasbourg in June 1989.[57] It will serve as a basis for further developments in that area.

A special case was the application for accession by Turkey made in 1987. In accordance with the Treaty,[58] the Commission formulated its Opinion.[59] The Commission stressed, in general terms, the vital importance of attaining the objectives laid down by the SEA and took the view that, unless there were exceptional circumstances, it would not be advisable to start negotiations before 1993 at the earliest on the accession of any country.[60]

The Community has an Association Agreement with Cyprus[61] and with Malta[62] and plans to establish a customs union for industrial products with Andorra. With Yugoslavia, the Community concluded a Co-operation Agreement in 1983[63] and has declared itself ready to examine the additional measures required to support the reforms being carried out in that country and to strengthen its co-operation with it.[64]

2.   The Gulf and Arabian Peninsula

The Maghreb (Algeria, Morocco, Tunisia) and Mashreq (Egypt, Jordan, Lebanon, Syria) countries and Israel are, because of their geographical proximity to the Community, of great importance to the development in trade. From the outset systems were set up to deal pragmatically with trade, to help remove the

[57] Bull. 12–1989, 13.
[58] EEC, Art. 237.
[59] Bull. 12–1989, 88.
[60] Twenty-third General Report (1989), 337. An association agreement was signed in 1963 (J.O. 1964, 3987). Because of the political situation in that country characterised by the absence of a pluralist parliamentarian democracy and lack of respect for human rights, the association during the last years "did no more than tick over" (Sixteenth General Report (1982), 253).
[61] O.J. 1972, L. 133/1.
[62] O.J. 1971, L. 61.1.
[63] O.J. 1983, L. 41/1.
[64] Bull. 4–1989, 68.

organisation of markets and production and improve the commercial and tariff machinery. However, the disparities of the systems created difficulties. The Council therefore decided to examine a "global approach" to the problems arising in the region. It would consist of a general Community policy covering trade, economic, technical and financial co-operation and also co-operation on labour. This global approach did not meet with great enthusiasm, but the Community pursued its efforts and over the years concluded agreements with all the countries of the region on that basis.

The first agreement was signed with Israel in 1975; it concerns free trade and co-operation.[65] With the other Mediterranean countries overall co-operation agreements were signed during 1976–77. They are all based on Article 238 of the Treaty and additional Protocols based upon Article 113 were concluded in the following years.

The countries concerned are Algeria,[66] Morocco,[67] Tunisia,[68] Egypt,[69] Lebanon,[70] Jordan[71] and Syria.[72]

On January 1, 1990 a Co-operation Agreement between the Community and the countries party to the Charter of the Co-operation Council of the Arab Countries of the Gulf (GCC) came into force. The agreement establishes free trade and provides for full liberalisation of trade after a transitional period.[73]

In this context mention should be made of the Euro-Arab Dialogue which was activated in December 1989.[74]

[65] O.J. 1975, L. 136/3, last modified O.J. 1987, L. 387/1.
[66] O.J. 1978, L. 263/1, last modified O.J. 1988, L. 288/2.
[67] O.J. 1978, L. 264/1, last modified O.J. 1988, L. 288/18.
[68] O.J. 1978, L. 265/1, last modified O.J. 1988, L. 288/34.
[69] O.J. 1978, L. 266/1, last modified O.J. 1988, L. 288/10.
[70] O.J. 1978, L. 267/1, last modified O.J. 1988, L. 288/26.
[71] O.J. 1978, L. 268/1, last modified O.J. 1988, L. 288/18.
[72] O.J. 1978, L. 269/2.
[73] O.J. 1989, L. 54/1.
[74] Twenty-third General Report (1989), 343.

3. Indian Sub-continent and South-East Asia

When the United Kingdom joined the European Communities, a Joint Declaration of Intent on the development of trade relations with Ceylon, India, Malaysia, Pakistan and Singapore was annexed to the accession Treaty. Consequently, agreements were signed with India in 1973,[75] Sri Lanka,[76] Pakistan[77] and Bangladesh[78] in 1975 and 1976.

A series of agreements on trade in textile products was concluded with Macao,[79] Korea,[80] Thailand,[81] Indonesia,[82] Singapore,[83] Hong Kong,[84] the Philippines[85] and Malaysia.[86]

A Co-operation Agreement was concluded with the States of the Association of South-East Asian Nations (ASEAN); it provides a framework for commercial, economic and development co-operation.[87]

4. China

A commercial and economic co-operation agreement was concluded with China in 1985 and another on trade in textile products in 1986.[88] However, relations between the Community

---

[75] A non-preferential framework agreement which was replaced in 1981: O.J. 1981, L. 328/5; others were later added on textiles and sugar cane: O.J. 1989, L. 72/28.

[76] On commercial co-operation (O.J. 1975, L. 247/1).

[77] O.J. 1976, L. 168/1 and O.J. 1986, L. 108/1.

[78] O.J. 1976, L. 319/1.

[79] O.J. 1979, L. 298/107 and O.J. 1987, L. 287/46.

[80] O.J. 1979, L. 298/67 and O.J. 1987, L. 263/38.

[81] *Ibid.* A co-operation agreement on cassava production, marketing and trade was concluded in 1982 (O.J. 1982, L. 219/52).

[82] O.J. 1979, L. 350/27.

[83] *Ibid.* at 99.

[84] O.J. 1980, L. 332/1.

[85] O.J. 1980, L. 371/1.

[86] O.J. 1981, L. 381/1.

[87] Indonesia, Malaysia, Singapore and Thailand. O.J. 1980, L. 144/1.

[88] O.J. 1985, L. 250/2 and O.J. 1986, L. 389/2.

and China were severely disrupted in 1989 as a result of the action taken by the Chinese authorities on June 4.

5. Latin America

With the countries of Latin America contacts are pursued both at the multilateral level and bilaterally. The former encompasses contracts with the Rio Group countries (Argentina, Brazil, Colombia, Mexico, Peru, Uruguay and Venezuela)[89]; the Contadora Group (Colombia, Mexico, Panama and Venezuela)[90]; the countries of Central America (Costa Rica, Guatemala, Honduras, Nicaragua and El Salvador), with whom the Community has concluded the EEC-Central American Co-operation Agreement[91]; and the Andean Group (Bolivia, Colombia, Ecuador, Peru and Venezuela). With some of those countries the Community has concluded bilateral agreements providing for wide-ranging commercial and economic co-operation: Brazil,[92] Uruguay,[93] Mexico[94] and Argentina.[95] Other agreements are more limited in scope: *e.g.* Peru.[96]

VI. RELATIONS WITH THE AFRICAN, CARIBBEAN AND PACIFIC COUNTRIES AND THE OVERSEAS COUNTRIES AND TERRITORIES

The main feature of the Community policy towards developing countries is the ACP-EEC Agreement, better known as the Lomé Convention.[97] It establishes commercial, industrial and

---

[89] Twenty-third General Report (1989), 349.
[90] Bull. 2–1989, 48.
[91] O.J. 1986, L. 172.
[92] O.J. 1983, L. 281/2.
[93] O.J. 1973, L. 333/2.
[94] O.J. 1975, L. 247/11.
[95] O.J. 1988, L. 24/59.
[96] O.J. 1987, L. 263/82.
[97] The Third Lomé Convention entered into force on May 1, 1986 and expired on February 28, 1990. The negotiations for the renewal were opened in Luxembourg in October 1988.

financial relations between the Community on the one hand, and 66 African, Caribbean and Pacific countries,[98] on the other. It is therefore a bilateral agreement.

This relationship grew out of a quite different set of links which existed when the Community was established. Most of the countries now "associated" with the Community were colonies at the time and the Member States had special responsibilities towards them. The Treaty provides for the association of "overseas countries and territories," in order to increase trade and to promote jointly economic and social development.[99] Consequently, countries which had special relations with Belgium, France, Italy and the Netherlands and after accession Denmark and the United Kingdom were associated with the Community. The Treaty provisions were drafted at a time when most of these overseas countries were still dependent but the principle of a special relationship was maintained after they gained independence.

For a first period of fivee years, the details and the procedures of the association were determined by an implementing convention[1] annexed to the Treaty.[2] This convention was replaced by an agreement negotiated between the Community and the emerging African and Malgasy States. Known as the Yaounde I Convention,[3] it still bears the marks of the paternalistic approach most

---

[98] Angola, Antigua and Barbuda, Bahamas, Barbados, Belize, Benin, Botswana, Burkina Faso, Burundi, Cameroon, Cape Verde, Central African Republic, Chad, Comoros, Congo, Djibouti, Dominica, Equatorial Guinea, Ethiopia, Fiji, Gabon, Gambia, Ghana, Grenada, Guinea, Guinea Bissau, Guyana, Haiti, Ivory Coast, Jamaica, Kenya, Kiribati, Lesotho, Liberia, Madagascar, Malawi, Mali, Mauretania, Mauritius, Mozambique, Niger, Nigeria, Papua New Guinea, Rwanda, St. Christopher and Nevis, St. Lucia, Dominican Republic, St. Vincent and the Grenadines, São Tomé & Principe, Senegal, Seychelles, Sierra Leone, Solomon Islands, Somalia, Sudan, Surinam, Swaziland, Tanzania, Togo, Tonga, Trinidad and Tobago, Tuvalu, Uganda, Vanuatu, Western Samoa, Zaire, Zambia, Zimbabwe, Namibia (once it is independent).

[99] EEC, Art. 131.

[1] This was of course a convention concluded between the Member States, not with the overseas countries.

[2] EEC, Art. 136.

[3] J.O. 1964, 1431 and 1490.

European countries nourished towards their former colonies. A second Yaounde Convention, similar to the first, came into force on January 1, 1971.[4] It did not apply to the United Kingdom, Ireland and Denmark until January 1, 1975.[5]

An entirely new agreement was signed at Lomé (Togo) on February 28, 1975, between the Community of 10 and 46 countries situated in Africa, the Caribbean and the Pacific.[6] It came into force on April 1, 1976[7] and expired on March 1, 1980. The Lomé II expired in 1985 and the Lomé III in 1990. The Lomé Conventions differ from the Yaounde Conventions in that they aim to establish a kind of partnership between the developing countries and the Community.

In respect of trade co-operation, the ACP countries enjoy, without reciprocity for the Member States, free entry into the Community for most of their agricultural products and for all industrial products originating in ACP countries. The Member States only have the guarantee that they will be treated not less favourably than any other industrialised country and that all of them will be treated equally.

An entirely new feature of the Lomé Conventions is the Stabilisation of Export Earnings (STABEX) and SYSMIN systems. STABEX is a mechanism assuring those ACP countries whose revenues derive mainly from a single product, a certain level of export earnings; to this end they are protected from income fluctuations due to the play of the markets or production hazards.[8] In 1989 this represented transfers to the amount of 315 million ECU. The second system, in the form of special loans, aims at remedying the harmful effects to the national economy of the situation in the mining sector.

The Lomé Conventions also provide for an undertaking by the Community to purchase from certain ACP countries, at guaran-

[4] J.O. 1970, L. 282/1; O.J. Sec. Ser. I(2) 7.
[5] Act of Accession, Arts. 109 and 115(1).
[6] O.J. 1976, L. 25/1.
[7] O.J. 1976, L. 85/1. Since it expired before the Lomé II Agreement became effective, transitional measures were adopted (O.J. 1980, L. 55/1). For Lomé III, see Bull. 11–1984, 7 and Eighteenth General Report (1984), 275.
[8] For details see Eighteenth General Report (1984), 285.

teed prices, cane sugar for an indefinite period and an undertaking from those countries to supply specific quantities annually; this is referred to as the Sugar Protocol.[9]

Another important element is the place assumed by industrial co-operation, with its Industrial Co-operation Committee and Industrial Development Centre. The purpose is to integrate firms and entrepreneurs into the EEC-ACP co-operation.

Mention must also be made of the Regional Co-operation; the Convention devotes considerable resources to it and contains provisions designed to encourage the ACP States towards greater solidarity, with the ultimate goal of genuine regional integration.[10]

The Lomé IV Convention was signed on December 15, 1989 and will remain in force for a period of 10 years commencing on March 1, 1990, with a renewable five-year financial protocol. It offers a number of innovations, the most important of which is support for structural adjustments (balance of payments, budget, public enterprises, debt burden, etc.) and includes a chapter on debt. In addition the ACP-EEC co-operation now covers cultural and social co-operation (population) and the development of services and environmental protection, (*e.g.* a ban on the movement of toxic and radioactive waste). The next emphasis will be on the private sector (investment, promotion, protection, support and financing, notably with risk capital) and on-the-spot enhancement of the value of ACP commodities through the development of processing, marketing, distribution and transport activities.

Finally, the Convention strengthens the provisions on human rights and respect for human dignity under which Article 5 specifies the various categories: non-discriminatory treatment, fundamental human rights, civil and political rights, economic, social and cultural rights. The same Article provides that financial resources may be allocated for the promotion of human rights in the ACP States through specific schemes.

The Community also contributes to the development of "non-associated" third countries; India has been the main recipient of

---

[9] For the Sugar Protocol see Twenty-third General Report (1989), 358.
[10] Twenty-third General Report (1989), 361.

the allocated financial aid. The aid programme is intended mainly for the most under-privileged sections of the population in the poorest countries. It has been running since 1976; the emphasis is on the rural sector and improving supplies of foodstuffs.[11]

1. Generalised Preferences[12]

While the Lomé Convention provides preferences for a particular group of developing countries, the Community also offers world-wide help in the form of generalised preferences, *i.e.* non-discriminatory tariff preferences for the import of manufactures and semi-manufactures and processed agricultural products from developing countries. In 1990 it was extended to Poland and Hungary while they are engaged in restructuring their economies (an estimated five years), since those countries are faced with problems similar to those of developing countries.[13]

The 1990 decisions concerning the preferences considerably improved the agricultural arrangements, the policy of differentiation in the industrial sector was continued, and finally, the quotas are now managed entirely by the Community. All industrial and agricultural quotas become zero-duty amounts, not divided among the Member States. The latter was done to comply with a ruling of the Court.[14]

---

[11] See Council Reg. on the implementation of the programme O.J. 1981, L. 48/8.

[12] The decision to offer tariff preferences was taken on the basis of an UNCTAD resolution and, as first among all the developed nations, was initiated by the Community in 1971 (O.J. 1971, L. 142) as a first series of implementing Regulations and Decisions. For 1990, see O.J. 1989, L. 383.

[13] Aid for economic restructuring (Operation Phare) was decided at the Western Economic Summit in Paris in July 1989. It provides financial help for: food aid, agricultural restructuring, improved access to markets, promotion of investment, vocational training and co-operation on the environment. 24 countries are associated in the programme and an initial amount of 300 million ECU is provided, while the EIB was asked to provide loans for up to 1 billion over a period of three years (Twenty-third General Report (1989), 331).

[14] Case 51/87 *Commission* v. *Council* September 27, 1988 (not yet published).

2. Commodities and World Agreements

The Community participates in the UNCTAD's integrated programme for commodities,[15] the Coffee Agreement,[16] the Cocoa Agreement,[17] the International Tropical Timber Organisation,[18] the Tin Agreement,[19] the United Nations Conference on Copper,[20] the International Natural Rubber Agreement,[21] the Jute and Jute Product Agreement[22] and the International Cotton Advisory Committee.[23]

3. Food Aid and Emergency Aid

For many years the Community has been implementing food aid programmes which allow it to distribute food to needy areas either directly or through international or non-governmental organisations.[24] This aid is financed by the yearly budget.

The Commission also allocates resources for emergency food aid following natural disasters. The same applies to emergency aid which goes mainly to victims of drought or civil war.

VII. Relations with International Organisations

The Treaty provides that the Commission shall "ensure the maintenance of all appropriate relations with the organs of the

---

[15] Sixteenth General Report (1982), 269.
[16] Bull. 2–1989, 50.
[17] Twentieth General Report (1986), 337.
[18] Bull. 5–1989, 71.
[19] O.J. 1982, L. 342/3.
[20] Bull. 2–1989, 50.
[21] O.J. 1988, L. 58/21.
[22] O.J. 1983, L. 185/4.
[23] Twenty-third General Report (1989), 370.
[24] *Ibid.* at 372.

United Nations, of its specialized agencies and of the General Agreement on Tariffs and Trade," and then adds that the Commission shall "maintain such relations as are appropriate with all international organisations."[25] In other words there is no limit set to the Community's activities in this field. Nevertheless, two other organisations are singled out for "appropriate forms of co-operation" (the Council of Europe)[26] and "close co-operation" (OECD).[27]

The organisations enumerated in the Treaty were of course the first ones the Community established relations with. There are, however, many others, of which a few are mentioned here: Economic and Social Council for Europe, Convention on the Law of the Sea, United Nations Environment Programme, International Monetary Fund and World Bank, International Atomic Energy Agency (already mentioned in the chapter on Energy), and the Conference on Security and Co-operation in Europe.[28]

VIII. THE COMMUNITY'S RIGHT OF PASSIVE AND ACTIVE LEGATION

With regard to diplomatic representation, the only relevant Treaty provisions are to be found in the Protocol on the Privileges and Immunities.[29] The Member States in whose territory the Communities have their seat, shall accord the customary diplomatic immunities and privileges to missions of third countries accredited to the Communities.[30] Reference can also be made to the Statement issued after the extraordinary meeting of the Council in January 1966, held in Luxembourg. It provides that the credentials of the Heads of Missions of non-member

---

[25] EEC, Art. 229.
[26] *Ibid.* 230.
[27] *Ibid.* 231.
[28] For details see the annual General Reports and the Bull.
[29] Annexed to the Merger Treaty.
[30] Protocol, Art. 17. For a list of the accredited missions, see "*Corps diplomatique accredité auprès des Communautés européennes,*" Directorate General External Relations.

States accredited to the Community will be submitted jointly to the President of the Council and the President of the Commission, meeting together for this purpose.

The representatives of the Community in third countries enjoy the same diplomatic immunities and privileges. This is the case also for the Community delegations to various International Organisations such as the GATT, the OECD, the United Nations and its Specialised Agencies.

Without it being more explicitly provided for in the Treaty, the Community thus exercises the right of active and passive legation.

IX. POLITICAL CO-OPERATION

In the final communiqué of the Conference of Heads of State or Government in December 1969, at The Hague, the Ministers of Foreign Affairs were instructed to study the best way of achieving progress in the matter of political unification within the context of enlargement.[31] At the request of the Ministers, the Davignon report was submitted and accepted in 1970.[32] The aim is to further political unification by co-operating in the field of Foreign Affairs.[33] In 1974 a second report was approved by the Heads of State or Government.[34] It was agreed that various meetings of Foreign Ministers would take place regularly and, within a Political Committee, the Political Directors of the Ministries of Foreign Affairs.

The SEA institutionalised this Political Co-operation by laying down provisions governing this activity; they were examined in

---

[31] Third General Report (1969), 489.

[32] Bull. 11–1969.

[33] The objectives of that co-operation are:
— to ensure, by means of regular consultations and exchanges of information, improved mutual understanding as regards the main problems of international relations;
— to strengthen solidarity between governments by promoting harmonisation of their views, and the alignment of their positions and, whenever it appears possible and desirable, joint action.

[34] Eighth General Report (1974), 7.

Chapter III "Institutions and other organs of the Community," under the Section devoted to the Council. It can indeed be argued that just as the European Council has been officialised by the SEA and become part of the institutional system of the Community, so the "European Political Co-operation"[35] now has its place among the Community bodies. The relationship between those two organs is extremely close, since foreign policy matters are usually discussed on the occasion of meetings of the European Council and of the Council, all three having the same President. The important element, however, is that this co-operation in the field of foreign relations seems indeed to lead towards political union. For the past years, the 12 Member States have increasingly stated their position on all major international events in joint declarations prepared by the machinery of the Political Co-operation. This was the case at the Madrid European Council (June 1989) with regard to the political developments in Eastern and Central Europe, especially in Roumania. The Strasbourg European Council (December 1989) expressed its desire to strengthen links with the Arab world. Other questions on which the Twelve expressed their views were: the Middle-East conflict, the situation in Lebanon, the tragic division of Cyprus, South Africa, Namibia, Angola, China, Iran (they condemned the incitement to murder Salman Rushdie and his publisher), Cambodia, Afghanistan (satisfaction at the withdrawal of the Soviet troops), Philippines (following the attempted coup d'état), Central America, Panama, the conflict in El Salvador and drug-trafficking in Colombia.

Those are just some examples of the many issues on which, through the Political Co-operation, the Member States were able to express a common or Community view.

Further Reading

J. McMahon, "The Renegotiation of Lomé: Inventing the future?" 140(1989) E.L.Rev.

---

[35] SEA, Art. 30, 10(a).

CHAPTER 8

COMMUNITY LAW

As was pointed out at the beginning of this book, the Treaties establishing the European Communities are more than classical international agreements creating mutual obligations between the High Contracting Parties. Indeed, by ratifying them the Member States intended to do more than that, although they most probably did not, at that time, foresee all the conclusions which the Court has, over the years, drawn from their specific nature. Hence the question: what is it that distinguishes those Treaties from other international agreements?

In the first place, they have created quasi-governmental bodies (the institutions) independent from the national public authorities and endowed with legislative, administrative and judicial sovereign rights which were transferred to them by the Member States. Furthermore, the Treaties lay down basic principles which are either worked out in the Treaties themselves or implemented by the acts of the institutions. Treaties and acts constitute a set of rules which directly, *i.e.* without interference or intervention, impose obligations upon, and consequently create rights for, the Member States and the natural and legal persons within the Community. The Treaties therefore present many analogies with national constitutions. It can therefore be said that, although they started out as international treaties, these texts have become the "Constitution" of the European Community.[1]

---

[1] The words "European Community" are used here in a global sense, encompassing the three Communities established by the three European Treaties.

As was shown, the rules embodied in the T
being referred to as "primary" Community la
being expanded, made specific, implemented, c
applied by the various acts and measures of the institutions
(known as "secondary" Community law). The European Treaties
have therefore, as was ascertained by the Court, established a
specific legal order. Indeed,

> "by creating a Community of unlimited duration, having its
> own institutions, its own personality, its own legal capacity
> and capacity of representation on the international plane
> and, more particularly, real powers stemming from a limita-
> tion of sovereignty or a transfer of powers from the States
> to the Community, the Member States have limited their
> sovereign rights, albeit within limited fields, and have
> created a body of law which binds both their nationals and
> themselves."[2]

It took years before all national courts and tribunals came to
share the view that the European Treaties create a separate legal
order. But at the time several of them were quick to agree, as
was the German Supreme Administrative Court. It stated that
Community law constitutes "a separate legal order, whose provisions belong neither to international law nor to the municipal law
of the Member States."[3]

1. Direct Applicability

Community law, being distinct from national law, is also independent from it. This means that rights can be conferred and

---

[2] Case 6/64 *Costa* v. *Enel* [1964] E.C.R. 585 at 593. It should be pointed out that
the unlimited duration only applies to the EEC and Euratom Treaties; the
ECSC Treaty has a duration of 50 years (Art. 97).
[3] C.M.L. Rev. 1967, 483.

obligations imposed directly by Community provisions, *i.e.* without interference or intervention from national authorities. There is indeed no necessity for Member States to intervene in order to ensure that decisions, regulations and, in certain cases, directives have binding effect throughout the Community.[4] Refering to regulations, the Treaty uses the words "shall be . . . directly applicable in all Member States."[5]

In addition, Member States are committed not to interfere with the application of Community law. This also follows from the Treaty which provides *inter alia* that Member States "shall abstain from any measure which could jeopardise the attainment of the objectives of this Treaty."[6]

More important than the acceptance of the "legal autonomy" of the Community legal order in regard to national law, is the understanding of its *raison d'être*. The European Treaties, it will be remembered, aim at establishing within the territories of the Member States a single market characterised *inter alia* by the basic freedoms and constituting a geographical area wherein Community rules apply with the same force and with exactly the same meaning and effect for all who operate therein."[7] Therefore, the very nature of the law created by the European Treaties implies uniform interpretation and application. Without those characteristics there can be no Community. Community law is either uniform in all the Member States or it is not. This does not mean that Community rules should not take into account the specificities of the various Member States or of their regions; as

---

[4] This is what is meant by s.2(1) of the European Communities Act of 1972: these provisions "are without further enactment to be given legal effect or use in the United Kingdom." In other words "reception" of Community law into the sphere of national law is not and cannot be required. Anyway reception is only required by those who adhere to the dualist theory, and furthermore "if one accepts, as is logical and in one view inevitable, that Community law is *sui generis* then, in strictness the monist/dualist argument is excluded, since it is an argument properly limited to international law strictly so called," which is not the case with Community law. John Mitchell, "British law and British membership," *Europarecht*, April–June 1971, 109.

[5] EEC, Art. 189(2).

[6] EEC, Art. 5.

[7] Case 6/64 *Costa* (n. 1, above) at 594.

long as the fundamental principles are safeguarded, the way of implementing them must be adapted. Indeed, applying the same rule to different situations constitutes a discrimination just as much as applying different rules to comparable situations.[8]

2. Direct Effect

If the consequence of direct applicability for the Member States is non-interference, for the citizens it means, in most cases, the possibility of invoking those Community rules in their national courts and tribunals. This allows them to protect the rights which those Community rules directly confer upon them.[9] Applicability of Community law must indeed be understood in two ways: on the one hand, the obligations and prohibitions (*i.e.* obligations to abstain) imposed upon national authorities, institutions and persons, and, on the other hand, the rights of those in favour of whom those obligations have been provided. Indeed, in law, every obligation has a right as its corollary, although this right is not always clearly specified. It is, of course, the same in Community law. For instance obligations imposed upon Member States, generally speaking, have as their corollary rights for the citizens of the Community. By prohibiting the Member States from hindering the free movement of goods, the Treaty grants the persons within the Community the right to move goods unhindered from one Member State to another.

It is this kind of right that the national courts and tribunals must, by virtue of the direct effect of most Community provisions, uphold in pursuance of the Treaty.[10] It is thus not only

---

[8] Case 52/79 *Procureur du Roi* v. *Debauve* [1980] E.C.R. 833 at 858(21) and Case 279/80 *Webb* [1981] E.C.R. 3305 at 3324(16).

[9] This was clearly stated by the Court in Case 43/75 *Defrenne* v. *Sabena* [1976] E.C.R. 455 at 474(24); the same was already apparent in Case 2/74 *Reyners* v. *Belgium* [1974] E.C.R. 631 at 651(25), although less clearly stated.

[10] EEC, Art. 5. This provision refers to "Member States," but this expression covers all the national authorities whether legislative, administrative or judicial. See Case 33/76 *Rewe* v. *Landwirtschaftskammer Saarland* [1976] E.C.R. 1989 at 1997(5).

regulations, which, because they are "directly applicable"[11] are, as such, suited to "grant to the citizens rights which the national tribunals are under obligation to protect,"[12] but all binding Community acts whatever their nature or form.[13] Consequently, the question concerning which provisions of Community law have direct effect should be put this way: "Which Community provisions which impose a clear and unconditional obligation upon a Member State, an institution or a person do not have direct effect?"[14] The answer is: only those which leave to the addressee of the obligation a discretionary latitude. For instance, with regard to Article 90(2), the Court stated that:

> "Its application involves an appraisal of the requirements, on the one hand, of the particular task entrusted to the undertaking concerned and, on the other hand, the protection of the interests of the Community. This appraisal depends on the objectives of general economic policy pursued by the States under the supervision of the Commission. Consequently . . . Article 90(2) cannot at the present stage create individual rights which the national courts must protect."[15]

In other words, the obligation is subject to a Commission appreciation and cannot therefore have direct effect.

[11] EEC, Art. 189. See above Chap. IV "Community Acts."
[12] Case 93/71 *Leonesio* v. *Italian Ministry for Agriculture and Forestry* [1972] E.C.R. 287 at 293(5).
[13] *e.g.* provisions of dirs., decs. or agreements; for directives, see Case 21/78 *Delkvist* v. *Anklagemyndigheden* [1978] E.C.R. 2327 at 2340(21); for decisions see Case 33/76 *Rewe* (n. 10 above) and for agreements see Joined Cases 21–24/72 *International Fruit Company* v. *Produktschap voor Groenten en Fruit* [1972] E.C.R. 1219 at 1227.
[14] Originally, the question was put the other way round: see Case 28/67 *Molkerei Zentrale Westfalen* v. *Hauptzollamt Paderborn* [1968] E.C.R. 143 at 153. See however Case 43/75 *Defrenne* (n. 9 above) at 471. If the acts were not clear and unconditional, nobody could establish what the exact obligation is and ask for it to be upheld; that goes without saying.
[15] Case 10/71 *Ministère Public Luxembourgeois* v. *Muller* [1971] E.C.R. 723 at 730 (14–16).

However, the Court made it clear that in cases where the latitude is limited in time, the expiration of the time-limit suffices to give direct effect to Community rules. This applies notwithstanding the absence of implementing regulations which were to be adopted by the institutions or by the national authorities. The Court found also that, even in the absence of any express reference to the possible action by the institutions, the Community provisions cannot be interpreted as reserving to the national legislature exclusive powers to implement those rules. Indeed, such implementation may be relieved by a combination of Community and national measures.[16]

The fact that the European Treaties have created a new legal order, directly applicable and conferring upon the citizens of the Community rights which the national courts must uphold, was not only ascertained by the Court, but also recognised from the beginning by most national jurisdictions. Indeed, in the first place, the judiciaries of all the Member States have implicitly recognised this fact for many years, by making extensive use of the possibility offered them by the Treaty to ask the Court for a preliminary ruling on questions concerning Community law raised before them.[17]

By referring those questions to the Court, they accepted that Community rules do apply within the territory of their jurisdiction and may confer rights which they must uphold.

In the second place, the fact that Community law constitutes a new legal order was recognised explicitly, years ago, by the highest national courts and tribunals. This was the case *inter alia* for the Italian Corte Costituzionale, the German Bundesverfassungsgericht and the Belgian Cour de Cassation. Although of historical value only at this stage of the development of Community law, these decisions were extremely important at the time when the novelty of those issues often resulted in provoking adverse reactions from national judges. All the implications of the autonomy of the Community legal order did not always

---

[16] Case 43/75, *Defrenne* (n. 9 above) at 480(68).
[17] EEC, Art. 177.

become immediately clear either. In many cases it was a lengthy process of adaptation and learning in which the Court played an important role.[18]

3. Precedence

In retrospect it might seem evident that the autonomy of the Community legal order, the necessity for its uniform interpretation and application in all the Member States automatically implies that Community provisions have precedence over national legislation in case of conflict. Since national courts and tribunals are under obligation, as was just seen, to apply Community rules alongside the provisions of national law, it is not unlikely that conflicts will result from this simultaneous application. The European Treaties contain no explicit provisions regarding the solution to be applied in such cases.[19] Attempts were therefore made to solve such conflicts in accordance with provisions of national law. However, few national legal systems provide for conflict rules of this nature.

In the United Kingdom, for instance, the European Communities Act 1972 provides for the necessary precedence by accepting the "legal effect" of Community provisions in the United Kingdom.[20] The same applies to the decisions of the European Court regarding the meaning or effect of any of the Treaties, or the validity, meaning or effect of any Community instrument.[21] In relation to statute law, this means that the directly applicable Community provisions shall prevail even over future Acts of Parliament, if the latter are inconsistent with those instruments. It also means that by ratifying the European Treaties, the United

---

[18] First General Report (1967), 563.
[19] One could, however, argue that EEC, Art. 5 constitutes a legal ground on which to base this precedence.
[20] European Communities Act 1972, s.2(1).
[21] *Ibid.*, s.3(1).

Kingdom, like any other Member State, must refrain from enacting legislation inconsistent with Community law.[22]

In the Netherlands, the Basic Law (Constitution) not only provides that the provisions of international treaties have precedence over existing national laws and regulations; it also specifies that the same applies to measures enacted by the institutions set up under those treaties and adds that this precedence applies in case of conflict between an existing Community rule and subsequent national law.[23]

The French Constitution provides, in general terms, that treaties or agreements, duly ratified or approved, shall, upon their publication, have authority superior to that of laws, subject, however, for each agreement or treaty, to its application by the other party.[24]

The German Constitution provides that the Federal Republic may, by legislation, transfer sovereign powers to inter-governmental institutions[25] and refers to the precedence of the general

---

[22] *Ibid.,* s.2(4) provides therefore that present and future enactments shall be construed and have effect subject to s.2. See *Hansard*, February 15, 1972, Vol. 831. This basic principle derives not only from the obligations explicitly accepted by the Member States when they became members of the Community, but, as was explained, from the very nature of the Community and Community law. Indeed, the existence of the Community depends upon the simultaneous and uniform application throughout the Community of all the provisions of the Treaties and the acts of the institutions. This was clearly stated over and over again by the Court. See, *e.g.* Case 83/78 *Pigs Marketing Board* v. *Redmond* [1978] E.C.R. 2347 at 2371(56) and Case 128/78 *Commission* v. *U.K.* [1979] E.C.R. 419 at 428(9).

[23] Dutch Constitution, Arts. 66 and 67; these provisions were incorporated in the Constitution in 1953.

[24] French Constitution of 1958, Art. 55. In a judgment of 1962, the French Cour de Cassation held that a contested action had been carried out under an EEC decision and regulation which are "acts regularly published and having acquired force of international treaties" (*Gazette du Palais*, December 9 to 11, 1970, 6–7). See also *Administration des Douanes* v. *Jacques Vabre* [1975] C.M.L.R. 336, where the French Supreme Court clearly stated that the Treaty has an authority greater than that of national acts and is binding on the national courts. See, however, the decision of the Conseil d'Etat, *Syndicat Général des Fabricants de Semoules* v. *Direction des Industries Agricoles* [1970] C.M.L.R. 395. It was only in October 1989 (31 years after the EEC Treaty came into force) that this French highest administrative jurisdiction finally recognised the precedence of Community law over national law!

[25] German Constitution, Art. 24(1).

rules of international law.[26] It is only with difficulty that one can equate Community measures with the latter.

The Italian Constitution is even less precise. It only provides that "Italy's legal system conforms with the general principles recognised by international law."[27]

These German and Italian texts and even the French Constitution form a rather meagre legal basis for the obligation that national courts should give precedence to Community law over national law in case of conflict between the two. And what about those Member States whose Constitution contains no provisions in this respect? Furthermore, in certain cases the above mentioned constitutional provisions were not considered by national judges as obliging them to accept the precedence of Community provisions over national rules.[28]

However, even in the case of the Dutch Constitution, which is so explicit about precedence, doubts might subsist as to the precise consequences. Furthermore, if the sole legal basis for supremacy of Community law over national law were national law itself, this supremacy would be at the mercy of the next constitutional amendment.

Other grounds had therefore to be found which would be accepted by all national jurisdictions without reference to their particular national legal orders. This ground was obviously the Community legal order itself. It was indeed accepted by all the Member States which "have adhered to the Treaty on the same conditions, definitively and without any reservations other than those set out in the supplementary protocols."[29] The Court has always considered that the wording and the spirit of the Treaty

---

[26] *Ibid.*, Art. 25.
[27] Italian Constitution, Art. 10(1).
[28] By a ruling of March 1, 1968 (*Recueil Dalloz-Sirey*, 1968, *jurisprudence*, 286) the French Conseil d'Etat ruled that a French court is bound to ensure the application of the national *lex posterior* to an existing Community rule, whatever the meaning and scope of Community law (Second General Report (1968), 453). The Commission considered this ruling incompatible with the legal obligations deriving from the Treaty (J.O. 1968, C.71). See also Cour de Cassation, October 22, 1970, *Contributions Indirectes* v. *Ramel* [1971] C.M.L.R. 315.
[29] Joined Cases 9 and 58/65 *San Michele* v. *High Authority* [1967] E.C.R. 1 at 30.

make it impossible for the Member States to accord precedence to a unilateral and subsequent measure over a legal system accepted by them on the basis of reciprocity. The Court also added that "the executive force of Community law cannot vary from one State to another in deference to subsequent domestic laws, without jeopardising the attainment of the objectives of the Treaty set out in Article 5(2) and giving rise to the discrimination provided by Article 7."[30]

Therefore, "the law stemming from the Treaty, an independent source of law, could not, because of its special and original nature, be overridden by domestic legal provisions, however framed, without being deprived of its character as Community law and without the legal basis of the Community itself being called into question."[31] This also applies, of course, with regard to national constitutional provisions. The Court states that the effect of a Community measure cannot be affected by allegations that it runs counter to fundamental rights as formulated by the Constitution of a State.[32]

To put it simply: either Community law stands by itself, is uniformly applied and has precedence over domestic law, or it does not subsist. This view is now generally accepted in all the Member States.[33]

The general principle of Community law's precedence over national law having been established, it is necessary to examine some of its more concrete consequences. As far as any national

[30] Case 6/64 *Costa* v. *ENEL* [1964] E.C.R. 585 at 594. This was once again emphasised by the Court in Case 128/78 *Commission* v. *U.K.* ("Tachographs") [1979] E.C.R. 419 at 429.

[31] *Ibid.* See also Case 11/70 *Internationale Handelsgesellschaft* v. *Einfuhr- und Vorratsstelle für Getreide* [1970] E.C.R. 1125 at 1134(3).

[32] *Ibid.* and Case 4/73 *Nold* v. *Commission* [1974] E.C.R. 491.

[33] It might be of interest to mention some of the earliest and most important rulings of national courts since they constitute essential steps towards recognition of the Community legal order and its implications. In Belgium reference must be made to a decision of 1971 of the Cour de Cassation in the case *Belgian State* v. *Fromagerie Franco-Suisse* ([1972] C.M.L.R. 373): the primacy of the Treaty results from the very nature of international treaty law. In France, Cour de Cassation, 1975, *Administration des Douanes* v. *Jacques Vabre et al.* (*ibid.*, 336).

court or tribunal is concerned, the Court has described its obligations as follows. Directly applicable rules of Community law are a direct source of rights and duties for all those affected thereby. The latter include any national court whose task it is, as an organ of a Member State, to protect, in cases within its jurisdiction, the rights conferred upon individuals by Community law. In accordance with the principle of precedence, Treaty provisions and directly applicable Community measures, by their coming into force, automatically render any conflicting provisions of current national law inapplicable.

It follows that every national court, in cases within its jurisdiction, must apply Community law in its entirety and protect the rights which the latter confers upon natural or legal persons. In other words, it must set aside any conflicting provision of national law, whether prior or subsequent to the Community provision. It is not necessary for the national court to request or await the prior setting aside of such national provisions by legislative or other means.[34]

As far as legislative bodies are concerned, the Court indicated that the principle of precedence precludes the valid adoption of new national legislative measures to the extent that they would be incompatible with Community provisions.[35]

As far as other national authorities are concerned, it is clear that respect for the precedence of Community law and the obligations resulting for Member States from the Treaty[36] not only prevent them from enacting measures which are incompatible with Community provisions, but also impose upon them the obligation to abolish all existing contrary measures, whatever their nature. Although these measures are inapplicable their maintenance gives rise to an ambiguous situation "by maintaining, as regards those subject to the law who are concerned, a

---

[34] Case 106/77 *Aministrazione delle Finanze dello Stato* v. *Simmenthal* [1978] E.C.R. 629 at 643–644 (14–18 and 21, 22, 24).

[35] *Ibid.*, at 17. See also Case 230/78 *Eridania* v. *Minister of Agriculture and Forestry* [1979] E.C.R. 2749.

[36] EEC, Art. 5.

state of uncertainty as to the possibilities which are available to them of relying on Community law."[37]

It follows from the preceding remarks that autonomy of the Community legal order, direct effect and precedence of Community rules over national measures all result from the particular nature of Community law.

A final aspect which needs to be mentioned in this respect is the reference by the Court to the usefulness[38] or effectiveness[39] of Community acts to justify the right of individuals to rely on obligations imposed by directives. Those acts are not directly applicable, since the choice is left to the national authorities as to the form and method of implementing the obligations imposed upon them. In other words, the implementation is left, within limits, to their discretion. Consequently, directives have no direct effect and persons cannot invoke them in national courts. However, the Court admits, as was seen before,[40] that provisions of directives can have direct effect, especially after the time-limit set for their implementation has elapsed. Similarly, interested parties have the right to ask national courts to determine whether the competent national authorities, in exercising the choice which is left to them, have kept within the limits of their discretionary powers.[41] However, whether national authorities have or have not exercised their discretionary power, *e.g.* to make a derogation, is a matter for the discretion of the legislative or administrative authorities of the Member State; it cannot, therefore, be subject to legal review on the basis of the provisions of the directive. "It is the duty of the national court before which the directive is invoked to determine whether the disputed national measure falls outside the margin of the discretion of the Member State."[42]

---

[37] Case 167/73 *Commission* v. *France* [1974] E.C.R. 359 at 372(41). See also Case 159/78 *Commission* v. *Italy* [1979] E.C.R. 3247 and Case 61/77 *Commission* v. *Ireland* [1978] E.C.R. 417 at 442.

[38] Case 51/76 *Nederlandse Ondernemingen* v. *Inspecteur der Invoerrechten en Accijnzen* [1977] E.C.R. 113 at 127(29).

[39] Case 38/77 *ENKA* v. *Inspecteur der Invoerrechten en Accijnzen* [1977] E.C.R. 2203 at 2211(9).

[40] See Chap. 4 "Community Acts."

[41] Case 38/77 *ENKA* (n. 39 above) at 2212(10).

[42] Case 51/76 *Nederlandse Ondernemingen* (n. 38 above) at 127(29).

4. Sources of Community law

As was previously indicated, the Community legal order has its
own sources, which consist not only of the European Treaties and
the acts of the institutions issued in pursuance of the powers
conferred upon them (regulations, directives, decisions and
agreements),[43] but also of the rules relating to the application of
this primary and secondary Community law. These rules comprise international law, in so far as applicable,[44] and the general
principles of law,[45] including the fundamental rights. The latter
play an important role, as the Court pointed out: "respect for
fundamental rights forms an integral part of the general
principles of law protected by the Court of Justice," and added
that "the protection of such rights, whilst inspired by the constitutional traditions common to Member States, must be ensured

---

[43] See above, Chap. 4 "Community Acts."
[44] Agreements concluded by the Community with third States or international
organisations (EEC, Art. 28), are, of course, governed by the rules of
international law. On the other hand, as the Court pointed out, when exercising
their rights to lay down Community rules, the institutions are not bound by
provisions of international law, unless the Community itself has assumed the
rights and obligations resulting for the Member States from international
agreements to which they are parties, and unless the provisions of those
agreements have direct effect within the Community: Joined Cases 21–24/72
International Fruit Company v. *Productschap voor Groenten en Fruit* [1972]
E.C.R. 1219 at 1226(8). See also *ibid.*, at 1227(18) and EEC, Art. 37(5) and
Joined Cases 89, etc./85 *Woodpulp Products* v. *Commission*, judgment of
September 27, 1988: "the conduct of the Commission is covered by the
territoriality principle as universally recognised by public international law."
As for Treaty precedence over agreements concluded between Member States
before its entrance into force, see Case 10/61 *Commission* v. *Italy* [1962] E.C.R.
1 at 10; see also EEC, Art. 219.
The precedence of Community law over all other applicable provisions,
including international law, is recognised by the European Communities Act
1972, ss.2(1) and (4).
[45] See Case 159/82 *Verli-Wallace* v. *Commission* [1983] E.C.R. 2711 at 2718(8)
and above, Chap. 3. "The Institutions and other organs," Court of Justice,
Grounds for annulment.

within the framework . . . and objectives of the Community."[46] A formulation of the fundamental rights is to be found, *inter alia*, in the Convention for the Protection of Human Rights and Fundamental Freedoms,[47] ratified by all the Member States. The Court has referred to this Convention in interpreting amongst other matters a Community provision concerning equality of treatment as regards membership of trade unions and the exercise of rights attached thereto.[48] Another formulation is to be found in the Joint Declaration by the European Parliament, the Council and the Commission of April 5, 1977 on fundamental rights.[49]

Thirty-three years ago, I drafted an article to be inserted in the Treaty Chapter on the Court of Justice, which would indicate the sources of law to be applied. Although different words would be used today, its basic indications still seem to be applicable:

"1. The Court whose function it is to ensure the rule of law in the execution of this Treaty, shall apply:
   (a) the provisions of this Treaty and of the judicial acts issued by the institutions;
   (b) the conventions to which the Community is a party or which are undertaken on its behalf;

---

[46] Case 11/70 *Internationale Handelsgesellschaft* v. *Einfuhr- und Vorratstelle Getreide* [1970] E.C.R. 1125 at 1134(4). See also Case 25/70 *Einfuhr- und Vorratstelle* v. *Köster* [1970] E.C.R. 1161 at 1176(36) where the Court found that a system of licences for import and export, involving a deposit, did not violate any right of a fundamental nature and Case 44/79 *Hauer* v. *Land Rheinland-Pfalz* [1979] E.C.R. 3727, where the Court examined whether a Community regulation violates the right of property and the free exercise of professional activity. Also the inviolability of the domicile in Case 46/87R *Hoechst* v. *Commission* [1987] E.C.R. 1549.

[47] Signed in Rome on November 4, 1950, it entered into force on September 2, 1953. In April 1979, the Commission adopted a memorandum on the accession of the Community to the Convention; this accession would bind the Community institutions and would imply recognition of the competence of the European Court of Human Rights (Bull. 4–1979, 16). See Case 4/73 *Nold* (n. 32 above) at 507(13).

[48] Case 36/75 *Rutili* v. *Minister for the Interior* [1975] E.C.R. 1219 at 1232(31–32).

[49] O.J. 1977, C.103 and Bull 3–1977, preliminary chap. See also the European Council Declaration of April 8, 1978 on Democracy (Bull. 3–1978, preliminary chap.).

    (c) the customary law of the Community;

    (d) the general principles of the law of the Community;

    (e) the municipal law of the Member States in case of explicit or tacit reference.

2. In case of reference to international law, the Court shall apply Article 38, paragraph 1, of the Statute of the International Court of Justice.

3. As auxiliary means for the determination of the applicable law, the Court shall apply the decisions of international tribunals, those of the Community and the doctrine."[50]

5. Application of National Law by the Court

The question of the applicability of national law by the Community institutions was raised on several occasions before the Court. The latter, however, decided that it lacked the competence to apply the internal law of the Member States.[51] Consequently, the Court cannot accept a claim that by taking a decision an institution has violated national law. Neither can the Court decide on the interpretation of a national provision.[52] Application of national law by the Court, however, takes place where the Treaty refers explicitly to national concepts.[53] This is the case, for instance, under Article 58 of the Treaty, which refers to companies and firms formed in accordance with the law of a Member

---

[50] P. S. R. F. Mathijsen, *"Le droit de la Communauté Européene du Charbon et de l'Acier; une étude des sources,"* Martinus Nijhoff, 's-Gravenhage, 1957, 193.

[51] See, *e.g.* Case 1/58 *Stork* v. *High Authority* [1959] E.C.R. 17; Joined Cases 36 –40/59 *Geitling* v. *High Authority* [1960] E.C.R. 423. See, however, Joined Cases 17 and 20/61 *Klöckner* v. *High Authority* [1962] E.C.R. 325 and Case 159/78 *Commission* v. *Italy* [1979] E.C.R. 3247.

[52] Case 78/70 *Deutsche Grammophon* v. *Metro* [1971] E.C.R. 487 at 498(3).

[53] See Case 50/71 *Wünsche* v. *Einfuhr- und Vorratstelle Getreide* [1972] E.C.R. 53 at 64(6).

State.[54] Also under Article 215 which provides that, in the case of non-contractual liability, the Community shall make good any damage caused by its institutions or servants "in accordance with the general principles common to the laws of the Member States." Similarly, when the Court is called upon to solve a question for which there are no Treaty provisions, it must solve the problem "by reference to the rules acknowledged by the legislation, the learned writings and the case law of the member countries."[55]

6. Conclusions

As shown by the foregoing considerations, the Community legal order grew and developed mainly at the hands of the Community judges.[56] Over the years, the Court has played an essential role in consolidating its autonomy *vis-à-vis* municipal and international law, by emphasising its originality and by imposing its precedence. It goes without saying that this task would have been impossible without the co-operation, understanding and adaptability of the national judges; for example by asking for preliminary rulings they gave the Court the opportunity to fulfil its task. But the Community Court was and still is the driving force.

It should be clear also that the task of the Court is not limited to applying, developing and interpreting Community law *stricto sensu*. According to the Treaty,[57] the Court shall ensure that "the law" is observed. The term "law" in this provision and as it is

[54] See, *e.g.* Case 18/57 *Nold* v. *High Authority* [1959] E.C.R. 41 at 48.
[55] Joined Cases 7/56 and 3–7/57 *Algera et al.* v. *Common Assembly* [1957–1958] E.C.R. 39 at 55. Another example is the definition of "misuse of power" (EEC, Art. 173) based on a comparative study by the Advocate-General of this concept in the municipal law of the Member States: Case 3/54 *ASSIDER* v. *High Authority* [1954–1955] E.C.R. 63 at 74.
[56] Of course, the Member States did also contribute to the consolidation and development of Community law; see, *e.g.* the Convention on the Law applicable to Contractual Obligations (O.J. 1980, L. 266/1).
[57] EEC, Art. 164.

understood by the Court refers to the concept of what is right, much more so than to anything that was described and analysed in the foregoing pages of this book. Seen in this light, the European Communities appear, beyond all the limitations, ambiguities, hesitations and conflicts, as a legal, political, social and economic system which, thanks to its balanced institutional structure and inherent potential, constitutes the only possible solution for Europe's problems and the only hope for its development.

At the time of finishing this fifth edition (May 1990), Europe is once more faced by a new challenge of as yet unforeseeable dimensions. The transformation of the East European countries from communism to market-oriented economies will require new initiatives and efforts in order for the Community to be able to assist the fledgling democracies in establishing their indispensable economic bases. The Community itself is caught at a difficult moment in its development: the completion of the internal market should be effective in two-and-a-half years, Economic and Monetary Union only exists as a blue-print and political union has not even reached that stage. They are, however, indispensable if the Community is to play an active role in the shaping of Europe in the 1990s.

Further Reading

R. Bieber, "On the Mutual Completion of Overlapping Legal Systems: The Case of the European Communities and the National Legal Orders" (1988) 13 E.L.Rev., 147.

F. Jacobs, *The Effect of Treaties in Domestic Law*, (1987) Sweet and Maxwell, London

J. Sterner, "How to Make the Action suit the Case: Domestic Remedies for Breach of EEC Law" (1987) 12 E.L.Rev., 102.

K. Wellens and G. Borchardt, "Soft Law in European Community Law" (1989) 14 E.L.Rev., 267.

INDEX